Aging in the Twenty-first Century

ISSUES IN AGING
VOLUME 5
GARLAND REFERENCE LIBRARY OF SOCIAL SCIENCE
VOLUME 1053

Issues in Aging

Diana K. Harris, *Series Editor*

Aging in the Twenty-first Century
A Developmental Perspective

Edited by
Len Sperry
Harry Prosen

Garland Publishing, Inc.
New York and London
1996

Library of Congress Cataloging-in-Publication Data

Sperry, Len.
    Aging in the twenty-first century : a developmental perspective / edited
by Len Sperry, Harry Prosen.
        p.   cm. — (Issues in aging ; vol. 5. Garland reference library of so-
cial science ; vol. 1053)
        Includes bibliographical references and index.
        ISBN 0-8153-2102-3 (alk. paper)
        1. Gerontology.   2. Geriatric psychiatry.   I. Prosen, Harry.   II.
Title.   III. Series: Garland reference library of social science ; v. 1053.   IV.
Series: Garland reference library of social science. Issues in aging ; v. 5.
HQ1061.S679 1996
305.26—dc20   96-20607
                                                                                    CIP

Printed on acid-free, 250-year-life paper
Manufactured in the United States of America

THIS BOOK IS DEDICATED TO OUR FRIEND AND COLLEAGUE, JEANNE M. FOLEY, PH.D., A NOTED DEVELOPMENTAL PSYCHOLOGIST AND RESEARCHER. IT IS BECAUSE OF HER GENERATIVE VISION AND SUPPORT THAT THE FOLEY CENTER FOR AGING AND DEVELOPMENT AT THE MEDICAL COLLEGE OF WISCONSIN WAS ESTABLISHED AND THIS BOOK WAS WRITTEN.

Contents

SERIES EDITOR'S FOREWORD

This series attempts to address the topic of aging from a wide variety of perspectives and to make available some of the best gerontological thought and writings to researchers, professional practitioners, and students in the field of aging as well as in other related areas. All the volumes in the series are written and/or edited by outstanding scholars and leading specialists on current issues of considerable interest.

Covering a wide range of topics, this collection of original essays deals with the consequences and challenges of our growing aging population on society. It emphasizes aging as a developmental process while addressing the future of the practice of geropsychiatry and geriatric psychotherapy. This book serves as a valuable resource to guide clinical training, practice, and research on aging into the next century and beyond.

Diana K. Harris
The University of Tennessee

FOREWORD

Gene D. Cohen

While Santayana admonished us about the risks of not paying attention to lessons of the past, there are similar risks in not contemplating the future. This is why books like *Aging in the Twenty-first Century: A Developmental Perspective* are so important; they help us to reexamine assumptions, failures, opportunities, needs, and gaps. *Aging in the Twenty-first Century*, moreover, adds phenomenological to clinical considerations in a broad view of geropsychiatric issues. Of course, in making predictions about the future, one should keep in mind the saying that "those who live by the crystal ball must learn how to eat ground glass." On the other hand, the twenty-first century is virtually upon us, making it less bold to build upon the ramifications of present trends in presenting perspectives on what might, should, and can be in the future of gerontology and geropsychiatry.

There are numerous conceptual vantage points from which one can view the nature and direction of progress in the areas of gerontology and geropsychiatry. One vantage point encompasses the continuum from basic to applied research; another spans biomedical and psychosocial domains of investigation; yet another focuses on studies ranging from a disease orientation to one of health promotion; still another moves from examinations of basic mechanisms of aging to age-associated problems for older adults. In all of these arenas of scientific inquiry, ideas and new knowledge about mental health and aging are burgeoning.

Cutting across all of the above domains of research on aging are three evolving and intersecting conceptual planes that are generating important new hypotheses and directions for geropsychiatric studies, clinical practice, and social policy (Cohen, 1992):

Differentiating mental illness in later life from normal aging changes: It was largely not until the mid-1970s—the fourth quarter of the twentieth century—that scientists and clinicians alike began with any depth to develop a more fundamental recognition that many of the negative mental changes experienced by older adults were, in fact, clinical manifestations of disease rather than inevitable consequences of aging per se. Long-standing myths and misinformation influenced how aging was perceived, blurring the distinction between clinical disorder and normal development in later life. If a negative change is perceived as inevitable—a normal development and not a clinical problem—a decision to seek solutions typically fails to follow. But once this distinction is made, the sense of both opportunity and responsibility to find solutions emerges.

Modifying mental illness in later life: By the 1980s, the distinction between aging and illness in later life had triggered an intense new wave of geriatric studies—in psychosocial as well as psychopharmacological arenas within geropsychiatry. Meanwhile the focus on differentiating normal development from clinical disorder in later life, as well as efforts to modify the latter in older adults, continues today with the promise of yet further progress with the turn of the century.

Modifying (enhancing) normal (mentally healthy) aging: In the 1990s, the quest to modify disorder began to expand into a quest to modify normal changes associated with aging as well—as reflected in the growth of research on health promotion and maintenance of function. This new direction aims not to diminish the importance of addressing disease and disability in later life, but to override denial of the potential for psychosocial growth and development—including creativity—with advancing years (Cohen, 1994a). This most recent orientation is relevant not only from a public health vantage point (how one balances approaches toward health promotion with disease intervention), but also from a social policy vantage point (how society views the role of older persons as a national resource rather than one-sidedly as a societal burden).

As we look toward the twenty-first century and its unfolding, certain other broad social trends and developments should be considered in efforts to anticipate the future of gerontology and geropsychiatry. One development is the expansion of the "geriatric landscape"; another is the emergence of a new, positive "intergenerationalism."

The geriatric landscape (Cohen, 1994b): The geriatric landscape refers to the growing number of settings where older persons both reside and receive treatment. These sites range from homes, to senior housing, to day programs, to continuing-care retirement communities, to assisted-living facilities, to nursing homes. In each of these settings, broad-based attention to well-being must address not only issues of health, but also of home—a combined health and humanities orientation representing a necessary interdisciplinary approach to the multidimensional factors influencing the course of later life.

Intergenerationalism (Cohen, 1995): Intergenerationalism is a newly coined positive "ism" reflecting the growing interest in intergenerational interaction and collaboration—contrary to negative stereotypes of intergenerational conflict misleadingly portrayed by popular media. Too often, when it comes to issues of aging, the popular media draw upon isolated anecdotes rather than aggregate data to push a predetermined point. But the aggregate data reveal strong, prevalent, and growing interest in intergenerational relationships. This important development, which will grow in the twenty-first century given baby boomer behavior, should begin to increase the pressure on policy makers to take a cohesive, family-oriented posture in policy deliberations, rather than a divisive we/they stereotyped stance.

Among the stereotypes of aging that will continue to change in the twenty-first century and influence policy and practice are those of the capacity to change and the significance of time in later life. Both are typically pejorative views—that, with aging, both the capacity to change and the amount of time become limited, thereby reducing personal opportunity and societal responsibility in older adults. But the more accurate picture was captured in the writing of that great observer of human nature, Somerset Maugham, in his classic work on later life, *The Summing Up*. Maugham's skills in observing behavior reflected those of his being both a gifted writer and a medical school graduate. He wrote, "I was at first amazed at Plutarch's description of the elder Cato (a Roman statesman) learning Greek at the age of 80; I am amazed no longer, for old age is ready to undertake tasks that youth shirked because they would take too long."

Developments in the twenty-first century are also likely to reflect the ramifications of some of William Carlos Williams's poetry. Though well known as a great poet, Williams was also a very fine physician. In his sixties, Williams suffered a stroke that precipitated a severe depression leading to a year of psychiatric hospitalization at the age of sixty-nine. He had to give up the practice of medicine and turned full-time to poetry; the poetry he completed in his late seventies led to a Pulitzer Prize. Williams wrote about "an old age that adds as it takes away." Relevant to gerontology and geropsychiatry in the twenty-first century, there are three important ramifications to Williams's poignant poetry: (1) Progress will continue in our understanding and approaches to disease and disability in later life (i.e., what is taken away); (2) progress will pick up pace in what can be maintained and even added in later life (i.e., issues of psychosocial growth and development and creativity in later life with relevance to the individual, family, and society); (3) progress will build on our recognition that in the face of loss, growth can occur: In treating what is taken away with aging, significant advances will be achieved in enhancing what can be added in old age.

REFERENCES

Cohen, G.D. (1992). The future of mental health and aging. In J.E. Birren, R.B. Sloane, and G.D. Cohen (eds.), *Handbook of mental health and aging,* 893–914. New York: Academic Press.

———. (1994a). Creativity and aging: Relevance to research, practice, and policy. *The American Journal of Geriatric Psychiatry,* 2(4): 319–321.

———. (1994b). The geriatric landscape—Toward a health and humanities research agenda in aging. *The American Journal of Geriatric Psychiatry,* 2(3): 185–187.

———. (1995). Intergenerationalism: A new "ism" with positive mental health and social policy potential. *The American Journal of Geriatric Psychiatry,* (3): 1–5.

PREFACE

AGING IN THE TWENTY-FIRST CENTURY

Len Sperry

Imagine, if you will, a hungry python foraging for food one day. The python spies a delectably plump but unsuspecting rabbit and proceeds to swallow it whole. Thoroughly satisfied with the catch of the day, the python stretches out and takes a long siesta, content to let nature take its course as the rabbit is slowly digested and moves down the python's now greatly distended digestive tract. Although this is the usual way pythons are nourished, this is no typical python. In fact, it is ninety miles long and about one mile high; when stretched out, he could connect the cities of Chicago and Milwaukee. Furthermore, the rabbit is no ordinary bunny, as it weighs a whopping seventy-six million tons. Each year the slowly digested rabbit moves about a mile farther down the python's length, getting smaller and smaller over the years. From a distance the python is quite a sight, for he has three humps: not only the bunny hump, but also gigantic mouse and squirrel humps, the results of previous meals.

However, there are few such observers around. And so this imposing presence—the rabbit-mouse-squirrel-within-python—is largely invisible to most, even though everyone is affected by it. Community leaders and residents are quick to note that their neighborhoods seem more crowded. Airlines find they have to reroute their flights, particularly as the hump of the python is some five miles high and wide. Motorists also find driving more difficult as there seem to be so many more hills and valleys. Legislators find themselves appropriating more and more funds to accommodate the change. On the other hand, the job market swells and the economy booms, so everyone who can takes credit for this seeming good fortune.

You might be thinking that this is an interesting story, but what does it have to do with aging, particularly developmental aging? Well, the rabbit represents the largest population "hump" the United States has ever—or may ever—know: that is, the "baby boomer" cohort, numbering some seventy-six million born between roughly 1946 and 1964. The mouse represents a cohort of forty-nine million born between 1927 and 1943, while the squirrel represents the fifty-five million Americans born between 1908 and 1926. The python represents these cohorts' expanded life spans and their attrition rates. Like the python, these cohorts, particularly the boomer cohort, were largely invisible to policy makers, bureaucrats, and even academics. There seemed to be little or no long-range planning in anticipation of how these cohorts would affect basic living patterns. Throughout the 1950s there was unprecedented building of new elementary schools to accommodate the bulging influx of students. The same phenomenon occurred in the early 1960s for high school construction and teaching staff expansion, and repeated itself a few years later for colleges and universities. As a result, there is a surplus of relatively new, unused, or underutilized schools today, as the current school-age cohort is half as large as the boomer cohort. This shortsightedness and reactivity is also reflected in current issues such as health care access and the impending Social Security crisis.

In many ways, the study of human development in psychology and psychiatry followed a similar pattern. Research and training grants and, subsequently, research and training in the areas of child and adolescent development constituted the focus of developmental psychology and psychiatry from the 1950s to the 1970s. Fortunately, these efforts did positively impact child rearing and parenting patterns for those born in the later boomer years and the subsequent "baby-bust" cohort. In the late 1970s and early 1980s, there was growing interest in adult (especially middle-age) development, but less research and training grant monies. However, as with child and adolescent development, the focus on adult development was largely a reactive undertaking rather than a result of proactive initiatives.

Will developmental aging suffer this same reactive fate? Were it not for visionaries such as George H. Pollock, David Gutmann, James E. Birren and Drs. Paul and Margret Baltes, the answer would probably be yes. These as well as other theorists and visionary researchers have been pioneers in the field of developmental aging. They have and continue to challenge myths and stereotypes of the elderly.

The Shift from Aging as Pathology to Developmental Process

Our current societal images of aging often reflect the conviction that aging is basically a pathological process, not to mention a medical, psychological, and economic problem. This belief fosters a number of myths about the elderly: that they are unhealthy, senile, unproductive, unattractive, and sexless. While research fails to support these myths, it does endorse the conviction that aging is a developmental process. When aging is viewed as such a process, positive and healthier images of aging result. Since images powerfully influence personal, corporate, and national decisions, it is crucial that our images of aging accurately reflect reality.

America and other industrialized nations are beginning to experience and take note of the impact of the increasing number of elderly. By the year 2010, it is estimated that 13.9 percent of Americans will be over the age of sixty-five. This group has already significantly redefined previous conceptions of childhood and adult development, as well as life styles, social policies, and cultural norms. They will surely change our current images of aging and influence clinical practice as well as research directives and methods. As the tide is shifting toward an aging future, health, mental health, and behavioral scientists need to understand this paradigm shift as well as influence these images and directions of change.

Until recently the focus of aging research and clinical practice has focused on decline and pathology. There are a number of fine research centers and training institutes investigating aging as a pathological process and training professionals to effectively treat pathology. What is desperately needed is clinical research and training in the processes and treatment of normal and healthy aging. Only when aging is understood in both its pathological and developmental dimensions can we have a truly mature science of geropsychiatry and geriatric psychotherapy. To meet the challenges of older adults in the twenty-first century, clinicians must understand and appreciate the developmental as well as pathological aspects of aging.

The Center for Aging and Development of the Medical College of Wisconsin was established in 1990 to study aging and its implications for the twenty-first century from the perspective of development, wellness, and health promotion, as well as from the perspective of decline, pathology, and rehabilitation.

One of the early initiatives of the center was to query experts on their predictions and projections about the developmental processes of aging and the practice of geropsychiatry and geriatric psychotherapy. The chapters that follow are the results of that query.

THE FUTURE OF GERONTOLOGY

Aging as a Developmental Process

Myths and Major Trends

Len Sperry

Growing old is typically viewed as a sad and negative occurrence, crossed with loss, poverty, loneliness, sickness, and impotence. Our images of the elderly are largely bleak and pessimistic: After age 65, the road turns downhill, with an ever-increasing slope, racing quickly toward death. This perception is projected by many institutions and values in our culture, especially by the media and advertising, where the experience of the elderly is distorted and discounted, if represented at all. In particular, ads seldom portray the elderly in a positive way, especially if the product relates to health, beauty, romance, or sexuality. Even television shows and magazines pitched to the elderly use younger persons in their advertisements and commercials. The powerful message that is being communicated is that the elderly are not worth writing about, nor are they interesting, beautiful, or sexy, nor do they deserve products created particularly for them.

When the elderly internalize this negative image of aging, they cannot help but feel left out and worthless. The message becomes "you must be young to be worthwhile."

Our culture is, to varying degrees, gerontophobic. We have a fear of aging and a prejudice against the old that clouds most of our perceptions about what it means to grow old in America. Far from portraying aging as a developmental process, aging is clearly viewed as a regressive phenomenon.

The purpose of this essay is to suggest that aging is indeed a developmental process, and that the elderly in general will be better served if theorists, clinicians, and researchers develop a more positive image of aging. This amounts to a paradigm shift in our thinking about the older adult (Pollock, 1986). To do so we must first confront the myths and misconceptions we have about aging and carefully consider the ever-increasing evidence that aging is in fact a developmental process. Six myths associated with aging are identified and refuted. Then five trends that clearly point to this more positive image of aging are reviewed.

There are a host of erroneous myths and aged-related stereotypes that pervade American culture. Such myths obscure the true later years of life and our images and expectations for happiness and health as we grow older. For a healthy aged America to arrive, many commentators (Dychtwald, 1986; Kra, 1986) believe it is essential for these myths be identified and refuted.

The first myth is that people over sixty-five years of age are old. Research does not provide biological or psychological support to connect the number sixty-five to the onset of old age (Baltes and Baltes, 1990). Sixty-five first emerged as a measure of old age in the 1880s when Chancellor Von Bismarck of Germany arbitrarily chose the sixty-fifth birthday as the age as which to retire some of his military personnel. In the not too distant future, we will likely think of old age as setting in at closer to ninety or one-hundred years rather than at sixty-five.

The second myth states that most older people are in poor health. While older persons may have chronic, controlled health problems as they age, they are not necessarily adversely affected or limited by them (Fries, 1990). Traditional notions about old age and health need to be rethought. Definitions that have more to do with functional abilities, levels of vigor and vitality, and an individual's own feelings of well-being will likely become the norm for health in the years to come.

The third myth says essentially that older minds are not as bright as younger minds. Of the thirty million Americans now over the age of sixty-five, only ten percent show any significant loss of memory and fewer than half of those show any serious mental impairment (Schaie, 1990). Thus it is a misnomer to say that senility is a disease. There are a few serious illnesses, such as Alzheimer's disease, that can produce the symptoms associated with senility, but there are more than 100 different conditions that can lead to such symptoms, most of which can be treated relatively easily. According to Robert Butler, the founding director of the National Institute of Aging: "the belief that if you live long enough you will become senile is just wrong."

The fourth myth is that older people are unproductive (Bengston and Dauneter, 1987). Research finds no consistent pattern to show superior productivity is the domain of any age group (Featherman, Smith, and Peterson, 1990). In fact, in the future, older workers will be considered not worn-out but seasoned veterans, not out-of-date but able to learn, and not ready to retire but open to more flexible and more productive work lives.

The fifth myth holds that older persons are unattractive and sexless

(Butler, Lewis, and Sunderland, 1991). Current research suggest that men and women can continue to experience sensual feelings and perform sexually into the later years. Sex, romance, and intimate relationships are likely to continue into the older years and may well become deeper, fuller, and more satisfying than previously.

The sixth myth suggests that all older persons are pretty much the same. Actually, persons in their later years tend to become more, not less, diverse (Butler, Lewis, and Sunderland, 1991). There is probably no age group more varied in physical abilities, personal styles, tastes, or financial capabilities than the elderly. And tomorrow's elderly will be different not only from one another, but from today's elderly as well.

In summarizing an important longitudinal study of human aging, Robert Butler reported:

> Evidence suggest[s] that many manifestations heretofore associated with aging per se reflect instead medical illness, personality variables, social-cultural affects. It is hoped that future research may further disentangle the contributions of disease, social losses, pre-distant personalities, so that we can know more clearly what changes should be resorted as age-specific. If we can get behind the facade of chronological aging we open up the possibility of modification through both prevention and treatment. (Butler, 1963)

Our negative view of aging and its concomitant gerontophobia is based on lack of information and a limited perspective on history. Education is needed to replace this negative view—and corresponding gerontophobia—with a more positive view of aging. This more positive view of aging as a developmental process is made possible by a number of emerging trends in the social and biological sciences.

FIVE MAJOR TRENDS

Changing Demographics

Throughout recorded history, only one in ten individuals could expect to live to be sixty-five years of age. For instance, in 1890 there were 2.4 million Americans over age sixty-five. Today the number is over 30 million and it is estimated that nearly 80 percent of Americans will live past that age. In the year 2000, approximately 45 million Americans will reach their sixty-fifth birthdays. That means that the elderly will represent 13 percent of the total population, well surpassing the number of teenagers. Today, there are

3.3 million Americans over the age of 85, and this is expected to rise to 15 million in the year 2050. Today, there are also about 45,000 Americans over the age of 100, and this is predicted to increase to about 5 million by the year 2080 (Menken, 1988).

What accounts for these major changes in demographics? Part is due to continued improvement in medical technology, but the major reason is that the post–World War II baby boomers—76 million babies born between 1946 and 1964—will become senior boomers. Because 20 percent of the baby boomers will have no children and 25 percent will only have one child, it is evident that we are shifting from a youthful to an aging culture, as a function of declining fertility and declining mortality.

The baby boom cohort—soon to become the senior boom cohort— will significantly change the image of aging that most of us presently hold. Just as they have redefined the earlier stages of life they have inhabited, the boomer cohort will change our conception of aging by revising and reshaping the popular habits, styles, and attitudes toward aging to better accommodate their needs and desires (Light, 1988).

The erosion of gerontocracy (the special status and rule by the elderly), whose decline Gutmann (1980) bemoaned when the founding generation of this country died, appears to be rapidly reemerging. In fact, if the American Association of Retired Persons (AARP) were to become an independent nation, it would constitute the thirtieth-largest nation in the world. The growing cultural, political, and economic power of today's elderly is significant, and offers only a very hint of the social, cultural, political, and economic clout they will likely exercise in the early decades of the twenty-first century.

Health, Status, and Well-Being

Throughout history, the major causes of illness and death have been natural disasters, infant mortality, and a variety of infectious diseases. Today, technological advances in public health and medicine have basically eliminated acute infectious diseases as a cause of premature death. Replacing infectious diseases has been a dramatic rise in the incidence and prevalence of life style-related and stress-related chronic degenerative diseases. Among the most common causes of death today are heart disease, cancer, stroke, and diabetes. These have become a primary obstacle to high-quality life and longevity among the elderly.

These chronic degenerative diseases, which count for a relatively long period of infirmity toward the end of life, represent the greatest health problems for the elderly (Fries and Crapo, 1986). Although there is little hope for cure of these diseases through traditional medical means, their onset can be postponed through modification of risk factors. As the onset is delayed to older ages and approaches the limit of the human life span, Fries and Crapo envision a society where individuals can expect to live in vigorous health to close to their projected life span of eighty-five years and then die after a brief period of illness.

Health promotion programs for the elderly have been pilot-studied in a variety of community, health care, and worksite settings. Perhaps the two most well-known longitudinal studies are the Baltimore Longitudinal Study of Aging (described in a subsequent chapter) and the Duke Normative Aging Study. Modifying diet, increasing fitness and exercise, reducing risk factors, and coming to terms with the emotional challenges of the later years have been shown to increase the overall health and well-being of the majority of participating elders (Dychtwald, 1986; Shock, Greulich, Andres, et al., 1984).

As longevity increases, it becomes clear that there are different subgroups among the elderly. Variations in health, rather than age, are responsible for perceived age differences, such that the frail impaired elderly female may have little in common with her more robust aged peers (Siegler and Costa, 1985). The challenge for gerontology in geriatric medicine is, then, to reduce risk factor profiles and disability during the middle and later years with a variety of wellness and health promotion measures, as well as traditional medical means. Because of the proven track record of long-term health care of the elderly in the provinces of Ontario, Manitoba, and British Columbia, it is incumbent upon us to carefully review the Canadian approach to health maintenance and promotion and learn from it (Kane and Kane, 1985).

Changes in Career and Work Patterns

With twenty-eight extra years added to life expectancy during the past century, the average American now has the choice not only of "growing old," but also of using these extra years to plan different life scenarios. Up until now, it was assumed that an individual would follow the "linear life plan," in which childhood and adolescence were a time of education and job preparation, followed by a career and family life, and then death. Longer life will allow more flexible life and career planning, which Best (1980) calls the "cyclic life plan." Individuals will now have the option of having several different careers and jobs in their lifetimes interspersed with periods of time off for further education or retraining, as well as planned sabbaticals and leaves of absence for extended leisure activities.

As American culture moves from a linear to cyclic career perspective, the way we work will change. Several social factors are converging that will allow many individuals to allow to continue working throughout the later years of their lives. First, since mandatory retirement has ended, more older Americans want to continue working. Now, they can opt for reduced work loads or more flexible schedules so as to combine work with leisure and continue to work into their eighth and ninth decades. Second, older Americans are getting healthier and work is becoming less physically demanding. This allows many of them to stay in the workplace at a time when a major shortage of new skilled workers is anticipated. Third, retirement as we now know it will probably not remain as it has been for much longer. Since the financial solvency and appropriateness of the Social Security system is being seriously questioned, it is quite likely that Social Security will be drastically changed in the near future. Assuming that Social Security benefits will only go to the very poor and disabled, and that other pension sources will be minimal, older Americans at the beginning of the twenty-first century may need to continue working to maintain their previous style of living.

Naisbitt and Aburdene (1990) reflect the shared belief of many futurists who envision that by the turn of the century, the purpose and arrangement of work will be redefined. The anticipation is that workers will have much more participation in job-related decisions, and also more options and control over both their personal and work lives so as to blend work, leisure, and retraining. Naisbitt and Aburdene cite a Rand Corporation study that predicts that by the year 2020, the average worker will need to be retrained up to thirteen times in his or her lifetime. It is believed that over the next three decades, more individuals will be involved with small entrepreneurial corporations or work independently than work for large hierarchical corporations. For one thing, there may not be as many jobs in hierarchical corporations in the years to come. Bengtson and Dauneter (1987) suggest that only 50 percent of those in the baby boom cohort who expect to move into top-level positions will actually get those positions, since in the years to come there will be "too many chiefs and not enough Indians." With jobs shifting more and more from the manufacturing to the service sector because of such changes as automation and robotics, the decreased need for generalists such as middle managers, and the movement towards team management and quality circles, corporations of the future are likely to be much more lean, with only a single layer of management overseeing the work of several groups or teams of specialists.

Changes in Family Patterns

Dramatic changes in the present structure and function of the American nuclear family is anticipated. Actually, the family has always been an evolving social institution changing to fit the social and economic climate of the time. It is anticipated that a shift from a nuclear, child-centered family toward a "matrix" family will occur. The new matrix family will be more adult-centered and span four to five generations (Riley, 1983; Butler, Lewis and Sunderland, 1991). Interpersonal relationships among the generations are less likely to be among parents and their young children and more likely to be among several generations of parents and adult children who essentially become peers.

It is estimated that the average American female will spend more years caring for her parents than she did caring for their children. Caring for the elderly members of matrix families at home will become a commonplace challenge for the matrix family. Currently, it is estimated that 80 percent of older Americans are cared for by their families at home (Menken, 1988). This percentage is likely to increase even more in the years to come.

Like child care today, it is anticipated that "parent care" will increasingly become a corporate responsibility. In the years to come, workers may be granted a specified number of parent care days as a standard benefit. Different kinds of insurance packages will likely offer coverage for the health needs of a worker's parents. Day care centers for the elderly may also become standard job benefits.

The divorce rate for individuals over the age of sixty is now increasing as rapidly as that of younger age groups (U.S. Bureau of the Census, 1989). It is anticipated that the baby boomers' casual attitude towards marriage will follow them into their later years, resulting in an even higher rate of divorce and marriage in the future. Since 80 percent of those who divorce remarry, and the number of Americans who have married three or more times has increased 56 percent in the past decade, serial monogamy may become the rule rather than the exception. Thus, as Americans age, they will have extended, multiple family bonds. In addition, they are also likely to have extended networks of close friends, work colleagues, and neighbors developed over their "extra" years of life, and because of their varied life and career patterns.

Recent Advances in Developmental Theory

Until very recently, developmental theory in psychiatry and psychology was, for all practical purposes, the study of psychological processes in children and adolescents. Even though there were few best sellers on adult development, such as Gail Sheehy's *Passages* and Erik Erikson's *Seasons of a Man's Life*, there has been only a modicum of systematic research on psychological development in the later years. Besides Erikson's theory of psychosocial stages (Smelser and Erikson, 1980) there have been relatively few theories of psychological development in the later years. Exceptions have been the works of Colarusso and Nemiroff (1981) and Levinson (1986). Colarusso and Nemiroff (1981) and Nemiroff and Colarusso (1989) offer several hypotheses as the basis for a psychodynamically oriented theory of adult development that they hope to elaborate in the future. These hypotheses are that development in adulthood is an ongoing, dynamic process; whereas childhood development is focused primarily on the formation of psychic structure, adult development is concerned with the continuing evolution of existing psychic structure and with its use; the fundamental developmental issues of childhood continue as central aspects of adult development but in altered forms; the developmental processes in adulthood are influenced by the adult's recent past as well as the adult's childhood past; development in adulthood is influenced by the body and physical changes; and, a central phase-specific theme of adult development is the normative crisis precipitated by the recognition and acceptance of the finiteness of time and the inevitability of personal debt.

Levinson (1986) conceptualizes a stage theory akin to Erikson in which there is a like structure with alternating periods of structure building and structure changing, which he calls "transitions." He and others have conducted extensive biographical interviews that form the empirical basis for the stage theory. Although Levinson has specified, with precision, the developmental period and the eras of early and middle adulthood, he has yet to do the same for the era of late adulthood. In time it is possible that developmental researchers like Levinson (1986) and Vaillant (1984) will follow their study cohorts into the later years and thus be able to elaborate the developmental stage of late adulthood.

Besides the epic research being done on stage theories of adulthood and aging, a number of other research efforts—often experimental and quasi-experimental studies—have been reported. The field of "psychology of aging" includes investigations on memory, cognitive processes, neuropsychology, and health psychology, but the mainstay of this field is the study of personality variables. Unfortunately, making generalizations about the findings on personality in the elderly is difficult. After an exhaustive review of recently reported research, Siegler and Costa (1985) cautioned that any generalizations are likely to be oversimplifications.

Furthermore, like Colarusso and Nemiroff (1981), Pollock (1986) has approached the study of the older adult from a psychodynamic perspective. In his longitudinal study of the mourning process, he concludes that the phenomenon of mourning serves as a necessary adaptation to the various losses sustained throughout life. In fact, Pollock believes that the mourning process is a basic mechanism for change in adulthood.

Unlike others who equate mourning with bereavement, grief, or a pathological condition, Pollock poses a more optimistic view. He describes "mourning-liberation" as an adaptative process to the experience of loss or change that begins early in life and extends throughout the life span, wherein its nature or completed form takes shape with the onset of psychological maturity (Pollock, 1987). Pollock believes that successful aging requires the ability to mourn what no longer exists in order to be liberated to invest energy in the present and future. Mourning, then, allows the individual to continue the developmental process of later adulthood (Pollock, 1986). Based on his extensive research, Pollock concludes that the mourning-liberation process is adaptational, developmental, and universal, extending throughout recorded history and across all cultures. Grief is described as an affect accompanying the mourning-liberation process in its early stages, while bereavement is a subclass of mourning-liberation related specifically to loss through death.

How does the mourning-liberation process operate? It is initiated by a change in internal organization resulting from reality, followed by a relinquishment of psychic investment in that which no longer exists. A transformation occurs when new and more neutral memories are established, which are preceded by a dissolution of the older, painful ones. Pollock describes four possible outcomes of the mourning-liberation process. The first is successful adaptation to loss or change with resolution of the disruption, followed by restoration with a realistic, new equilibrium. A second is an arrest of the process at any point in the life span. These arrests have been found to be reversible with psychotherapy. Third is a fixation at particular development points without arrest. Fixations are commonly seen in anniversary reactions. The fourth outcome is the pathological mourning reaction. The inner loss associated with this outcome cannot be healed without treatment (Pollock, 1987).

In short, Pollock believes that each developmental phase of life involves the mourning-liberation process. As individuals develop, separate, and differentiate themselves, the mourning for what has been given up liberates them to move on to the next developmental phase. A more complete account of Pollock's research is found in his two-volume work, *The Mourning-*

Liberation Process (1989). Besides heralding change in the way theorists and researchers conceptualize mourning, Pollock's view has important implication for the practice of psychotherapy with older adults. Whereas many previously believed that the elderly were poor candidates for psychotherapy, Pollock and others have convincingly shown that age itself does not preclude psychoanalytic treatment (Pollock, 1986). In fact, Pollock has successfully worked in psychotherapy with individuals over the age of 100! Thus, previous misconceptions and pessimism about the meaning of loss in old age and the utility of psychotherapy has given way to a more optimistic, developmental view.

A second line of developmental theory involves cohort or generational differences. Social gerontology considers cohort differences of great significance (Uhlenberg, 1988). Cohort differences are due to membership in a birth year-defined group that is socialized to certain beliefs, attitudes, and personality dimensions that remain constant for that group and distinguish it from other such groups. A related term is generational cohort. Strauss and Howe (1991) have developed a generational cycle theory consisting of recurring generational patterns. Each cycle has few patterns and begins with an idealistic generation that grows up as indulged youth after a political or economic crisis; comes of age, inspiring an awakening; fragments into narcissistic rising adults; cultivates principles as midlife moralizers; and emerges as visionary adults. They are followed by a reactive generation that grows up as underprotected and criticized youth during a period of spiritual awakening, become midlife pragmatists and family-oriented conservatives, but finally undemanding elders. Next is the civic generation, that comes of age by overcoming a secular crisis, unites into a heroic and achieving cadre of rising adults, builds institutions as powerful midlifers, and as elders are attacked during the next awakening. They are then followed by an adaptive generation, that grows up suffocated as children of crisis, comes of age as conformists, produces the indecisive mediators of the next awakening, and ages into other-directed elders. The next generation is idealist and the cycle repeats.

Strauss and Howe report that when linear social trends are stripped away, similar human dramas repeat over and over. They note that the majority of today's elders—those born between 1901 and 1924—are a civic generation. They have successfully managed to get things done and get their needs met. Today they are busy senior citizens, possessing considerable civic pride and political clout, as well as a sense of public entitlement. They are also a security-conscious group who learned that "God helps those who help themselves" during the Depression, settled into safe urban and suburban neighborhoods, and later exchanged hard work and corporate loyalty and commitment for lifelong employment (Light, 1988). As a cohort, this generation appears to have a relatively lower prevalence of anxiety syndromes, but a correspondingly higher rate of depression (Blazer, Hughes and George, 1987).

On the other hand, the adaptive generation—those born between 1925 and 1942—were the unobtrusive children of the Depression and war, the conformists called the "Lonely Crowd," and the youngest marrying generation in U.S. history. They have experienced considerable insecurity during their formative years: the cold war and the "age of anxiety," and more recently the brunt of the massive layoffs and job losses due to merger and takeover mania. Following them are an idealist generation of baby boomers who for all their individualism, self-reliance, instant gratification, and introspection have generally short-term commitments to social institutions like church or synagogue, work and family. Thus, as Bellah et al. (1985) suggest, the boomers' individualism and lack of long-term commitment may become a source of loss of meaning and bitterness as opportunities shrink and expected entitlements do not materialize. It is predicted that this generation may experience increasing insecurity as they turn sixty-five around the year 2010, about the time a major secular crisis is likely, according to the generational cycle theory (Strauss and Howe, 1991).

Several other advances in developmental theory have been described by Birren and Bengston (1988) in their edited text, *Emergent Theories of Aging*. In addition to describing four dimensions of developmental biological theories of aging, they concentrate on twelve dimensions of developmental, psychological, and sociocultural theories of aging. Among other things, these advances account for the resurgence of interest in psychotherapy with the elderly.

CONCLUDING NOTE

It has been argued that a more positive view of aging is needed, in which aging is conceptualized as a developmental process. Accordingly, six currently held myths and misconceptions about aging were identified and discounted. Then five major trends that support a developmental perspective were described. Furthermore, it was noted that these trends have influenced the resurgence of interest in psychotherapy with older adults. Essentially, changing demographics fueled by increased longevity and the aging of the baby boom generation, along with major changes in the institutions of work and the family, are creating the basis for a social transformation heretofore unknown in America. Those involved with health and mental health theory, research, and clinical services would do well to anticipate and plan for these changes with such a developmental perspective.

REFERENCES

Baltes, P., and Baltes, M. (1990). Psychological perspectives on successful aging. In P. Baltes and M. Baltes (eds.), *Successful aging: Perspectives from the behavioral sciences* 1–34. Cambridge, England: Cambridge University Press.

Bengtson, V., and Dauneter, D. (1987). Families, work and aging: Implications of disordered cohort flow for the twenty-first century. In R. Ward and S. Tabin (eds.) *Health in aging: Sociological issues and policy direction,* 212–229. New York: Springer.

Bellah, R., Madsen, R., and Sullivan, W., et al. (1985). *Habits of the heart.* Berkeley: University of California Press.

Best, F. (1980). *Flexible life scheduling.* New York: Praeger.

Birren, J., and Bengston, V. (eds.). (1988). *Emergent theories of aging.* New York: Springer.

Blazer, D., Hughes, D., and George, L. (1987). The epidemiology of depression in an elderly community population. *The Gerontologist,* 27:288–287.

Brink, T. (1979). *Geriatric psychotherapy.* New York: Human Services Press.

Butler, R. (1963). The facade of chronological aging. *American Journal of Psychiatry,* 119:235–242.

Butler, R., Lewis, M., and Sunderland, T. (eds). (1991). Aging and mental health. 4th ed. New York: Merrill.

Colarusso, C., and Nemiroff, R. (1981). *Adult development: A new dimension in psychodynamic theory and practice.* New York: Plenum.

Dychtwald, K. (1986). The aging of Americans: Overview. In K. Dychtwald (ed.), *Wellness and health promotion for the elderly,* 3–19. Rockville, MD: Aspen.

———. (1989). Age-wave: *The challenge and opportunities of an aging America.* Los Angeles: Jeremy Tarcher.

Featherman, D., Smith, J., and Peterson, J. (1990). Successful aging in a post-retired society. In P. Baltes and M. Baltes (eds.), *Successful aging: Perspectives from the behavioral sciences,* 50–93. Cambridge, England: Cambridge Unversity Press.

Fries, J. (1990). Medical perspectives upon successful aging. In P. Baltes and M. Baltes (eds.), *Successful aging: Perspectives from the behavioral sciences,* 35–49. Cambridge, England: Cambridge University Press.

Fries, J., and Crapo, L. (1986). The elimination of premature death. In K. Dychtwald, (ed.), *Wellness and health promotion for the elderly,* 139–149. Rockville, MD: Aspen.

Gutmann, D. (1980). Observations on culture and mental health in later life. In J. Birren and R. Sloane (eds.), *Handbook of mental health and aging,* 217–239. Englewood Cliffs, NJ: Prentice-Hall.

Kalish, R. (1975). *Late adulthood: Perspectives on human development.* Monterey, CA: Brooks/Cole.

Kane, R., and Kane, R. (1985). *A will and a way: What the United States can learn from Canada about caring for the elderly.* New York: Columbia University Press.

Karpf, R. (1982). Individual psychotherapy with the elderly. In A. Horton (ed.), *Mental health interventions for the aging,* 21–49. New York: Praeger.

Kra, S. (1986). *Aging myths.* New York: McGraw-Hill.

Larson, D., Whanger, A., and Busse, E. (1983). Geriatrics. In B. Wolman (ed.), *The therapist's handbook,* 2nd ed., 287–324. New York: Van Nostrand Reinhold.

Lazarus, L. (ed). (1984). *Psychotherapy with the elderly.* Washington, DC: American Psychiatric Press.

Levinson, D. (1986). A conception of adult development. *American Psychologist*, 41:3–13.

Light, P. (1988). *Baby boomers*. New York: Norton.

Menken, J. (1988). *Aging America: Trends and projections, 1987–88 edition*. Washington, DC: U.S. Department of Health and Human Services.

Naisbitt, J., and Aburdene, P. (1990). *Megatrends 2000*. New York: Morrow.

Nemiroff, R., and Colarusso, C. (1989). *The race against time: Psychotherapy and psychoanalysis in the second half of life*. New York: Plenum.

Pollock, G.H. (1986). The psychoanalytic treatment of older adults with special reference to the mourning-liberation process. In J. Masserman (ed.), *Current psychiatric therapies*, 87–98. Orlando, FL: Grune and Stratton.

———. (1987). The mourning-liberation process in health and disease. In *Psychiatric clinics of North America*, 345–354. Philadelphia: W.B. Saunders.

———. (1989). *The Mourning-Liberation Process*. 2 vols. Madison, CT: International Universities Press.

Riley, M. (1983). The family in an aging society: A matrix of latent relationships. *Journal of Family Issues*, 4:321–340.

Schaie, K. (1990). The optimization of cognitive functioning in old age. In P. Baltes and M. Baltes (eds.), *Successful aging: Perspectives from the behavioral sciences*, 94–117. Cambridge, England: Cambridge University Press.

Shock, N., Greulich, R., Andres, L., et al. (1984). *Normal human aging: The Baltimore longitudinal study of aging*. Washington, DC: U.S. Department of Health and Human Services.

Siegler, I., and Costa, P. (1985). Health behavior relationships. In J. Birren and K. Schaie (eds.), *Handbook of the psychology of aging*, 144–166. 2nd ed. New York: Van Nostrand Reinhold.

Smelser, N., and Erikson, E. (eds.). (1980). *Themes of work and love in adulthood*. Cambridge, MA: Harvard University Press.

Strauss, W., and Howe, N. (1991). *Generations: The history of America's future, 1584 to 2060*. New York: William Morrow.

Uhlenberg, P. (1988). Aging and the societal significance of cohorts. In J. Birren and V. Bengston (eds.), *Emergent theories of aging*, 405–425. New York: Springer.

U.S. Bureau of the Census. (1989). *Marital status and living arrangements*. Washington, D.C.: U.S. Government Printing Office.

Vaillant, G. (1984). The study of adult development at Harvard Medical School. In S. Mednick, M. Harway, and K. Finello (eds.), *Handbook of Longitudinal Research*, 315–327. New York: Praeger.

GERONTOLOGY RESEARCH IN THE TWENTY-FIRST CENTURY

SOME WISHFUL THINKING

David Gutmann

I am a psychologist with specialties in clinical and developmental psychology. As such, I am no prophet. Indeed, like most social scientists, I find it hard to understand what is going on in front of my nose, much less predict with any accuracy such matters as the shape of gerontological research in the year 2010. Like the remembered past, the imagined future is a screen for fantasy: a picture of the possibilities that we either fear or hope for. So, instead of dignifying my fantasies with the title of "predictions," I will instead tell you about my wishes and fears—identified as such—for the future of research in gerontology, and particularly in my field of geropsychology. In effect, I will be commenting on current tendencies in the field that I would like to see amplified, and those that I would not mind seeing suppressed.

We have entered the age of the victim; in the social sciences, the age of "victim-babble." The field of geropsychology is no exception: The aged have been inducted into the mystique of victimhood. They are portrayed, almost exclusively, as victims of their failing bodies, on the one hand, and of a "youth-centered" culture, on the other. True enough, the human body may appear to be programmed for eventual mortality; but much modern research shows us that the body and its systems do not begin the long slide into death during the period of aging itself. Instead, the "third age" (the era when direct parental responsibilities decrease) is marked by selective losses in certain physical domains, but also by long-term stability in others. The cardiac capacity to respond to emergency situations in the "fight or flight" mode decreases, but the physical capacity to act effectively and with satisfaction under relatively stable and protected conditions persists more or less unimpeded across the third age. It is during the relatively brief period of rapid, pre-mortal decline, or termination—not aging per se—that the principle of selective degradation is lost, and all major systems move together towards their mortal end. However, in geroclinical practice, the phenomenon of termination is made retroactive over the relatively stable period of aging. In effect, the signs of normal physical aging are too often misinterpreted, treated as though they were the stigmata of termination.

I am particularly troubled by the absence of a truly developmental conception of elderhood. In most species, individuals do not long outlive the procreative period of life. The general rule in nature is that individuals rear their own offspring to the point where these can become procreant, and then the parents die. We are one of the few species that has been granted a third season of life, the third age, relatively free of direct parental responsibility. This third age is not an accident, a modern by-product of good nutrition or Medicare; indeed, it is in the most rugged mountain environments, those furthest from clinics and Medicare, that we are most apt to find longevous people and even centenarians. The third age, the last twenty or so years of our three score and ten, granted to the average human appears to represent a relatively unique species adaptation, the outcome of a special evolutionary process. Species adaptations are replayed as patterns of individual growth; individual development recapitulates, within the individual lifespan, the long journey of species evolution. Accordingly, on the individual level, the attainment of elderhood must represent the outcome of a special developmental process.

The evidence for a developmental framework of the third age is read clearly enough in the historical and cross-cultural record; logical necessity requires that we move to a developmental perspective in regard to the study and understanding of elderhood. If we are to have a true science of gerontology, one that can lead to useful applications, then the question, "Why aging?" must be raised in regard to all the major domains—physical, psychological, and social—that bear on the aging process. Meanwhile, though the literature of humanistic psychology is full of sentimental psychobabble about the "growth of wisdom" and "serenity" in later life, we are still enormously far away from any precise understanding. I submit that current directions in personality research—particularly those coming from the reigning schools of social and humanistic psychology—can only retard the necessary movement toward a truly developmental psychology of late adulthood. Unfortunately, for reasons which I will attempt to explain, the dominant schools of psychology can neither study nor even acknowledge the evolutionary component that is intrinsic to any passage—early in life or late in life—of human development.

The foregoing can be better understood if we consider a short but profound statement by the great anthropologist Ralph Linton (Kardiner and Linton, 1945): "In some ways each man is like all other men; in some ways each man is like some other men; and in some ways each man is like no other man."

Linton's first level, concerning the ways in which each man is like all other men, refers to the human species as a distinct entity, with certain defining appetites and potentials; it also refers to the generic human characteristics that contribute to species survival—and to its particular problems. Specifically, the first level refers to human biopsychology: the reservoir of elemental appetites and developmental possibilities that underwrite the physical survival of the individual and, through sexual reproduction, the species as a whole. When Kipling wrote, "the colonel's lady and Rosie O'Grady are sisters under the skin," he was exploring, poetically, the implications of Linton's first level. In addition, Linton's first level concerns the interface at which psyche and soma meet, where the requirements of our bodies for nourishment, for comfort, for pleasurable sensation, and for propagation resonate and extend themselves in fairly standard ways through the psychological system. Thus, under conditions of group panic, group excitement, or group hunger, the learned distinctions of gender, social class, and individual history fade away. Auschwitz is a poor place to study individual differences; it is a good place to study aspects of what I will call Level I functioning.

Paradoxically, Linton's first level finds its best metaphor in geophysics, in the continental plates that shift and grind in their slow march deep below the earth's surface. These plates have never been directly observed, and their very existence can only be inferred from surface phenomena. Nevertheless, any discussion of particular earthquakes or volcanic activity that does not take these subsurface structures and their associated tectonic forces into account would not be seriously considered.

Linton's second level—"each man is like some other men"—refers to the collective and cultural frameworks of human existence. A society includes those individuals who either share common understandings, or, at the very least, share common ways of communicating their diverse understandings. At this level, which I will call Level II, we also look for the trained capacities that individuals devote to preserving the social order and to preserving themselves, in their own minds and in the eyes of their fellows, as social beings. In sum, seen from this level, the individual no longer appears to be driven by some innate nature, but by imposed conformities: the language, values, laws, and customs of a particular human group.

Linton's third level, concerning the ways in which "each man is like no other men," refers to the unique as distinct from the social self, to the means by which we preserve—again, for others and for ourselves—our sense of specialness and individuality. I will call this Level III.

Taken together, these three stations of selfhood trace the arc of any major sequence in human development. Thus, Level I represents the peremptory or tectonic phase of development; the phase of diffuse excitation that will not be denied and that shakes up the individual's physical and psychological establishment. Level I activity finds expression in the preverbal symbolism of body language, parapraxes, and dreams. Such stimulation urges the individual toward those psychosocial habitats in which the surgent tensions can be relieved, and in which the emerging potentials can find their appropriate sponsors. The maturing individual pushes proactively into facilitating habitats that vary according to the individual's age and stage of development: The earliest habitats consist entirely of the mother, or some maternal equivalent, but become more complex, more peopled, with the passage of time. Thus, such developmental contexts become increasingly complex in their organization, personnel, and physical range. As development proceeds, social habitats grow to include primary caretakers, then teachers, peers in the schoolyard or playing field, potential mates, and even enemies encountered on the battlefield.

These habitats vary across societies in their furnishings and their particular personnel: In some societies, the baby is received by a wet nurse rather than by a biological mother; teachers may be found in a religious seminary, in a military school, or in a progressive "classroom without walls." But across societies, the essential structure and sequencing of habitats/contexts remains the same: We meet the mother/wet nurse before we encounter the teacher; and we usually do our stint in school and on the playing field before we seek out or get sent to the battlefield. And again, no matter how they dress or speak, the significant others encountered in the habitat take up, in various ways, the task of fitting the individual to the average demands of the local psychosocial habitat: to introduce the individual to the local language, the local proprieties and conformities, the proper expression of acceptable emotions, the local myths and rituals, and the accepted ways of demonstrating that one is an accredited member of the "people." The raw appetites and unformed potentials of the tectonic phase lead to the special habitat in which particular appetites may be satisfied or emerging capacities sharpened. Nonetheless, in all passages of human development, the task of training potentials into the executive capacities that serve person and society is conceded to the conditions of social nurture: the models, instructors and intimates who turn one into a Level II individual—a person who is like some others.

In the psychosocial habitat, the appetites, and urgent potentials that drive the individual there are muted in favor of the outer, contextual demands and pressures set by the models, teachers, and intimates encountered there. But the tectonic energies of Level I do not completely subside within the habitat. Irrational needs, as well as expectations, preferences, and transferences formed in other settings, will continue to direct the individual's choices among available activities, and among the models, teachers, and intimates that prove most congenial. In other words, within the general setting of the habitat, using its standard raw materials, maturing individuals construct a unique, idiosyncratic arrangement of intimates, associates, favorites, and enemies. Out of the standard materials of the habitat, each person makes a private arrangement—a niche—unique to that person. The niche is the special "life structure" (Levinson et al., 1978) that marks that person as being like no one else. The Level III niches form within the arena of Level II; but the process that leads to increased differentiation is still driven by the urgencies that characterize Level I.

I have already used the term "tectonics"; and dynamic geology does provide us with an apt metaphor for understanding of typical processes in human development and the particular contribution of Level I phenomena to them. Thus, the creation of a landscape begins with powerful events, usually, the collisions or subduction of continental plates: These determine the gross features—the fault lines, the mountain ranges, the plateaus, the volcanoes, and rift valleys of the basic landscape. The surrounding atmosphere of wind, water, and water vapor, energized by the sun's heat, eventually erodes the gross geological features, and also determines the placement of ice caps, oceans, lakes, river valleys, and river canyons. Thus, plate tectonics are not entirely responsible for the Grand Canyon. These subsurface forces caused the land to rise into hills, but it was the rain-fed, cascading Colorado River that cut a new bed through the lifted lands. Finally, the character of local rock and strata determined Level III phenomena—the special features of canyon bend, color, and depth that signify the "one and only" Grand Canyon to us. In order to understand that great creation, in all its uniqueness, we do need a theory of hydraulics, to understand the canyon-cutting power of descending waters; we also need to know the geology of sedimentary stone, to understand particular rock formations. Still, if plate tectonics had not done the essential work, the canyon-creating action of water on rock would never have taken place.

Similarly, as we consider the myriad outcomes of human development in the form of ego executive capacities, and complex life structures, we should never forget the raw peremptory phase. However, in the social sciences generally, and in the study of human development particularly, we increasingly ignore Level I, the tectonics of personality formation. More and more, attention is concentrated exclusively on Levels II and III. In effect, we focus on the psychological forces and influences that are available to consciousness, even though these may shape the form, quality, and direction of our thought. Bruno Bettelheim once remarked to me that psychoanalysis was going out of fashion because people do not like to be reminded that "They are not the masters even in their own mental house." To consider Level I phenomena causes, in effect, a narcissistic wound.

Level I phenomena are also discredited by strict methodologists: They are hard to measure. But again, the science of plate tectonics could also be criticized, and on the same grounds: Nobody has ever seen a continental plate, much less observed its movement. The slow crawl of such plates can only be inferred from obscure surface traces. Nevertheless, as noted earlier, the theory of plate tectonics helps us to relate many seemingly unrelated—though measurable—surface phenomena. It would be hard to imagine a contemporary study of a particular earthquake or a suddenly active volcano that did not relate these phenomena to local tectonic forces.

But in the social sciences, the forces that originate in our dynamic human nature are denied, and, in the name of political correctness, all influence over human behavior is conceded to the variables of our social nurture: class, cohort, and economic circumstance. From this basically politicized point of view, there are no universals: Boys are more aggressive than girls, and go gleefully to battle, not because they are intrinsically more competitive, but because they have played for too long with toy soldiers instead of dolls. Not only does this kind of thinking lead to silly conclusions, not only does it stretch the data of human experience out of shape, it also denies the contribution of the body to the mind and soul, and rams a mind-body dichotomy into the very heart of the social sciences. Furthermore, even when Level I phenomena are not completely denied, they are too frequently misread. The same mistaken thinking that leads to the denial of the sensate body, leads us to study Level I phenomena—unconscious motives and appetites— with tools that were originally crafted to the study of Level II and Level III phenomena. Thus, contemporary psychologists typically use self-report instruments—those that register the individual's conscious self-presentation and public relations—to study asocial, unconscious motives. Instruments crafted to study social conformity and individual self-image are misapplied to study the kinds of conflictual appetites that, precisely because they violate social norms, are usually kept out of consciousness. To continue our geologic metaphor, this is equivalent to studying subsurface phenomena, such as earthquakes, with instruments crafted for the study of surface phenomena, such as hurricanes. An anemometer cannot do the work of a seismograph.

Translated into gerontological practice, this kind of false scientism has retarded the development of a sophisticated developmental psychology of aging. For example, Costa and McCrae (1976) have used self-report questionnaires to isolate what they assert to be essential personality traits (neuroticism, for example, and "openness"), and they find no change in the ratings of these variables across the whole adult life span. Their conclusion: There is no so called "mid-life crisis," and measurable—and, by their logic, essential—personality traits are fixed across the whole adult life span. But the Costa-McCrae doctrine is refuted by studies based on the more subjective but also more sensitive projective tests; these psychic seismographs routinely pick up the tracings of orderly change in later life at the covert layers of personality.

But instruments that study the unconscious in its own idiom are, like the unconscious itself, suspect in conventional psychology; and so we move to a picture of adult personality in which all determining power is conceded to contextual influences, and the possibility of true development in the later years is ruled out. Costa and McCrae can only tell us that "open" individuals remain so; they cannot tell us about age change in sensitivity—what are older individuals open to? And what do they close off? As Michael Lind (1991) recently noted, all theories having to do with the evolutionary and biopsychological capacities of the human body—Darwinism, for example, and more recently, sociobiology—are routinely disregarded by the humanities; and as the social sciences and psychology become more "humanistic," they too have ignored the charged, sensual body. The result is the oversocialized and overculturalized view of the person that dominates the social sciences today. The body has been driven out of our theories of psychological growth, and our methods and instruments confirm the antisomatic prejudices. But Freud taught us that repression does not wipe out powerful appetites and their associated fantasies; instead, these go underground, to return in the form of neurotic symptoms.

An equivalent process is taking place in geropsychology: The developmental role of the appetitive body is denied, but the forgotten body returns in our gerontology texts as a portrait of pathology, a collection of decaying organs, and the source of organic depressions. When we overlook the body in its more forceful aspect, when we deny the tectonics of Level I, our picture of aging inevitably becomes one of dissolution rather than development. And no amount of sentimental prating about "wisdom" and "serenity" in later life can compensate for the absence of a truly developmental psychology of later life.

Now I will briefly report some of the findings, pertaining exclusively to the Level I or universal aspects of the aging process, that have been developed by my students and me. All findings are based on cross-cultural and clinical investigations utilizing open-ended interviews and projective instruments with male subjects. This selection summarizes research previously reported at greater length (Gutmann, 1987).

Content analysis of "naturalistic" interviews, projective test responses, and artistic productions reveals that, regardless of society, as men age there is a tectonic shift in their definitions of basic pleasure in the oral or "pregenital" direction. This "oral shift" of personality represents more than increased appreciation of groceries in later life. The new orientation towards satisfaction is developmental in nature in that it has modal reach as well as zonal specificity: High scores on the oral dimension correlate, across cultures, with passive themes in dreams and in Thematic Apperception Test (TAT) stories, and with visual eroticism. That is, as predicted by psychoanalytic libido theory, the pleasure in seeing and looking increases in step with heightened concerns around food. Furthermore, these changes are essentially psychological in nature in that they correlate with life stage rather than age per se. Thus, as men and women emerge from the period of parental emergency, they are liberated from the stringent discipline of parenthood, and they can begin to live out and reexperience the pleasures that were kept on hold, for the sake of the children, during their time of active child rearing. As the oral appetites revive, there is an associated return to the maternal figures—the mother in the past, and the wife in the present—most directly associated with oral pleasure. Older men routinely transform the wife into "Mom."

Again, the surgent changes of the postparental period can lead to new growth, to the maturation of new executive capacities, or to new vulnerabilities, and even to late-onset psychopathology. Thus when we investigate the lives of men who have become clinical casualties in the later years, we find that a man who never adequately separated—in the psychological sense—from the mother, cannot separate from his wife, even when she creates a rupture by refusing the "Mom" status that these mother's sons would impose on her. When the ascendant wife, newly liberated from child care, refuses the maternal role, the "oral" husband, intolerant of the imposed separation, often develops symptoms, usually of a psychosomatic nature. In effect, these men say to their liberated wives, "If you will not mother me, at least take care of my ailing heart, my diseased liver, or my needy stomach."

In sum, Level I data concerning the tectonics of the male life cycle help us to understand the sources of developmental change in the later years, but also the predispositions to late-onset psychopathology. Armed with such understanding, we can intervene more effectively in these disorders.

Thus, research into the neglected terrain of Level I opens up new domains and new answers to the problems and possibilities of the aging psyche. Getting back to the title question, I would like to see Level I research finally legitimized for geriatrics—and before the year 2010.

REFERENCES

Costa, P.T., and McCrae, R.R. (1976). Age differences in personality structure: A cluster-analytic approach. *Journal of Gerontology,* 31:564–570.

Gutmann, D. (1987). *Reclaimed powers.* New York: Basic Books.

Kardiner, A., and Linton, R. (1945). *The psychological frontiers of society.* New York: Columbia University Press.

Levinson, D.J., Darrow, C.N., Klein, E.B., Levinson, M.H., and McKee, B. (1978). *Seasons of a man's life.* New York: Knopf.

Lind, M. (1991). The 2 cultures (continued). *Commentary,* 92 (N2):31–35.

The Psychology of Adulthood and Aging

Comments on "Wishful Thinking"

Dan P. McAdams

I am happy to comment briefly on David Gutmann's "Wishful Thinking" for geropsychiatry in the twenty-first century as manifest in the preceding chapter and in his provocative book, *Reclaimed Powers: Toward a New Psychology of Men and Women in Later Life* (Gutmann, 1987), from my own standpoint as a personality and developmental psychologist. My remarks come out of my own observations of how psychologists have studied the course of "normal" (that is, nonclinical) adulthood over the past fifteen years and my own recent contributions to this empirical and theoretical literature.

Gutmann asserts that the dominant approaches in contemporary psychology are poorly positioned to explore what he terms Level I phenomena in adulthood and aging; that is, the basic level of human nature at which adults reveal their fundamental commonalities, rooted in biology and the unconscious. By contrast, explorations of Level II proceed apace (e.g., McCrae and Costa, 1990), as psychologists continue to count and classify so that they may determine ways in which each adult is like some other adults; in other words, ways in which adults may be grouped into types or along the lines of traits. At Level II, psychologists examine individual differences that, for the most part, are a product of culture and learning. Finally, Level III reveals how each individual adult is unique, like no other adult. Researchers such as Levinson (1978) have explored this terrain through such concepts as the individual life structure. All three levels are related to each other in complex ways, Gutmann maintains. Yet if psychologists continue to reject Level I, their efforts at understanding will fail.

From my own vantage point, I would include within Level I, various approaches that conceptualize the adult life course as a well-defined sequence of transitions. One need not focus exclusively on biology or the unconscious to produce a theory of adulthood that centers on how all adults are alike.

Indeed, in certain respects the psychosocial theories of Erikson and Levinson speak to Level I concerns in delineating a sequence of stages or eras through which adults pass on their journeys through life, journeys that are shaped by both biology and society. In the realm of cognitive development, Labouvie-Vief echoes Carl Jung and certain dialectical theorists in suggesting that men and women move from an "acquisitive and focused mastery of symbol systems" in early adulthood to "a focus on inner dynamics, on private experience, on the continuity of autobiographical memories" after midlife (Labouvie Vief, DeVoe, and Bulka, 1989, p. 425).

Erikson, Levinson, Labouvie Vief, and other "stage theorists" (e.g., Gould, Kohlberg, Loevinger, Havighurst) propose normative sequences in personality, social, and cognitive development during the adult years—sequences potentially applicable to all (or most) adult lives. These theorists are primarily concerned, therefore, with how a particular adult is like all other adults. These Level I perspectives tend to be criticized, as I see it, not so much because they emphasize nature over nurture but because they tend to sweep away variations from the normative sequence. Many researchers and practitioners do not like the idea that there is one and only one pathway through adulthood: one encompassing sequence of stages, stances, eras, or seasons. In addition, many find it difficult to believe that adults really change all that much, as much as stage models suggest. While I sympathize, therefore, with Gutmann's concern that Level I approaches are being ignored, and while I applaud his own attempts to explore Level I through such projective assessments as the Thematic Apperception Test (TAT), I do not think that psychologists' skepticism about these perspectives reflects their tendency to deny the body and the intrapsychic mysteries buried in human nature. To the contrary, it seems to me that biological approaches are on the ascendency in personality and developmental psychology overall, reflecting the mounting influence of sociobiology and behavior genetics (cf. Buss, 1984; Scarr, 1987).

Level II in Gutmann's analysis refers to individual differences in personality and cognitive functioning in adulthood. As I see it, Level II approaches tend to view adulthood from the perspective of the stability of features. Trait approaches, such as the influential "Big Five" model of personality dispositions (McCrae and Costa, 1990), conceive of the adult as a configuration of discrete features: bipolar, linear dimensions such as "extraversion vs. introversion" or "neuroticism vs. emotional stability." Adults may be rank-ordered along fundamental trait continua, typically according to self-report ratings. An impressive body of research shows that these rank orderings remain relatively stable across the adult life span (cf. Conley, 1985; McCrae and Costa, 1990). In other words, if a person tends to be relatively extraverted (say, seventy-fifth percentile) at age twenty-five, he or she is likely to be relatively extraverted (again, around the seventy-fifth percentile) at age fifty. Furthermore, few age differences in mean level of traits appear in either cross-sectional or longitudinal studies. According to McCrae and Costa (1990), "The data suggest to us that personality change is the exception rather than the rule after age 30; somewhere in the decade between 20 and 30, individuals attain a configuration of traits that will characterize them for years to come" (p. 10).

In the same way that Level I perspectives are not necessarily rooted in biology or the unconscious, Level II viewpoints do not presuppose cultural or learning explanations for traits. It would seem to be just as plausible to suggest that a particular adult is like some other adults for reasons of biology as for reasons of socialization, and indeed most sophisticated perspectives today would argue for an interaction of the two. Furthermore, influential studies of identical and fraternal twins published in the 1980s (cf. Tellegen et al., 1988) provide compelling evidence for genetic influences on traits. As much as 50 percent of the variance in ratings of most personality traits appears to be a function of genetic inheritance, with the remaining variance attributable to nonshared environment effects and measurement error (Dunn and Plomin, 1990). Explanations for individual differences that rely on socialization and culture are viewed with increasing skepticism in many circles. Contrary to Gutmann, I do not think that psychologists today are painting a "picture of adult personality in which all determining power is conceded to contextual influences." I do not think that we need to fear an "oversocialized and overculturalized view of the person that dominates the social sciences today." If anything, the fear in the year 2000 may go in the other direction, as more and more psychologists today seem willing to consider the possibility that, in the realm of traits at least, biology is (almost) destiny.

Level III addresses how a particular adult is like no other adult. In Gutmann's words, this is the level whereby we each express "our sense of specialness and individuality." As I see it, this is the level that subsumes the critical domain of human identity and the self. Here I add some of my own wishful thinking. Beyond the normative sequences of transitions (stages) and the individual stability of features (traits), there is a third realm of human functioning that concerns how each adult defines who he or she is in the world, as an individuated person in a social context who strives to find meaning, pattern, unity, and purpose in life. If stages spell out a normative series of changes for all adults and if traits specify how each adult brings to life a characteristic signature of personality style, then identity is the adult's construction of a self that renders the stages, the traits, and all else that is salient in the adult's world personally meaningful. While I support Gutmann's call for a more concerted examination of Level I, I believe that Level III has suffered at least as much neglect and rejection. Yet the exquisitely nuanced patterning of the single life in context should not be solely the subject of the biographer or the poet. There is room here for the social sciences if they are willing to focus unswervingly on the person; on the evolving meanings of the single adult life in cultural and historical context.

Like David Gutmann's, therefore, my own wish list is something of a projective test, reflecting my own intellectual agenda and professional investments. My own empirical work of late falls within Level III, as I have begun to explore in detail the the identity-conferring life stories that adults construct to provide their lives with unity and purpose (cf. McAdams, 1990). Thankfully, I also see other social scientists moving in the direction of Level III. Recent investigations of life scripts (Tomkins, 1987), life tasks (Cantor, 1990), possible selves (Ryff, 1991), and dialogical selves (Hermans et al., 1992) point to a resurgence of interest among personality and developmental psychologists in the unique patterning of individual lives. Furthermore, the growing acceptance of qualitative and interpretive methodologies (e.g., Denzin, 1989; McAdams and Ochberg, 1988) provides researchers with golden opportunities to explore the richness and complexity of women's and men's lives in a systematic and scientific manner.

My wish for the twenty-first century is that these trends will continue, that their attendant conceptualizations and methodologies will mature, and that psychologists will begin to explore the linkages and relationships among Gutmann's three levels: linkages and relationships that may arise when each of the three is given its appropriate scientific due.

REFERENCES

Buss, D.M. (1984). Evolutionary biology and personality psychology: Toward a conception of human nature and individual differences. *American Psychologist*, 39:361–377.

Cantor, N. (1990). From thought to behavior: "Having" and "doing" in the study of personality and cognition. *American Psychologist*, 45:735–750.

Conley, J.J. (1985). A personality theory of adulthood and aging. In R. Hogan and W. Jones (eds.), *Perspectives in personality*, 81–116, Vol. 1. Greenwich, CT: JAI Press.

Denzin, N.K. (1989). *Interpretive biography*. Newbury Park, CA: Sage.

Dunn, J., and Plomin, R. (1990). *Separate lives: Why siblings are so different*. New York: Basic Books.

Gutmann, D. (1987). *Reclaimed powers: Toward a new psychology of men and women in later life*. New York: Basic Books.

Hermans, H.J.M., Kempen, H.J.G., and van Loon, R.J.P. (1992). The dialogical self: Beyond individualism and rationalism. *American Psychologist*, 47:23–33.

Labouvie-Vief, G., DeVoe, M., and Bulka, D. (1989). Speaking about feelings: Conceptions of emotion across the life span. *Psychology and Aging*, 4:425–437.

Levinson, D.J. (1978). *The seasons of a man's life*. New York: Ballantine.

McAdams, D.P. (1990). Unity and purpose in human lives: The emergence of identity as a life story. In A.I. Rabin, R.A. Zucker, R.A. Emmons, and S. Frank (eds.), *Studying persons and lives*, 148–200. New York: Springer.

McAdams, D.P., and Ochberg, R.L. (eds.) (1988). *Psychobiology and life narratives*. Durham, NC: Duke University Press.

McCrae, R.R., and Costa, P.T., Jr. (1990). *Personality in adulthood*. New York: Guilford Press.

Ryff, C.D. (1991). Possible selves in adulthood and old age: A tale of shifting horizons. *Psychology and Aging*, 6:286–295.

Scarr, S. (1987). Distinctive environments depend on genotypes. *Behavioral and Brain Sciences*, 10:38–39.

Tellegen, A., Lykken, D.J., Bouchard, T.J., Jr., Wilcox, K.J., Segal, N.L., and Rich, S. (1988). Personality similarity in twins reared apart and together. *Journal of Personality and Social Psychology*, 54:1031–1039.

Tomkins, S.S. (1987). Script theory. In J. Aronoff, A.I. Rabin, and R.A. Zucker (eds.), *The emergence of personality*, 147–216. New York: Springer.

Explorations in Generativity in Later Years

Dan P. McAdams

Shirley Rock* looks like a battle-scarred veteran of the Chicago streets. A tough-talking, chain-smoking, late-middle-aged woman who cuts an intimidating first impression, Shirley reports that she spent her late twenties and early thirties raising two children and running a number of extremely profitable brothels. The other den mothers at the Girl Scout meetings had no idea that Shirley doubled as a madame, or that she was deeply involved in organized crime, or that she would eventually do time in a state penitentiary, some of it in solitary confinement or, as she puts it, "in the hole." Today, at age fifty-seven, Shirley is a church minister for an inner-city congregation, having received her "call from God"—her words—at the age of fifty-one, one year later than her grandmother prophesied long ago when she told the ten-year-old Shirley, "God will call you home when you are fifty." Most of her work is what the church deems "social ministry," involving her in a wide range of activities ultimately aimed at serving the poor. She is responsible for establishing a neighborhood food pantry through which needy children and families are able to obtain free food, and she coordinates a series of "warming centers"—city shelters for the homeless. Shirley's is a life story about a bold sinner whose bold actions on behalf of the oppressed and the underprivileged—especially those of the younger generation—bespeak a creative and powerful sense of *generativity*.

In a very different way for perhaps very different reasons, Betty Swanson is just as generative. Betty occasionally does volunteer work at the food pantry that Shirley organized. But Betty is better known in the community as "the T-shirt lady." A couple of years ago Betty decided that the students enrolled in her twelve-year-old son's school needed appropriate

---

*Shirley Rock and other names for participants in this research are all pseudonyms. The cases are drawn from McAdams, D.P. (1993). *The stories we live by: Personal myths and the making of the self*. New York: William Morrow and Company.

clothing for gym class. She designed an elegant school logo, made arrangements to have the T-shirts and gym shorts made, and established a distribution and payment plan. Now school sweatshirts and jackets may also be purchased. When her son enrolled in the school, the cafeteria provided no lunch menus. Children found out what they were going to eat each day when they arrived at school. Betty felt that parents should know what was going to be served for lunch well in advance, so that they could make informed decisions concerning when their children were to bring bag lunches to school and when they were to purchase a hot lunch. Fighting intense opposition from the cafeteria employees and the school administration, Betty established a program to address this need, and now at the beginning of each month she sends a menu to each parent. In 1989, the parent-teacher organization voted Betty "Mother of the Year." Betty's accomplishments are impressive but perhaps not all that dramatic until one learns that some of her doctors are surprised that she is not yet dead. In the last ten years, Betty has suffered a massive stroke, two major heart attacks, and brain damage from an accident in which she fell out of a window and landed on her head. Once an accountant who was well paid for her work with numbers, she can no longer add or subtract. She is able to walk only with assistance from others; she speaks very slowly; and for each active day in her life—wherein, say, she attends church, or collects T-shirt orders, or volunteers time at the food pantry—she must rest in bed for two days afterward.

Daniel Kessinger is a forty-eight-year-old community organizer and executive director of a mental health agency. He has been married for twenty-five years. His wife, Lynette, is a social worker. They have a daughter in second grade. From his early involvement in the American civil rights movement through his two-year stint in the Kennedy Peace Corps to his current work as one who, in his words, "builds things and organizations that institute the values I have," Daniel has constructed a personal identity that is dominated by what I call a *generativity script*. A disarmingly unassuming man in public, he is not modest in private about his achievements, commitments, and aspirations. He believes that much of what he has accomplished he has done on his own. He sees himself as being similar in ways to Martin Luther King, Jr. But when asked if he sees King as a hero, Daniel answers, Not really. Um, to me, he's more like a colleague," Daniel remarks. "My life theme is creating a better world."

Generativity in Adulthood

Shirley Rock, Betty Swanson, and Daniel Kessinger are three of almost ninety adults that my associates and I have interviewed in the last three years as part of a large research project on generativity and adult development. The purpose of this chapter is to describe our recent and current explorations into the measurement and meaning of generativity in adult lives. I believe that our work on generativity may serve as a model for integrative life-span research in the 1990s and beyond. On a conceptual level, the work moves beyond "trait" (e.g., McCrae and Costa, 1990) and "stage" (e.g., Levinson, 1978) theories to articulate an interactional model of generative lives that explains both continuity and change in the adult years while emphasizing social context, social construction, and the profound effect of narrative in adult lives. On a methodological level, our work on generativity employs state-of-the-art quantitative measures administered to relatively large samples as well as in-depth qualitative investigations of particular adult lives in context.

The work begins with a theory, and the theory begins with Erik Erikson. Over forty years ago, Erikson (1950) introduced the concept of generativity in the context of a life-span theory of personality development. According to Erikson, generativity is "primarily the concern in establishing and guiding the next generation" (1963, p. 267). In Erikson's stage model, the polarity of *generativity vs. stagnation* is the psychosocial centerpiece of the seventh of eight major developmental stages, the stage loosely associated with the middle adulthood years. In the ideal Eriksonian scenario, the adult approaches the issue of generativity after resolving earlier developmental issues of adulthood: identity vs. role confusion (stage five) and intimacy vs. isolation (stage six). As Erikson conceived it, once the adult has consolidated a sense of who he or she is (identity) and established long-term bonds of intimacy through marriage and/or friendships, then he or she is psychosocially ready to make a commitment to the larger sphere of society as a whole and its continuation, even improvement, through the next generation. In generativity, the adult nurtures, teaches, leads, and promotes the next generation while generating life products and outcomes that aim to benefit the social system and promote its continuity from one generation to the next.

From Erikson's point of view, generativity may be expressed in bearing and raising children, in that parents are actively involved in providing for the next generation as epitomized in their own offspring. But not all parents are especially generative, Erikson maintained, and generativity is by no means limited to the domain of parenthood. One may be generative in a wide variety of life pursuits and in a vast array of life settings, as in work life and professional activities, volunteer endeavors, participation in religious and political organizations, neighborhood and community activism, friendships, and even one's leisure-time activities. Some of Erikson's most compelling examples of generativity appear in his psychobiographical explorations of the lives of Martin Luther and Mahatma Gandhi, both of whom appear to have been their most generative in the bright light of public action rather than in the private realms of friends and family.

Since Erikson introduced the term, generativity has been variously described as a "need," "drive," "concern," "task," and "issue." It has been couched in terms of biological and instinctual imperatives (a drive to reproduce oneself), philosophical and religious longings (a search for transcendence, symbolic immortality), developmental tasks (a stage in normal growth), and societal demands (the integration of the adult into a productive niche). It has been identified with behavior (child rearing), with motives and values (concern for preserving what is good and making things better), and with a general attitude toward life and the world (having a broad perspective, understanding one's place in the sequence of generations). Unlike personality traits such as extraversion (Eysenck), developmental stages such as formal operations (Piaget), and social processes such as causal attributions (Heider), generativity is not readily construed as a single, structured concept located "within" the individual. It is rather more like the construct of attachment (Bowlby) and certain other relational and multiply-contextualized constructs that require the scientist and the practitioner to operate on multiple levels and to take into consideration the particular relation or fit between the person and environment.

The construct of generativity links the person and the social world, existing as a configuration of characteristics arranged in a particular psychosocial space. Beginning with this insight, I have developed a new theory of generativity (McAdams and de St. Aubin, 1992) that draws upon some of Erikson's ideas while incorporating the important contributions of Kotre (1984), Becker (1973), Browning (1975), and earlier work of my own on life stories in adulthood (McAdams, 1984, 1985, 1987, 1990; McAdams, Ruetzel, and Foley, 1986). As Figure 1 shows, I view generativity as a configuration of seven psychosocial features constellated around the personal (individual) and cultural (societal) goal of providing for the next generation. I will briefly describe each of the seven features and then move to a discussion of how the model has generated different kinds of empirical research.

In Figure 1, Box 1 is labeled *cultural demand*. One of the reasons that generativity emerges as a psychosocial issue in the adult years is that society comes to demand that adults take responsibility for the next generation in their roles as parents, teachers, mentors, leaders, organizers, "creative ritualizers" (Browning, 1975), and "keepers of the meaning" (Vaillant and Milofsky, 1980). Generativity is prompted by the developmental expecta-

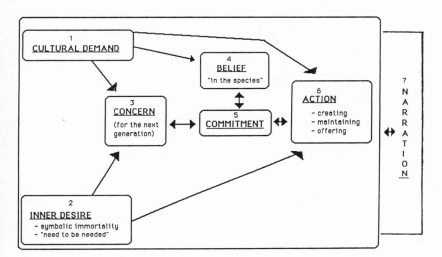

Figure 1. A model of generativity.

tions encoded in cultural demand. The demand is normative and age-graded. As adults move through their thirties and forties, those who are unable or unwilling to assume responsibility for the next generation, usually through family or work, are considered to be "off time" (Neugarten and Hagestad, 1976) and at odds with the "social clock" (Helson, Mitchell, and Moane, 1984). In addition to such developmental expectations, furthermore, the feature of cultural demand includes the many and varied occupational, ideological, and life-style opportunities and resources, as well as the constraints, that a particular society offers the adult to shape and motivate his or her generative inclinations. The feature of cultural demand in generativity, therefore, encompasses a wide spectrum of factors and forces external to the individual, and much of this domain remains unexplored in contemporary psychological and sociological research.

A second major source of generativity is *inner desire* (Box 2 in Figure 1). Generativity is frequently described in motivational terms as a need, instinct, or drive that produces a want or desire. Two kinds of desires have typically been identified: a desire for symbolic immortality and a desire to be needed by others. Kotre (1984) defines generativity as the "desire to invest one's substance in forms of life and work that will outlive the self" (p. 16). McAdams (1985) has invoked Becker's (1973) concept of "heroism" in describing generativity as partly the creation of a self-defining legacy that may be offered to society and to succeeding generations as a "gift." As such, adults desire to defy death by constructing legacies that live on. In addition, the generative adult expresses a "need to be needed" (Stewart, Franz and Layton, 1988, p. 56), a desire to nurture, assist, or be of some important use to other people. These two desires appear to be derivatives of two general motivational tendencies in human lives, aptly described by Bakan (1966) as *agency* and *communion* (cf. McAdams, 1988; Wiggins and Broughton, 1985). The desire for immortality appears to be one manifestation of agency: a tendency to assert, expand, and develop the self in a powerful and independent way. The desire to be needed by others appears to be one expression of communion, as the general tendency to relate to others in loving, caring, and intimate ways, even to be at one with others.

Cultural demand and inner desire combine to promote in adulthood a conscious *concern* for the next generation (Box 3 in Figure 1). Thus, developmental expectations about making a contribution to the next generation and inner desires for agentic immortality and communal nurturance come together in adulthood to influence how the person cares for and about the development of the next generation. Writes Erikson, "care" is "the widening *concern* for what has been generated by love, necessity, or accident" (1964, p. 131). Adults may translate their conscious concern into generative *commitment* (Box 5), taking responsibility for the next generation by making decisions and establishing goals for generative behavior. Commitment may be enhanced, or undermined, by what Erikson has called a "*belief* in the species" (1963, p. 267; Van de Water and McAdams, 1989). Belief in the species (Box 4) is a basic and general belief in the fundamental goodness and/or worthwhileness of human life specifically as envisioned for the future. To believe in the (human) species is to place hope in the advancement and betterment of human life in succeeding generations, even in the face of strong evidence of human destructiveness and deprivation. When such a belief is lacking, the adult may find it difficult to make a strong commitment to generative action, for it may appear that a generative effort may not be very useful anyway.

Guided by commitment—which itself is a product of cultural demand, inner desire, generative concern, and belief in the species—generative *action* (Box 6 in Figure 1) may be expressed in any of three loosely related guises: *creating*, *maintaining*, or *offering*. One meaning of generative behavior is to generate things and people—to be creative, productive, and fruitful, to "give birth," both literally and figuratively. Indeed, Stewart, Franz and Layton (1988) identify "productivity" as one of four main themes in generative content of personal documents, and McAdams (1985) emphasizes that generativity, unlike simple altruism or general prosocial behavior, involves the creation of a product or legacy "in one's own image," a powerful extension of the self. Equally generative is behavior that involves the conservation, restoration, preservation, cultivation, nurturance, or maintenance of that which is deemed worthy of such behavior, as in nurturing children, preserving good traditions, protecting the environment, and enacting rituals (in school, home, church) that link generations and assure continuity over time (Browning, 1975; Erikson, 1982). Finally, generative behavior sometimes involves the seemingly selfless "offering up" of that which has been created or maintained, passing something or someone on to (or as part of) the next generation as a gift, granting the gift its own autonomy and freedom (Becker, 1973; McAdams, 1985). For example, the truly generative father is both a self-aggrandizing creator and a self-sacrificing giver. Biologically and socially, he creates a child in his own image, working hard and long to promote the development of that child and to nurture all that is good and desirable in the child. But he must eventually grant the child her own autonomy, letting go when the time is right, letting the child develop her own identity, make her own decisions and commitments, and ultimately create those offerings of generativity that will distinguish that child as someone who was "given birth to" in order to "give birth to."

The last feature of generativity is *narration* (Box 7 in Figure 1). I conceive of generativity within the larger context of a life-story theory of adult identity (McAdams, 1985, 1987, 1990, 1993). According to this view, the adult defines him- or herself in society by fashioning a personal myth or life story that provides life with unity, purpose, and meaning. The process of identity development in adulthood, therefore, is the gradual construction and successive reconstruction of a personal myth integrating one's perceived past, present, and anticipated future while specifying ways in which the individual fits into and distinguishes him- or herself within the social world. Rather than viewing identity as residing neatly within a well-demarcated stage for late adolescence and young adulthood (à la Erikson), I suggest that identity development is *the* major psychosocial issue for the preponderance of one's adult lifetime, and generativity is incorporated within it as one of many different and important aspects. Contrary to Erikson, I do not conceive of identity and generativity as developmental stages. Rather, in the encompassing psychosocial context of an evolving personal myth (identity formation and reformation), an adult constructs and seeks to live out a *generativity script*, specifying what he or she plans to do in the future in order to leave a legacy of the self for future generations.

The generativity script, then, is an inner narration of the adult's own awareness of where efforts to be generative fit into his or her own personal history, into contemporary society and the social world he or she inhabits, and, in some extraordinary cases, within the scope of society's own encompassing history. The generativity script, which may change markedly over the life course, functions to address the narrative need in identity for a "sense of an ending" (Charme, 1984; Ricoeur, 1984), a satisfying vision or plan concerning how, even as one's life will eventually end, some aspect of the self will live on through one's generative efforts. The generativity script enables the personal myth (identity) to assume the form of "giving birth to." As Erikson writes, in midlife and later, the adult is increasingly likely to define him- or herself as, "I am what survives me" (1968, p. 141).

Quantitative Assessments of Concern, Commitment, and Action

To date, my associates and I have developed and validated three quantitative measures of generativity and have employed these measures in a number of studies of normal, well-functioning adults. With respect to the theory of generativity sketched in Figure 1, the three measures focus respectively on the features of generative concern, generative commitment, and generative action.

To assess individual differences in the extent to which adults are consciously *concerned* with making a contribution to the next generation, my students and I (at Loyola University of Chicago, 1987–1989) developed a twenty-item self-report scale entitled the Loyola Generativity Scale (McAdams and de St. Aubin, 1992). For each item on the scale, the adult is asked to rate the extent to which he or she agrees with or endorses the sentiment expressed. Derived from a careful reading of the major theoretical writings on generativity, the scale includes items such as: "I try to pass along the knowledge I have gained through my experiences" and "I feel as though my contributions will exist after I die." The scale exhibits good internal consistency and temporal stability (two indices of reliability), and it does not appear to be strongly associated with the tendency simply to say good things about the self, or what psychometricians call the response set of "social desirability." Scores on the Loyola Generativity Scale (LGS) appear to be modestly positively associated with independent self-report measures of nurturance, empathy, dominance, affiliation, and achievement, and with self-report assessments of life satisfaction. In other words, adults scoring highly in generative concern tend also to report high levels of motivations toward helping others, empathizing with others, leading others, engaging others in friendly relationships, and achieving goals in life, and they tend also to be relatively well satisfied with their lives (Guyot et al, 1991; McAdams and de St. Aubin, 1992; de St. Aubin and McAdams, 1995; Nestor, 1989).

LGS scores are modestly associated with parental status, but only for men. In one study, fathers scored higher than other men on generative concern, even after age and marital status were controlled (McAdams and de St. Aubin, 1992). With respect to mothers, however, generative concern does not appear to be linked to parental status. Generative concern does appear to be implicated, however, in the degree of involvement both mothers and fathers show in their children's educations. In a survey of over 350 parents whose children attend public and private schools in Chicago, Nakagawa (1991) found that LGS scores predicted the extent to which parents were actively involved in their children's education, even after demographic factors such as family income and parental education were controlled. Parents scoring high on generative concern, as assessed on a short form of the LGS, were more likely to attend parent-teacher meetings, volunteer to work in the schools, help in fund-raising, work on school committees, and so on, compared to parents scoring low on generative concern. By contrast, psychological measures of locus of control and self-esteem were unrelated to parental involvement.

In the first systematic study in the psychological literature of age differences in generativity (McAdams, de St. Aubin, and Logan, 1993), we administered measures of generativity and other psychological factors to 152 adults in three discrete age cohorts living in Evanston, Illinois. The three age groups were young adults (between the ages of twenty-two and twenty-seven), midlife adults (aged thirty-seven to forty-two), and older adults (aged sixty-seven to seventy-two). The three cohorts represent a random stratified sampling of residents in this heterogeneous, middle- to upper-middle-class community. Figure 2 shows the results for the LGS. As might be expected from the literature on generativity, midlife women show higher levels of generativity than their younger and older counterparts. The results for men, however, do not fit this pattern, with young and midlife men showing comparable levels, followed by a sharp dropoff among older men.

To assess generative *commitment*, we asked adults in the Evanston sample to list their ten most important "personal strivings" (McAdams, de St. Aubin, and Logan, 1993). Following a procedure developed by Emmons (1986), personal strivings are described as "the things you typically or characteristically are trying to do in your everyday life" and "the objectives or goals that you are trying to accomplish or attain." Emmons has argued that reports of personal strivings provide a useful vehicle for assessing individual differences in the goals and objectives to which adults feel commitment in their daily lives. In our study, we asked each adult to write a sentence about

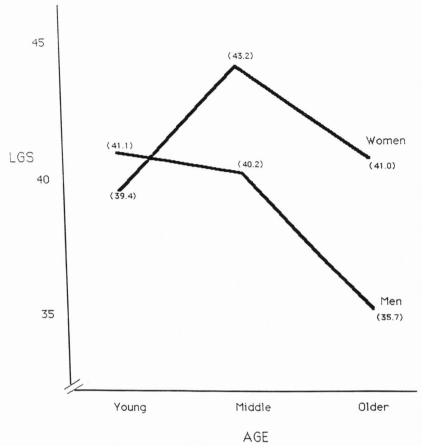

Figure 2. *Generative concern by age and sex. From McAdams, de St. Aubin, and Logan (1993).*

each striving, and then we coded each sentence for three themes of generativity: (1) involvement with younger people or members of the next generation; (2) providing care or help for others; and (3) engaging in creative activities and/or attempting to act in such a way as to make a significant contribution to society. Verbatim examples of a few especially generative strivings are reproduced in Table 1.

Table 1. Examples of Generative Strivings

I typically try to . . .

manage my business to have enough profit to send my son to college.

help my daughter-in-law who now has terminal cancer.

not waste food by giving extra to a shelter.

assist a candidate running for election.

be supportive to my friends.

agitate for justice and peace in my neighborhood and in the world.

write creatively, be it plays, musicals, songs, letters, etc.

teach my students in a way that imparts skills but also gives them a deeper sense of being a professional.

create new programs at work.

be a good father.

help people commit their lives to God.

explain teenage experiences to my son and help work through difficult situations.

imagine a better world, a positive future.

accomplish something worthwhile in my work and personal life that benefits and helps protect the environment.

be kind to my employees.

restore confidence and self-esteem in a son who went bankrupt.

make my oldest daughter, a teacher, realize she can't change all things for all people; she's an idealist.

The results of our research show a positive correlation between generative commitments, as assessed via strivings, and generative concern, as indexed in scores on the LGS. As one might predict, adults who show high levels of conscious concern for the next generation also tend to have more daily goals and objectives associated with generativity. The relationship between age cohort on the one hand and generative commitments (strivings) on the other is shown in Figure 3. As can be seen, midlife and older adults show significantly higher levels of generative commitments compared to younger adults. There is no dropoff among the elderly. Indeed, the group with the highest levels of generative commitments, as assessed via strivings, are the elderly women.

With respect to generative *action* or behavior, we administered a behavior checklist consisting of fifty items phrased as behavioral acts. Of the total, forty acts were chosen to suggest generative behaviors and ten were chosen as acts that appeared irrelevant to generativity. Examples of purported

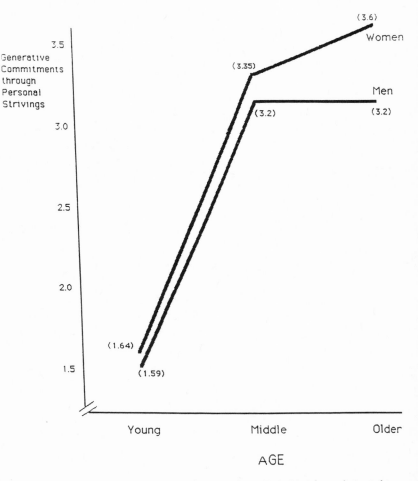

Figure 3. Generative commitments by sex and age. From McAdams, de St. Aubin, and Logan (1993).

generative acts include "taught somebody a skill," "read a story to a child," "attended a neighborhood or community meeting," "donated blood," and "produced a piece of art or craft." The generative acts covered a wide spectrum and included some acts that would be expected to have a very low base rate (e.g., "invented something," "became a parent"). By and large, each act corresponded to one of the three main behavioral manifestations of generativity: creating, maintaining, or offering. Examples of acts purportedly unrelated to generativity included "went to see a play or movie," "participated in an athletic sport," and "purchased a new car or major appliance."

On the behavior checklist, the adult responds to each act by specifying how often during the previous two months he or she has performed the given act. The adult marks a "0" if the act has not been performed during the previous two months, a "1" if the act has been performed once during that period, and a "2" if the act has been performed more than once during the previous two months. In two different studies (McAdams and de St. Aubin, 1992; McAdams, de St. Aubin, and Logan, 1993), we have collected act frequencies for generativity and found that the scores on generative action from the behavior checklist are positively and strongly correlated with scores on the LGS. In other words, people with strong concerns for the next generation tend to act in ways commensurate with those concerns.

Figure 4 displays age cohort results from our Evanston sample. As

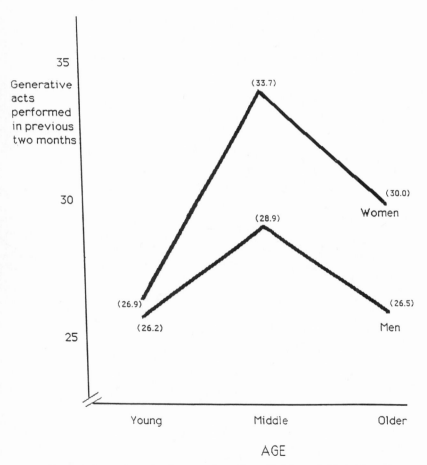

Figure 4. Generative action by age and sex. From McAdams, de St. Aubin, and Logan (1993).

can be clearly seen, generative actions tend to peak in midlife for both men and women, with young adults and older adults showing significantly lower scores than their midlife counterparts. In addition, there is a nonsignificant trend for women to score slightly higher on generative acts than men. The trend is especially apparent when comparing the relatively high scores for midlife and older women to the scores shown by midlife and older men.

In sum, new quantitative methodologies for assessing individual differences in generativity converge nicely on this multiply-manifested construct from three different angles: generative concern, generative commitments, and generative action. Midlife adults (aged thirty-seven to forty-two) appear to display higher levels of generative behavior (frequency of generative actions) in daily life than younger adults in their mid-twenties and older adults in their late sixties and early seventies. A similar curvilinear trend in generative concern reveals itself for women, but not as clearly for men. When it comes to generative commitments, however, older adults show levels that equal or exceed those shown at midlife. Young adults, by contrast, show very low levels of generative commitments, suggesting that they have yet to structure their daily lives in terms of goals and projects linked to strong generative commitment. In addition, the new measures of generativity predict such personally significant phenomena as life satisfaction, empathy, and nurturance needs, as well as such socially valuable behaviors as parents' involvement in their children's education.

Generative Narration: The Social Construction of Generative Lives

The concept of *narration* in generativity refers to the way in which an adult makes sense of his or her generative efforts in the context of his or her self-defining life story, or personal myth. In recent years, a growing number of social scientists and clinical practitioners have entertained the possibility that human beings, especially when they reach adulthood, tend to define themselves in terms of integrative and animating stories (Bruner, 1986; Charme, 1984; Feinstein and Krippner, 1988; Hermans, Kempen, and van Loon, 1992; Linde, 1992; Schafer, 1983; Shotter and Gergen, 1989; Spence, 1982). An emerging "narrative psychology" explores what Sarbin (1986) deems "the storied nature of human conduct." The central proposition of my own life-story model of adult identity is that contemporary adults find unity and purpose in their lives through the ongoing construction and elaboration of an integrative narrative of self. The philosopher Alasdair MacIntyre puts it well:

The unity of a human life is the unity of a narrative quest. Quests

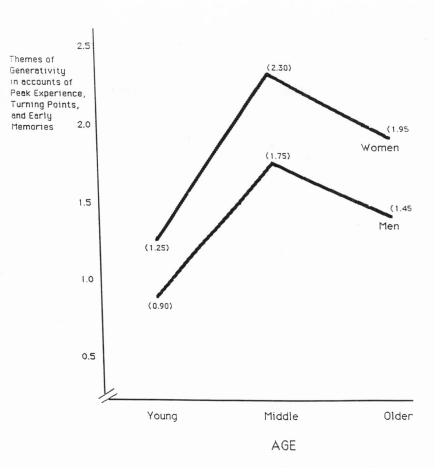

Figure 5. Generative narration by sex and age. From McAdams, de St. Aubin, and Logan (1993).

sometimes fail, are frustrated, abandoned, or dissipated into distractions; and human lives may in all these ways also fail. But the only criteria for success or failure in a human life as a whole are the criteria of success or failure in a narrated or to-be-narrated quest. (1984, p. 219)

We were able to get an initial peek into the kinds of narratives adults construct about generativity in the Evanston sample (McAdams, de St. Aubin, and Logan, 1993) and in a second sample of approximately eighty adults (McAdams and de St. Aubin, 1992) by collecting from each participant detailed written accounts of three personally meaningful experiences.

Following a procedure developed in McAdams (1982, 1985; McAdams, Booth, and Selvik, 1981), we asked each subject in the study to describe in detail (1) a peak experience (a high point in one's life), (2) a turning point (an episode of important transformation), and (3) an earliest memory. We conceived of each account as a narrative reconstruction of a significant autobiographical event rather than a perfectly accurate replay of the past. Our interest in analyzing these responses was in how adults make sense of the past through stories peopled with characters, rather than what actually happened in the past per se.

We coded each of the three accounts for five themes of generativity:

1. *Creating:* The character creates a new product or outcome or manifests creative skills in life.

2. *Maintaining:* The character puts forth effort to sustain an ongoing project, product, or tradition.

3. *Helping and Offering:* One character offers help, assistance, guidance, mentoring, and so on to another.

4. *Intergenerational Involvement:* The character becomes meaningfully involved with members of another generation, as in the younger generation (typically children or subordinates) or the older generation (typically parents, grandparents, or superiors).

5. *Symbolic Immortality:* The character expresses concern or interest in becoming involved with a phenomenon that is enduring, even immortal.

Our results showed that themes of generativity were positively associated with generative concern, generative strivings, and generative actions. Adults who tended to be concerned about the next generation, who made generative commitments, and who performed generative behaviors in daily life also tended to reconstruct key events from their past in ways accentuating generativity themes. In addition, generative reconstructions of the past were clearly associated with age cohort, as can be seen in Figure 5. Midlife adults were most likely to conceive of their pasts in generative terms, followed by older adults, and finally young adults. In addition, women were significantly more likely to provide narratives suffused with generativity themes than were men.

Most recently, our explorations of narrative and generativity have moved in the direction of intensive interviewing of especially generative adults and their less generative peers. We have chosen approximately fifty adults who have distinguished themselves through paid or volunteer work for their generative contributions to society. These include a select group of schoolteachers (a number of whom have won awards for excellence in teaching), psychotherapy mentors (who train junior therapists on a purely voluntary basis), and men and women who are significantly involved as volunteer workers in and organizers of an urban food pantry that dispenses free food to needy families and children. In addition, most of the adults comprising our "high-generativity" sample score relatively high on our paper-and-pencil measures of generative concern (the LGS) and generative actions (behavior checklist). We have also interviewed approximately thirty adults comprising a "contrasting sample"—well-functioning and psychologically healthy men and women who have *not* distinguished themselves in generativity through paid or volunteer work. In addition, adults in the contrasting sample tend to score in the middle-to-low ranges on the LGS and generative behavior checklist. The contrasting sample has been chosen to match closely the high-generativity group with respect to mean age, family income, and occupational status. Overall, approximately half of the participants in the study are male, half female. Ages range from twenty-five to seventy-two with a mean of approximately forty-three.

Each participant is administered a battery of personality tests and participates in a two-hour life-story interview. In the interview, we solicit information concerning the major chapters in the person's life story, the key events (what I call "nuclear episodes"—high points, low points, turning points in the story), the significant characters, major conflicts and tensions, plans for the future, the personal ideology that provides a backdrop for the action, and the central theme or message. In analyzing the lengthy interview transcripts, we are centrally concerned with discerning the characteristic way in which the adult constructs a sense of self—what William James (1892/ 1963) called "the Me"—through narrative forms. In that we are examining lives that differ centrally on the issue of generativity, we are especially interested in how particularly generative people construct a life narrative that makes sense of their generativity. What narrative strategies do they employ to assimilate the material of their remembered lives to meaningful story forms? How do they understand their own development? What kinds of experiences from the past do they highlight? What central tensions emerge? How do they see family, society, the global environment? What kinds of ultimate concerns in the domains of religion, ethics, and politics animate their narratives?

Our analyses of these rich case histories are still in progress. What I will describe below are some initial impressions of the material that appear promising but that have not as yet been cross-validated in a systematic way.

So far we have been especially struck by four narrative constructions that appear again and again in the stories given by highly generative adults but that manifest themselves with much less frequency in the contrasting sample.

The first of these is a *childhood sense of being chosen*. Especially generative adults, like Daniel Kessinger and Betty Swanson from this chapter's opening, tend to reconstruct their childhood years as a time in which they experienced special positive treatment or exposure from their social environments. As they reconstruct it in personal myth, either an extremely warm and supportive family or a powerful system of beliefs and values provides them with a secure base upon which they can build their identities. In the case of Daniel Kessinger, the first chapter of his life story is not especially positive in an emotional sense. He reports that he was a relatively lonely child, more comfortable with books than friends. But he was immersed in a powerful ideological setting that laid the groundwork for a value system that continues to guide him even today. The first thing he says in his interview is that he was raised in the 1950s in an "Adlai Stevenson–type, liberal democratic household." He goes on to explain in great detail just what this characterization of his family is all about. "This is the most important thing you can know about me," he says. "It is fundamental to my identity and to the generativity script that I have constructed for my past, present, and anticipated future." In life stories of especially generative adults, like Daniel, there appears to be a positive force of some kind—a person, a relationship, a value system—that seems to single out the child and say to him or her, "You are different and special. There is something uniquely good about you."

With respect to childhood, especially generative adults tend to suggest that from an early age onward they were intimately aware that human lives should be immersed in an "ecology of care." Compared to our contrasting sample, high-generativity adults are more likely to identify early experiences in which they became acquainted with death, sickness, disability, discrimination, or special human needs that required a concerted effort of care from responsible adults. People are supposed to care for each other, they suggest, and certain people, through no fault of their own, require more care than do others. The responsibilities of care even extend to strangers, some narratives imply.

Especially generative adults tend to recall specific instances from their past in which a casual acquaintance or total stranger did something very nice or kind for them. Surely such events are actually more common in the lives of some people than others, and it is indeed possible that gratuitous acts of kindness may have some long-term causal influence on personality development. However, we tend to view these reports in reconstructive, narrative terms. Especially generative adults, therefore, have a certain kind of story to tell, a story in which people care about people, in which some people require more care than others, and in which they themselves have been the beneficiaries of care from an early age on. Reconstructions about the "kindness of strangers," as Tennessee Williams might put it, fit the story. That is why they are recalled, told, and integrated into the self.

A second feature is *unwavering conviction*. We are finding that especially generative adults rarely describe periods in their lives in which they doubted that they were doing the right thing. They rarely appear to struggle with the ambiguities of right and wrong. This, combined with a sense of being chosen, suggests that they see their destiny as guided, supported, or even directed by something larger and deeper than the self. "Why do I do what I do?" an especially generative teacher asks. "Because it is what I have been chosen to do. It is me. I can't explain it any further." In his interview, Daniel Kessinger struggles with the question concerning why he does what he does. He concludes that, ultimately, he does not know for sure. "I'm not exactly sure where all this comes from," he says. Similarly, Shirley Rock describes her personal odyssey from organized crime to the ministry as the journey down a path that was carved out before she even began. "At some level," she reports, "I always knew what was right for me. I always knew I would be a minister. In fact, I think I always was. Even as a madame, I was doing ministry, of a sort." There is mystery here, a mystery that comes from knowing deep in your heart what you should be doing with your life but not knowing why you know it.

Especially generative adults mythologize the past to suggest that they have been "called" to do what they do. The call is clear and unambiguous, even if its source is obscure. They do not need to struggle to hear it or understand it. In *The Protestant Ethic and the Spirit of Capitalism*, Max Weber (1920/1958) described the concept of "calling" as a man's or woman's unwavering conviction that he or she has been put on earth to perform a uniquely self-defining and self-justifying task. The calling is larger than the person, and beyond his or her control. It is a destiny to which one must submit, a gift (or curse) that one must accept. The rhetoric of the calling is surprisingly prevalent in the life stories of especially generative adults, equally prevalent among those who profess conventional religious beliefs and those who have little or no involvement with conventional religion. As the urban minister, the community organizer, and the T-shirt lady, respectively, Shirley Rock, Daniel Kessinger, and Betty Swanson all construct their lives as scripts of commitment though which they are true to their own unique, transcendent, and self-validating callings.

A third feature is manifest in numerous narrative examples of *turning bad things into good*. Through childhood loneliness, Daniel tells us, he learned self-sufficiency. His bad relationship with his own father has resulted in his investing more heavily in his current project of being a good father for his second-grade daughter. Because he did not wish to participate in what he believed to be an especially bad war—the Vietnam war—he joined the Peace Corps, went to India, and really discovered his life calling. From the standpoint of a liberal Democrat like Daniel Kessinger, the election of Ronald Reagan to the American presidency in 1980 was surely "bad." But Daniel turns it into a "good" in his personal myth. Because of the rise of conservatism in the 1980s, Daniel redoubled his efforts to get liberal candidates elected on the local level. As the Reagan administration cut funding for the programs Daniel initiated, he worked harder to get money from private foundations. As more and more Americans sank beneath the poverty line in the early 1980s, Daniel built a food pantry. In Daniel's personal myth, because there are such vexing problems facing humankind, Daniel is freed up, in a sense, to build organizations that institute the values he has. Again, the bad turns into good.

The transformation of bad into good suggests a "redemptive" quality to human life. To "redeem" is to make good, or make better, to "save" the good and renounce or expel the bad. Especially generative adults utilize a great deal of redemptive imagery in their life stories. This kind of narrative form appears to have deep and intricate relationships to the concept of generativity, even as expressed in the common perceptions of childbirth and raising children, as well as in archetypal stories of generativity from myth and folklore.

The prototype of biological generativity is childbirth (Kotre, 1984). Childbirth provides a vivid example of how pain and suffering ultimately give way to pleasure, joy, and satisfaction, as labor and delivery result in the emergence of a new life. Similarly, parenting is often conceived as a difficult and challenging endeavor requiring personal sacrifice, patience, and a host of other less than desirable experiences that ideally and ultimately pay some sort of positive dividend in the form of a job well done, a child well taught, a loving and productive family, and so on. Other forms of technological and cultural generativity—as in teaching, community service, artistic production, and so on—require hard work and sometimes difficult commitments, but these ventures in generativity are sustained by the hope of future reward, development, progress, and fulfillment. Again, the expectation is that positive outcomes will result from sustained and difficult effort. Proximal suffering is justified in light of a distal good. Negative experiences may be redeemed (rescued, made better, transformed into good things) by positive end results. Indeed, the negative may be necessary for the positive to occur. Suffering may "build character" or enhance "empathy"; things may be made better by first being made bad.

In mythology and folklore, stories of generativity are filled with the imagery of redemptive experience. For example, the ultimate progenitors for the Israelite people—Abraham and Sarah, in the book of Genesis—must endure many long years of childlessness (bad) before they are blessed with the birth of Isaac, the son (good). The Israelites must wander forty years in the wilderness (bad) before they are able to enter the promised land and claim their rightful destiny as the chosen children of God (good). A most illuminating story from the mythology of ancient Greece is the myth of Demeter and Persephone. Demeter is the generative goddess of grain and fertility, and Persephone is her beloved daughter. One day, Persephone is swallowed up by the earth and seized by Hades, lord of the underworld. Stricken with grief and rage, Demeter lashes out against the earth and causes a most dreadful famine. Zeus, king of Olympus, eventually intervenes and forces Hades to return the lost daughter to her mother. But Demeter soon learns that her daughter has made the mistake of tasting forbidden food while she was in captivity. As a result, Persephone must return every year to the underworld, where she must live with Hades for about four months. These months, therefore, become the season of winter, during which Demeter mourns her lost daughter and the earth is barren and cold. But at the end of winter, Persephone rises up from the underworld, and the earth is blessed with springtime abundance.

In sum, the Demeter story depicts a cycle of suffering (deprivation, going down under) followed by fulfillment (enhancement, coming back up). One may contrast this myth to the parallel story of Icarus, the young boy who fashioned wings to fly but who fell crashing into the sea when the heat of the sun melted the wax in the wings. In the Icarus story, one goes up or is enhanced only to fall down and become deprived. Robert May (1980) has argued that the Demeter story is a characteristically feminine myth (detectable even in the Thematic Apperception Test (TAT) stories written by women and girls) whereas the Icarus legend depicts an essentially masculine pattern. It would seem more sensible, however, to suggest that the Demeter story tells us something about mature generativity, whether it be masculine or feminine. After all, Demeter is a mature and generative goddess of fertility and grain, whereas the Icarus story depicts the insouciance of youth. The Demeter story elaborates an essentially redemptive quality of mature generativity, detectable in the narrative reconstructions of personal experiences provided by especially generative adults. These adults, therefore, are likely to see their lives and understand their world from the mythic frame of turning bad things into good. Like Demeter, their suffering is given meaning by eventual enhancement. And enhancement is given meaning by prior suffering.

Finally, a fourth theme is the life stories of especially generative adults is the *confrontation between power and love*, or more technically, between what Bakan (1966) calls agency and communion. Generativity seems to challenge adults to deal creatively with competing motivational tendencies. The theoretical literature on generativity identifies two contrasting personal motivations for generativity. One is an agentic desire for symbolic immortality, as in the idea of generating products and outcomes that will outlive the self (Kotre, 1984). The second is a communal desire to be needed by others, what Erikson calls a "need to be needed." The tension between the agentic, creating aspect of human life and the communal, offering aspect is vividly apparent in the personal myths of a good number of highly generative adults. The same tension is not nearly as apparent, however, in the interviews done with adults in the contrasting sample.

In the case of Daniel Kessinger, the conflict between agency and communion—power and love—is perhaps most apparent in his current role as father. Daniel describes his daughter, Samantha, as bright and very talented, but she is not as disciplined as Daniel would like. She does not work at things as hard as he did when he was a child. "I have known kids who have a lot less ability than she has but who will ultimately do more with what they have, just because they work at it." As the good father, what should he do? How hard should he push her to achieve? He says, "I kind of get caught between one end of the scale and the other. One end is having real high standards about everything, and on the other end is, well, you know, being almost an anarchist, anti-establishment, letting her do what she wants to do."

The conflict of parenting is doubly significant in Daniel's personal myth. First, the conflict reveals the common problem in generativity: the problem of letting the creation be what it wants to be. A man who builds things that institute his own values—creations in his own image—has a hard time giving those creations up, letting them go, making what Becker (1973) calls an "offering" of his heroic gifts. The agentic mode of generativity conflicts with the communal mode. When does the creator ease up? When does he cut back on his efforts to control? A seven-year-old daughter needs guidance and direction, for sure. But how much? It is hard to know, as Daniel readily acknowledges.

Second, the conflict between agency and communion connects to issues of value and lifestyle in Daniel's personal myth. Daniel says that he has always been politically very liberal but personally very conservative. He believes strongly in both approaches. They are both right for him. But in Daniel's personal myth, political liberalism is tied up with social activism, community organizing, healing the sick, representing the poor. It connects to his rebellion against the establishment in high school, to his confrontations with the Ku Klux Klan when in college, to the rational problem-solving he showed in the Peace Corps in India, to his inherent reasonableness in dealing with social issues, in which he has always taken pride. In his own personal myth, Daniel's political liberalism is expressed in the public actions of a boldly independent man, a powerful agent who has found his own way in the world, who has chosen his own path. The agentic quality of political liberalism is reinforced for Daniel in the Unitarian Church:

> The Unitarians basically believe that each individual works out their own religious posture and their own path and their own way. And there's a side of me which obviously sees a lot of merit to that. On the other hand, I don't think that when everything in the whole religion brings it back to the individual you have a very good thing. This doesn't bring out the best in human beings. I could never be a Christian because I don't believe the myth. But there are some elements in Christianity that help people go beyond the individual. They bring out a collective commitment. The individual doesn't just stand alone. Part of me likes that a lot.

The part that likes it is the conservative, communal part. Unlike many of his counterculture peers who came of age in the 1960s, Daniel has never been comfortable with the unbridled expression of human individuality in interpersonal relations. After all, he has been married to the same woman for twenty-five years. He owns a home; he is raising a family; he is saving money for Samantha's college education. He wants her to have all the opportunities that the American middle class can provide. He sees communal merit in traditional Christianity, even though he cannot accept it for himself. In Daniel's life story, the split between agency and communion subsumes what Daniel perceives to be his dual nature as a liberal at work and a conservative at home.

Agency or communion? Power or love? Work or home? Control or surrender? The opposition is always there. In Daniel Kessinger's life story, the tension between agency and communion pushes the plot forward. As his identity becomes richer and more integrated over time, Daniel finds that agency and communion confront each other again and again, at increasingly complex levels. It is a confrontation that very generative people often seem to face, each person in his or her own unique way. It is perhaps among those who fashion the best and most enduring gifts for the next generation that we witness the most momentous conflicts between creating and giving, between controlling and letting go, between standing alone and being with others. But it is in these generative narrations that adults best justify their time on this earth, as mature men and women who can see past their own endings to the beginnings of a better world in the future.

NOTE

Much of the research described in this chapter has been supported by a grant from The Spencer Foundation. The author would like to thank Rachel Albrecht, Ed de St. Aubin, Karen Dicke, Gina Logan, Beth Mansfield, Tom Nestor, Janet Shlaes, Dinesh Sharma, Carol Stowe, and Donna Van de Water for their involvement in and help with the generativity research conducted at Loyola University of Chicago and Northwestern University between 1987 and 1992.

REFERENCES

Bakan, D. (1966). *The duality of human existence: Isolation and communion in Western man*. Boston: Beacon Press.

Becker, E. (1973). *The denial of death*. New York: Free Press.

Browning, D.S. (1975). *Generative man: Psychoanalytic perspectives*. New York: Dell.

Bruner, J. (1986). *Actual minds, possible worlds*. Cambridge, MA: Harvard University Press.

Charme, S.T. (1984). *Meaning and myth in the study of lives: A Sartrean perspective*. Philadelphia: University of Pennsylvania Press.

de St. Aubin, E., and McAdams, D.P. (1995). The relations of generative concern and generative action to personality traits, satisfaction/happiness with life, and ego development. *Journal of Adult Development*, 2:91–112.

Emmons, R.A. (1986). Personal strivings: An approach to personality and subjective well-being. *Journal of Personality and Social Psychology*, 51:1058–1068.

Erikson, E.H. (1950). *Childhood and society*. New York: Norton.

———. (1963). *Childhood and society*. 2nd ed. New York: Norton.

———. (1964). *Insight and responsibility*. New York: Norton.

———. (1968). *Identity: Youth and crisis*. New York: Norton.

———. (1982). *The life cycle completed*. New York: Norton.

Feinstein, D., and Krippner, S. (1988). *Personal mythology: The psychology of your evolving self*. New York: St. Martin's Press.

Guyot, G.W., Shelton, C., Jackson, N., and Clayton, J. (1991). Empathy, generativity and prosocial behavior in adults. Unpublished manuscript, Regis College, Denver, CO.

Helson, R., Mitchell, V., and Moane, G. (1984). Personality and patterns of adherence to the social clock. *Journal of Personality and Social Psychology*, 46:1079–1096.

Hermans, H.J.M., Kempen, H.J.G., and van Loon, R.J.P. (1992). The dialogical self: Beyond individualism and rationalism. *American Psychologist*, 47:23–33.

James, W. (1892/1963). *Psychology*. New York: Fawcett.

Kotre, J. (1984). *Outliving the self: Generativity and the interpretation of lives*. Baltimore, MD: Johns Hopkins University Press.

Levinson, D.J. (1978). *Seasons of a man's life*. New York: Ballantine.

Linde, C. (1992). *Life stories: The creation of coherence.* New York: Oxford University Press.

MacIntyre, A. (1984). *Beyond virtue.* 2nd ed. South Bend, IN: University of Notre Dame Press.

May, R. (1980). *Sex and fantasy: Patterns of male and female development.* New York: Norton.

McAdams, D.P. (1982). Experiences of intimacy and power: Relationships between social motives and autobiographical memory. *Journal of Personality and Social Psychology,* 42:292–302.

———. (1984). Love, power, and images of the self. In C.Z. Malatesta and C.E. Izard (eds.), *Emotion in adult development,* 159–174. Beverly Hills, CA: Sage.

———. (1985). *Power, intimacy, and the life story: Personological inquiries into identity.* New York: Guilford Press.

———. (1987). A life-story model of identity. In R. Hogan and W. Jones (eds.), *Perspectives in personality,* 15–50, Vol. 2. Greenwich, CT: JAI Press.

———. (1988). Personal needs and personal relationships. In S. Duck (ed.), *Handbook of personal relationships: Theory, research, and interventions,* 7–22. New York: Wiley.

———. (1990). Unity and purpose in human lives: The emergence of identity as a life story. In A.I. Rabin, R.A. Zucker, R.A. Emmons, and S. Frank (eds.), *Studying persons and lives,* 148–200. New York: Springer.

———. (1993). *The stories we live by: Personal myths and the making of the self.* New York: William Morrow.

McAdams, D.P., Booth, L., and Selvik, R. (1981). Religious identity among students at a private college: Social motives, ego stage, and development. *Merrill-Palmer Quarterly,* 27:219–239.

McAdams, D.P., and de St. Aubin, E. (1992). A theory of generativity and its assessment through self-report, behavioral acts, and narrative themes in autobiography. *Journal of Personality and Social Psychology,* 62:1003–1015.

McAdams, D.P., de St. Aubin, E., and Logan, R.L. (1993). Generativity among young, midlife, and older adults. *Psychology and Aging,* 8:221–230.

McAdams, D.P., Ruetzel, K., and Foley, J.M. (1986). Complexity and generativity at mid-life: A study of biographical scripts for the future. *Journal of Personality and Social Psychology,* 50:800–807.

McCrae, R.R., and Costa, P.T., Jr. (1990). *Personality in adulthood.* New York: Guilford Press.

Nakagawa, K. (1991). *Explorations in the correlates of public school reform and parental involvement.* Ph.D. diss., Northwestern University.

Nestor, T. (1989). *Celibacy and generativity.* Master's thesis, Loyola University of Chicago.

Neugarten, B.L., and Hagestad, G.O. (1976). Age and the life course. In R.H. Binstock and E. Shanas (eds.), *Handbook of aging and the social sciences,* 35–55. New York: Van Nostrand Reinhold.

Ricoeur, P. (1984). *Time and narrative.* Vol. 1. Chicago: University of Chicago Press.

Sarbin, T.R. (1986). The narrative as a root metaphor for psychology. In T.R. Sarbin (ed.), *Narrative psychology: The storied nature of human conduct,* 22–44. New York: Praeger.

Schafer, R. (1983). *The analytic attitude.* New York: Basic Books.

Shotter, J., and Gergen, K.J. (eds.) (1989). *Texts of identity.* London: Sage.

Spence, D.P. (1982). *Narrative truth and historical truth: Meaning and interpretation in psychoanalysis.* New York: Norton.

Stewart, A.J., Franz, C., and Layton, L. (1988). The changing self: Using personal documents to study lives. In D.P. McAdams and R.L. Ochberg (eds.), *Psychobiography and life narratives,* 41–74. Durham, NC: Duke University Press.

Vaillant, G.E., and Milofsky, E. (1980). The natural history of male psychological health: IX. Empirical evidence for Erikson's model of the life cycle. *American Journal of Psychiatry*, 137: 1348–1359.

Van de Water, D., and McAdams, D.P. (1989). Generativity and Erikson's "belief in the species." *Journal of Research in Personality*, 23: 435–449.

Weber, M. (1920/1958). *The Protestant ethic and the spirit of capitalism*. New York: Charles Scribner's Sons.

Wiggins, J.S., and Broughton, R. (1985). The interpersonal circle: A structural model for the integration of personality research. In R. Hogan and W. Jones (eds.), *Perspectives in personality*, 1–47, Vol. 1. Greenwich, CT: JAI Press.

NORMAL HUMAN AGING TODAY AND TOMORROW

INSIGHTS FROM THE BALTIMORE LONGITUDINAL STUDY OF AGING[1]

Len Sperry
Caroline McNeil

Launched in 1958, the Baltimore Longitudinal Study of Aging (BLSA) is one of America's longest-running scientific examinations of human aging in the United States. Its aims are twofold: (1) to measure the usual or universal changes that occur as people age, and (2) to learn how these changes are interrelated with the diseases that sometimes accompany aging (Shock et al., 1984). BLSA involves both study participants who are monitored biannually and scores of investigators, from the National Institute of Aging Gerontology Research Center (GRC) and other academic centers around the world, who analyze the BLSA data. The first part of this chapter describes the study, which has challenged a number of stereotypes of aging, while the second highlights some key findings about aging that have emerged from the longitudinal data.

THE STUDY

Ranging in age from their twenties to their nineties, BLSA participants come from every part of the United States. Some have been with the study since its inception. But every year new volunteers of all ages join the BLSA, attracted by the opportunity to learn more about themselves and the satisfaction of being part of a major scientific enterprise.

The overall goal of the study is to describe systematically the process of aging. Often called a study of "normal aging," the BLSA is examining the usual and universal changes that affect all people as they age, changes that can be attributed to aging per se, rather than to a disease or to specific environments. It is a longitudinal rather than a cross-sectional study (Fozard, Metter, and Brant, 1990).

One of the BLSA's objectives is to relate aging processes to one another. It is a study of transitions: not only the transitions of normal aging, but the transitions from the usual aging process to the disease processes that sometimes accompany aging. Transitions occur with aging not only in organs and tissues, but also in cells and molecules. Three overall themes characterize research with BLSA data. First are the longitudinal changes; second is the relationship between health and disease, and third is the fundamental biology of aging (Shock et al., 1984).

Challenging Stereotypes of Aging

In general, two major conclusions have emerged from the BLSA: 1) aging cannot be linked to a general or universal decline in all physical and mental functions, and 2) there is no single, simple, pattern to human aging (Shock et al., 1984).

Consider heart function: It was once thought that resting cardiac output always declined with advancing age. However, studies with BLSA data have shown that when aging hearts are carefully screened and found free of disease, their cardiac output at rest is comparable to that of younger people (Swinne et al., 1992).

Psychological stereotypes are also retreating in the face of BLSA data. It was once believed that personality altered as people grew older. According to one popular image, age brought crankiness; according to another, people became mellower with age. Neither view has held up under scientific scrutiny. The fact is that human personality remains remarkably stable. A person who is cheerful and optimistic when young usually stays that way throughout life. Someone who is irritable and impatient in early life keeps those traits with advancing age (McCrae, 1989).

BLSA data also show that aging is a highly variable, individualized process. For example, studies have shown that in some people glucose tolerance begins to decline in the mid-thirties. The rate of decline, however, differs markedly among individuals (Elahi, Clark, and Andres, 1990). In the GRC's Laboratory of Clinical Physiology, researchers have found that three factors—fatness, distribution of fat on the body, and physical inactivity—account for many of these individual differences.

Studies of osteoporosis and osteoarthritis are done in a section of the GRC's Laboratory of Clinical Physiology. Data from BLSA bone scans help show when and how fast the loss of bone mass occurs at various ages (Sherman et al., 1992). The Dual Energy X-Ray Absorpimeter (DEXA) test is playing an important role in the BLSA's Perimenopausal Initiative, which is examining three major factors—hormones, bone density, and body composition—and how they are affected by menopause. This study is examining what precisely happens before, during, and after menopause in 100 white and 100 African-American women.

This study will show how obesity is related to estrogen levels and how hormone levels interact with bone turnover, which increases during menopause. Because the BLSA participants in this particular study come to Baltimore every three months, the Perimenopausal Initiative will be able to track closely the changes that occur during menopause and provide more insight than has been available up to now. Data from the Perimenopausal Initiative will also be used to measure changes in cholesterol and other fats in the blood as women pass through menopause.

Similarly, BLSA data on the links between hearing loss and three other factors—smoking, alcohol use, and high blood pressure—is suggestive that high blood pressure in women may be linked in some way to a loss of hearing (Morrell and Brant, 1991).

Even within a single individual, organ systems can change at different rates. This suggests that several processes are at work in aging. These include genetic, life-style, and environmental factors, and because they differ so widely among individuals, no two people age in the same way. In fact, individual differences increase as we age, according to studies which show that older people differ from each other to a greater degree than do younger people.

The Origins of BLSA

In 1958, Nathan Shock was the chief of the Gerontology Branch, now the GRC, of the National Institutes of Health. A pioneer in the relatively young science of gerontology, he had developed the branch into the largest institution in the Western Hemisphere devoted entirely to studies of aging (Deeg, 1989).

Shock was approached by William Peter, a retired medical missionary and officer of the United States Public Health Service. Then in his seventies, Dr. Peter wanted to make arrangements to bequeath his body to science when he died. Shock had for some time been convinced of the need to study healthy volunteers living at home in their own communities. Up until then, most aging research had been carried out in hospitals or institutions, where illness could mask normal age changes.

Dr. Peter became the BLSA's first volunteer. As Dr. Shock began building the scientific framework, Dr. Peter embarked on a personal quest to find others. He organized an intensive word-of-mouth campaign, starting with his own family, friends, and neighbors. Each of the early recruits was asked to find friends and acquaintances, and by 1967, more than 500 people had signed up. In 1978 the study was expanded to include women (Migdal, Abeles, and Sherrod, 1981). Inclusion of women was inevitable and necessary because of the need to study conditions like osteoporosis, which is especially common among older women. As the study passed its thirty-fifth anniversary in 1993, it included about 500 women and nearly 700 men. Its goal is to expand still further, with new recruitment efforts focusing on women and minorities.

THE BLSA: VOLUNTEERS, RESEARCHERS, AND DATA

Volunteers

BLSA data come from more than 1,100 volunteers aged from their twenties to their nineties who return every two years for two-and-a-half days of testing. In 1993, there were 675 active male participants and 503 active female participants. Recruitment goals call for more women in the perimenopausal period and more African-American men and women. Since 1958, the BLSA has had 2,331 volunteer participants, of whom 600 have died. Approximately 175 participants have withdrawn during the period from 1958 to 1994, which is an extremely small percentage for a longitudinal study (Gunby, 1994).

Assessments

Data are collected on over 100 variables, including heart, lung, and kidney function; immune function; metabolism and endocrine function; body composition; sensation; cognition; personality factors; and dietary history.

Researchers

The BLSA data are used by numerous researchers and students, including scientists who are affiliated with the GRC and with collaborating institutions. Pre- and postdoctoral students, faculty, and scientists from other academic centers collaborate, either at the GRC or at their own institutions. More than 250 scientists and physicians received research training or collaborated with GRC staff scientists in the study's first thirty-five years.

Research Resources

BLSA data are stored in information archives, tissue banks, and serum banks. Data sets associated with specific procedures are stored for ongoing and future longitudinal studies by GRC scientists and collaborators. Frozen skin and fibroblast samples are stored at The National Institute of Aging's Aging Cell Repository, where they are available to qualified researchers. Frozen blood serum is stored at the GRC for research by National Institute of Aging (NIA) scientists and collaborators.

Most of the BLSA tests are designed to assess the physical changes that come with age. Following are a few of the key findings that have emerged to date on the aging body.

Cardiovascular Changes: Assessment

The treadmill tests have shown, over the years, that the older heart adapts to the effects of age. While it is unable to increase its perfusion rate during exercise as much as a younger heart, it makes up for this by expanding to a greater extent, delivering more blood per heartbeat. In other words, the healthy, exercising older heart increases its output in a somewhat different but just as efficient manner as the younger heart. On the other hand, coronary artery disease (CAD) does increase as people age (Lakatta, 1992a). Studies using BLSA treadmill data show that CAD may be much more prevalent than previously thought.

In one study, 233 men were given a thallium treadmill test. While more than half of the men in their seventies had evidence of CAD, most had had no overt signs or symptoms of heart disease. In contrast, conventional clinical histories and resting electrocardiograms had a much lower detection rate, finding CAD in only 22 percent of the men in the same group. The findings suggest that this kind of exercise screening could be more effective than standard clinical criteria in detecting CAD (Fleg et al., 1990).

Cardiovascular Changes: Risk Factors

Other studies with BLSA data have yielded new information on cholesterol and cardiovascular disease (CVD). High blood cholesterol, according to these findings, remains a significant risk factor for cardiovascular disease, even into very old age. Earlier studies of cholesterol and CVD, including those used to establish cutoff points for treatment of high cholesterol, had focused primarily on middle-aged men. BLSA data show that individuals ages sixty-five to ninety-six with high cholesterol levels continue to be at increased risk. Even in men without evidence of coronary artery disease, cholesterol levels were a risk factor. The finding suggests that preventive measures, such as a prudent diet, continue to be important into old age (Sorkin et al., 1992).

Skeletal and Joint Changes

Bones continually lose cells and replace them throughout the adult life span, but around age thirty-five, the rate of bone loss speeds up, gradually gaining on and outstripping bone growth. Among women, bone loss speeds up again around the time of menopause. On the average, as women age they lose more than half the density of the top of the femur or hip bone, and 42 percent of the density of vertebrae in the lower back (Plato, Fox, and Tobin, 1994). Men lose bone also but at a lower rate.

Ongoing studies with BLSA data are looking for factors involved in bone loss. One study found that the rate of bone loss is similar for young and old men. In the young men, the rate of bone turnover was high; in the older men it wasn't. Differences like these are intriguing because they provide new clues to the biological mechanisms that differ between young and old, mechanisms that may eventually explain how some diseases, like osteoporosis, develop with age.

Arthritis is another focus of GRC scientists, who are studying hand and knee X-rays to see if certain risk factors—body fat or bone density, for example—can be linked to arthritis (Plato and Tobin, 1990). So far, excess fat and body composition have been associated with arthritis of the knee in women, and bone density does not appear to be a factor.

Changes in Physical Fitness Status

Oxygen use during exercise, perhaps the best measure of physical fitness, declines as people age. In each decade of adult life, otherwise healthy people experience a 5 to 10 percent decline in physical fitness by this measure. But like many age-associated changes, this decline in oxygen use is not inevitable. Older athletes maintain higher levels of oxygen consumption, for example, than people who are less active.

Researchers once thought that the decline in oxygen use was linked to decreases in thyroid function as people grew older. But a recent BLSA study showed that a major reason oxygen use declines is that muscle mass is also declining. Muscle tissue consumes the vast majority of oxygen during exercise, and when it declines, oxygen use and, subsequently, physical fitness also decline.

A related study has provided a clue to why, at any age, men have about a 20 percent higher measure of oxygen use than women. It was hypothesized that the smaller amount of lean muscle mass in women could account for the supposed gender differences in physical fitness. The study compared oxygen consumption to total muscle mass rather than total body weight. Body weight has traditionally been used in calculating oxygen consumption. Gender differences disappeared, suggesting that women's smaller muscle mass, not lower levels of physical fitness, may be the major factor in their lower oxygen consumption (Fleg and Goldberg, 1990).

Weight Changes and Longevity

While lean muscle tissue generally declines with age, the other side of the body composition coin is fat, which tends to increase with age. BLSA data and other studies have shown that where fat builds up on the body may have something to do with health. Fat around the waist, which is more common among men than women, goes with an increased risk for heart disease and diabetes. Fat around the hips, more common among women, does not. The BLSA's longitudinal data demonstrate that across the adult age span, increasing fatness around the abdomen is associated with lower glucose tolerance, increased blood pressure, and shifts in levels of cholesterol and other fats (Lakatta, 1992b).

In addition, individuals who are excessively obese or thin do not live as long as those with medium weights. BLSA participants who gained a moderate amount of weight over the years have lived longer, in general, than those who remained youthfully slim. These findings are now reflected in the ideal weight/height ratios recognized by the National Academy of Sciences and the federal government's Department of Health and Human Services and Department of Agriculture.

Changes in Lung Capacity

In one BLSA test, volunteers fill their lungs with air and then force it out through tubes with variously sized openings. Known as spirometry, this measures lung capacity or pulmonary function. Over the years, spirometry has revealed that lung capacity declines with age and that the decline occurs regardless of other factors, such as how large the lungs were to begin with or how much an individual exercises. Essentially, about 40 percent of lung capacity is lost between ages twenty and eighty, a decline that appears to be universal and due, therefore, purely to aging (Tockman, 1992). Lung capacity, however, can be lost more quickly because of smoking or a disease. Analyses of BLSA data have linked low lung capacity to subsequent illness and death, particularly to ischemic heart disease in BLSA men.

Changes in Metabolism: Glucose Tolerance

The ability of the body to metabolize sugar—glucose tolerance—declines with age and can lead to diabetes. But not always. In fact, BLSA data have shown that lower levels of glucose tolerance at older ages are often not associated with diabetes. The data challenged the standards in use in the 1960s for diagnosing diabetes, saying they were too stringent at older ages. Use of these old standards resulted in the overdiagnosis of diabetes in middle-aged and older people. New standards were developed and the number of false positive tests for diabetes has dropped significantly since then (Andres, 1981). BLSA data also show that worsening glucose tolerance at older ages is linked to intrinsic aging processes and to life-style factors such as increasing fatness and physical inactivity (Elahi, Clark, and Andres, 1990). Furthermore, it was learned that the problem is not insulin secretion; it is that cells are not as sensitive to the insulin as they were at younger ages (Shimokata et al., 1991). BSLA researchers developed the glucose clamp technique, which enables researchers to fix or "clamp" the glucose concentration level in the blood at a specified level. The glucose clamp provides a standardized, reproducible method of studying the body's response to glucose in people who are young and old, thin and fat, diabetic and nondiabetic.

Changes in Metabolism: Nutritional Factors

Many BLSA participants do not eat the recommended dietary allowances (RDAs) of some vitamins and minerals. Even in this well-nourished and health-conscious population, vitamin B6, magnesium, and zinc intake is low among substantial numbers of men and women; iron intake is inadequate among many younger women; and calcium intake is low in women of all ages.

GRC researchers have found that BLSA participants with higher vitamin C levels also have high levels of HDL2-cholesterol, the "good" cholesterol that seems to protect against plaque buildup in the arteries. Vitamin C is one of the vitamins, along with beta carotene and vitamin E, that are known as antioxidants.

Antioxidants have been shown to reduce oxygen free radicals. Various studies around the country suggest that these vitamins may help protect against heart disease, cataracts, cancers, and other conditions that are more common with advancing age. Researchers at the BLSA are planning to examine longitudinal data for correlations between antioxidants and these or other diseases.

BLSA participants periodically keep diaries of what they eat and over time these have revealed significant changes in diet (Sobell et al. 1989). Today, for example, participants on the average are consuming fewer cholesterol-rich foods and more dietary fiber than they were in the 1950s and 1960s. These changes will be related to trends in disease incidence as the BLSA progresses.

Life-Style Changes

The complex interplay between life style and aging is an important focus of research at the BLSA. For example, about 75 percent of BLSA men reported smoking in 1958, compared to 16 percent in the early 1990s. Participants also report drinking fewer alcoholic beverages in the later years of the study.

Researchers are also looking at how participants spend their time, through an activity questionnaire that has been filled out by each participant since 1966. The findings are complex. It was found that older men are less active than younger men. Over time, however, all age groups have reported increased levels of physical activity (Fleg and Goldberg, 1990).

Recently, researchers found significant changes with aging in time use among BLSA participants. Not surprisingly, men report less time spent in child-rearing activities than women, but that trend is changing with time. After retirement, both men and women report more time spent socializing and in quiet activities; time spent in vigorous activity declines on the average.

The BLSA's lifestyle and activity studies have taught researchers that it is impossible to describe aging within an individual without taking into account the era during which aging occurs; aging from sixty to seventy years old was different in the 1950s than it is in the 1990s.

Hearing Changes

Declines in hearing can begin in the twenties but often go unnoticed because it is only the high-frequency tones that become harder to hear at first. Most individuals are not aware of hearing problems until low-frequency tones, which are more common in speech, become difficult to hear. On the average, low-frequency hearing begins to fade between the ages of sixty and seventy (Fozard, 1990).

Men lose their hearing more than twice as fast as women, according to a study that tracked results of BLSA hearing tests on volunteers of all ages. GRC researchers found that both men and women had a gradual loss of hearing with age, but after age thirty, men's average rate of loss speeded up until it was about twice that of women (Morrell and Brant, 1991).

This finding confirmed previous cross-sectional studies showing that women on the average have more sensitive hearing at all ages and that men's hearing declines more quickly. But this study suggests that the earlier studies may have seriously underestimated men's rate of hearing loss, particularly for younger men. BLSA researchers have been examining whether various factors—noise exposure, high blood pressure, systemic illness, or drug use—account for these differences between the sexes (Brant et al., 1992).

Vision Changes

Vision tends to decline with age, even without an eye disease such as cataracts or glaucoma. However, the ability to detect fine detail changes little until one's seventies.

The eye's lenses—three of them—become more cloudy and harden as we age, making it more difficult to see nearby objects, and leading in some cases to cataracts that block vision completely (Fozard, 1990). One BLSA study tested the theory that this cloudiness was linked to heart attack or coronary artery disease, but found no association. Another study using BLSA data found that volunteers who had higher levels of calcium and vitamin E in blood samples had a lower risk for cataracts in one of the three lenses.

Contrast sensitivity—the ability to see differences between light and dark—declines with age along with other measures of eyesight. Contrast sensitivity, however, may be a better gauge of how we see. BLSA studies have shown that participants' reported difficulties with vision, particularly glare and seeing peripheral objects, correlate with their scores on the BLSA's contrast sensitivity test (Schieber et al., 1991). Contrast sensitivity may be more useful in predicting difficulties with vision while driving, for instance, than the vision tests currently in use. Not surprisingly, transportation agencies are beginning to pay attention to these findings.

Changes in Health Status

Overtime, the overall number of medical diagnoses recorded in BLSA participants increases almost fivefold—from two to more than nine—from the twenties to the nineties. Yet the pattern varies tremendously from one class of diagnoses to the next. Essentially, there is no simple relationship between health and aging. Individuals have different genes, different life styles, different environments. All of this adds up over time to differences in aging (Fozard et al., 1992). In fact, older participants are much more heterogeneous in terms of their health than are younger participants.

When asked to rate their own health, most BLSA participants of all ages choose "good" or "excellent" over "fair" or "poor." Fewer older participants, however, choose "good" or "excellent." These self-reports of health status have been linked to other factors. One is a person's number of medical diagnoses and another is disposition; people who score higher on "neuroticism" in personality testing tend to report poorer health.

BLSA studies show that measure of health can have different meaning in different age groups. For instance, one study identified a group of participants in their eighties who had no cancer, heart disease, or stroke. In a cross-sectional analysis, medical profiles of these men in their eighties were compared to a group of men in their sixties who were also free of these diseases. However, the men in this second group did develop cancer, heart disease, stroke, and other medical problems by the time they were in their eighties. The lesson was that one cannot assume equal health in persons of different ages just because their medical profiles are similar—more evidence that the proper study of aging and health requires a longitudinal study (Fozard et al., 1992).

Cognitive Changes

While it is true that some mental skills do begin to decline at about age seventy, these changes are highly variable. More than a quarter of BLSA volunteers over age seventy show no decline in memory. Some continue to perform well on the cognitive tasks as they move into their eighties (Fozard et al., 1992).

The brain, like the heart, may do more adapting and less declining with age than previously thought. For instance, when faced with a problem-solving task, older volunteers may draw on different capacities to complete the task. They may not use memory as well as a younger person but rather draw upon a greater reservoir of information and experience to solve the problem. At least up to age seventy, there is little or no decline in problem solving.

Moreover, when mental skills do decline, it may be later than commonly believed. In BLSA studies of "vigilance"—the ability to respond to infrequent and unpredictable stimuli—men who are sixty-five or older appear to be as vigilant, or more so, than those who are younger. After age seventy, vigilance declines sharply in many people, and more time is needed to respond to the stimuli (Giambra, Camp, and Gordsky, 1992). This suggests that a reduction in the ability to react is a true effect of aging, though it may occur at a later age than was once believed.

Some gender differences have emerged in BLSA studies of mental functioning (Giambra, 1989). Women, for example, do better at remembering words, and men have higher scores when it comes to immediate recall of numbers. However, men and women have similar rates of decline for the most part. They forget sentences at identical rates, and older men and women recall fewer sentences after twenty-four hours than younger men and women.

Searching the longitudinal data for early markers of Alzheimer's disease, BLSA researchers have discovered that immediate visual memory may begin to fail before this devastating disorder is detected by other methods (Schieber et al., 1991). GRC's Laboratory of Personality and Cognition is also studying changes in the structure and function of the brain. Using magnetic resonance imaging and positron emission tomography, this study will follow a group of BLSA volunteers for a period of years to learn whether changes in visual memory and other mental functions can be linked to changes in brain structure or function.

Personality Changes

BLSA studies have produced conclusive evidence that age does not alter personality, even in the face of serious physical problems. By following older men and women over many years, the GRC's Laboratory of Personality and Cognition has exploded one stereotype after another. As BLSA participants age, they are no more conservative or cranky or prone to complaining about their health than they were when young.

The Five-Factor Model of personality used at the GRC, which has been adopted by many researchers elsewhere, divides personality into five dimensions labeled neuroticism, extroversion, openness, agreeableness, and conscientiousness. Costa and McCrae (1990) have found that the dimensions of neuroticism and extroversion are powerful predictors of psychological well-being, even when the personality factors were measured years earlier. That is, people who scored high on measures of neuroticism when young tended to have low levels of well-being later in life; those with higher extroversion scores were more likely to report greater well-being later.

The ability to cope with stress does not decline with age, according to BLSA data. Personality traits help determine how one copes with a stressful situation. Extroversion, in one study, was linked to coping strategies labeled "rational action, "positive thinking," "substitution," and "restraint." "Open" individuals were more likely to use humor in dealing with stress, "closed" individuals more likely to use faith (McCrae and Costa, 1989a). The choice of coping strategies depended on both enduring personality traits and the specific situation to which people were responding.

BLSA findings on the stability of personality have laid the groundwork for studies of personality change. There is some evidence that personality change is among the earliest markers of dementia. Studies are now exploring what specific aspects of personality change with the onset of Alzheimer's disease. Like many BLSA findings, the constancy of personality offers a new perspective on aging (McCrae, 1989).

NOTE

1.   This chapter has been adapted with permission from "With the Passage of Time: The Baltimore Longitudinal Study of Aging", written by Caroline McNeil and published by the National Institute on Aging, October, 1993 (NIH Publication

No. 93-3685). Grateful acknowledgement is extended to James Fozard and Freddi Karp of the National Institute of Aging for facilitating publication of BLSA data in this book.

REFERENCES

Andres, R. (1981). Aging, diabetes, and obesity: Standards of normality. *The Mount Sinai Journal of Medicine*, 48(6):489–495.

Brant, L.J., Metter, E.J., Gordon-Salant, S., et al. (1992). Modifiable factors affecting age-related hearing loss. In H. Bouma and J.A.M. Graafmaans (eds.), *Gerontechnology: Studies in health technology and informatics*, 265–270. Vol 3. Amsterdam: IOS Press.

Costa, P.T., Jr, and McCrae, R.R. (1990). Personality disorders and the five-factor model of personality. *Journal of Personality Disorders*, 4:362–71.

Deeg, D. (1989). *Experience from longitudinal studies of aging*. Nijmegen, The Netherlands: Netherlands Institute of Gerontology. (Also, Chap. 4, The Baltimore Longitudinal Study, 67–82.)

Elahi, D., Clark, B., and Andres, R. (1990). Glucose tolerance, insulin sensitivity, and age. In H.J. Armbrecht, R.M. Coe, and N. Wongsurawat (eds.), *Endocrine function and aging*, 48–63. New York: Springer-Verlag.

Fleg, J.L., Gerstenblith, G., Zonderman, A.B., et al. (1990). Prevalence and prognostic significance of exercise-induced silent myocardial ischemia detected by thallium scintigraphy and electrocardiography in asymptomatic volunteers. *Circulation*, 81:428–36.

Fleg, J.L., and Goldberg, A.P. (1990). Exercise in older people: cardiovascular and metabolic adaptations. In W.R. Hazzard, R. Andres, E.L. Bierman, and J.P. Blass (eds.), *Principles of geriatric medicine and gerontology*, 85–100. 2nd ed. New York: McGraw-Hill.

Fozard, J.L. (1990). Vision and hearing in aging. In J.E. Birren and K. Schaie (eds.), *The handbook of the psychology of aging*, 150–170. 3rd ed. New York: Academic Press.

Fozard, J.L., Metter, E.J., Brant, L.J. (1990). Next steps in describing aging and disease in longitudinal studies. *Journal of Gerontology*, 45:116–127.

Fozard, J.L., Metter, E.J., Brant, L.J., et al. (1992). The physiology of aging: Keynote address. In H. Bouma and J. Graafmaans (eds.), *Technology and aging: Proceedings of the First International Conference on Gerontechnology*. The Netherlands: Eindhoven.

Fozard, J.L., Mullin, P.A., Giambra, L.M., et al. (1992). Normal and pathological age differences in memory. In J.C. Brocklehurst, R.C. Tallis, and H.M. Fillit (eds.), *Textbook of geriatric medicine and gerontology*, 94–109. 4th ed. London: Churchill-Livingston.

Giambra, L.M. (1989). Sex differences in sustained attention across the adult lifespan. *Journal of Applied Psychology*, 74:91–95.

Giambra, L.M., Camp, C.J., and Gordsky, A. (1992). Curiosity and stimulation seeking across the adult life span: Cross-sectional and six to eight year longitudinal findings. *Psychology and Aging*, 7:150–157.

Gunby, P. (1994). Graying of America stimulates more research on aging associated factor. *Journal of the American Medical Association*, 272: 1561–1566.

Lakatta, E.G. (1992a). Cardiovascular function in aged adults. In D.P. Zipes and D.J. Rowlands (eds.), *Progress in cardiology*, 77–91. Philadelphia: Lea and Febiger.

Lakatta, E.G. (1992b). Interaction between nutrition and aging: Summary effects on the cardiovascular system. *Nutrition Review*, 50 (12):419–420.

McCrae, R.R. (1989). Age differences and changes in the use of coping mechanisms. *Journal of Gerontology*, 44:161–169.

McCrae, R.R., and Costa P.T. (1989a). Different points of view: Self-reports and ratings in the assessment of personality. In J.P. Forgas and M.J. Innes (eds.), *Recent advances in social psychology: An international perspective*, 429–439. Amsterdam: Elsevier Science Publishers.

McCrae, R.R., and Costa, P.T. (1989b). Rotation to maximize the construct validity of factors in the NEO Personality Inventory. *Multivariate Behavioral Research*, 24: 107–24.

Migdal, S., Abeles, R.P., and Sherrod, L.R. (1981). *An inventory of longitudinal studies of middle and old age*. New York: Social Science Research Council.

Morrell, C.H., and Brant, L.J. (1991). Modeling hearing thresholds in the elderly. *Statistics in Medicine*, 10:1453–464.

Plato, C.C., Fox, K.M., Tobin, J.D. (1994). Skeletal changes in human aging. In D.E. Crews and R.M. Garruto (eds.), *Biological anthropology and aging: Interdisciplinary, cross-cultural, and comparative approaches*. Oxford: Oxford University Press.

Plato, C.C., and Tobin, J.D. (1990). Bone loss and osteoarthritis: Diseases of normative aging processes. *Collegium Antropologicum*, 14:57–67.

Schieber, F., Fozard, J.L., Gordon-Salant, S., and Weiffenbach, J.M. (1991). Optimizing sensation and perception in older adults. *International Journal of Industrial Ergonomics*, 7:133–162.

Sherman, S.S., Tobin, J.D., Hollis, B.W., et al. (1992). Biochemical parameters of bone mineral density in healthy men and women. *Journal of Bone and Mineral Research*, 7:1123–1130.

Shimokata, H., Muller, D.C., Fleg, J.L., et al. (1991). Age as independent determinant of glucose tolerance. *Diabetes*, 40:44–51.

Shock, N., Grevlich, R., Andress, R., et al. (1984). *Normal human aging: The Baltimore Longitudinal Study*. Washington, DC: U.S. Department of Health and Human Services.

Sobell, J., Block, G., Koslowe, P., et al. (1989). Validation of a retrospective questionnaire assessing diet 10–15 years ago. *American Journal of Epidemiology*, 130:173–187.

Sorkin, J., Andres, R.A., Muller, D., et al. (1992). Cholesterol as a risk factor for coronary heart disease in elderly men: The Baltimore Longitudinal Study of Aging. *Annals of Epidemiology*, 2:59–67.

Swinne, C.J., Shapiro, E.P., Lima, S.D., and Fleg, J.L. (1992). Age-associated changes in cardiac performance during isometric exercise in normal subjects. *American Journal of Cardiology*, 69:823–826.

Tockman, M.S. (1992). Aging of the respiratory system. In W.R. Hazzard (ed.). *Principles in geriatric medicine and gerontology*, 160–199. New York: McGraw-Hill.

The Self in Later Years of Life

Changing Perspectives on Psychological Well-Being

Susan M. Heidrich
Carol D. Ryff

Introduction

Thinking about old age—what we can expect and how we will fare—most commonly elicits a checklist of unpleasant or distressing events. These include changes in health and physical functioning, widowhood, death of friends and family members, perhaps a change in residence or loss of income, and loss of roles such as parent, spouse, and worker. The impression is that negative events multiply as one grows older and inevitably lead to loneliness, isolation, and unhappiness. This may be especially true for older women who live longer than men and are more apt to be widowed, poor, and have chronic health problems that interfere with being able to live independently (Jette and Branch, 1981; Strickland, 1988; Van Nostrand, Furner, and Suzman, 1993; Verbrugge, 1985).

Yet empirical studies consistently demonstrate that the elderly are no worse off, and often better off, than younger adults when it comes to mental health and psychological well-being. For instance, the elderly report higher levels of life satisfaction, morale, well-being, and happiness and lower levels of depression and anxiety than younger adults (Idler and Kasl, 1991; Larson, 1978; Markides and Lee, 1990; Okun et al., 1982). The majority of older people rate their health as good or excellent, as do younger adults. Older individuals say they are healthier, happier, and coping better than physicians or nurses or other more "objective" indices might indicate. And, in fact, an older person's subjective health rating is more predictive of future morbidity and mortality than are objective ratings (Idler, 1993). Furthermore, the elderly report fewer stressful life events than younger adults, and they perceive these events as less stressful than younger adults do. These paradoxical findings have led to a search for explanations of how aging individuals manage to maintain high levels of psychological well-being when faced with the negative events of old age.

Our formulation of positive psychological functioning is drawn from diverse theoretical literatures, including formulations of life-span development, which postulate progressions of growth across the life course; clinical conceptions of maturity, individuation, and self-actualization; and mental health conceptions targeted at the "presence of wellness" versus "absence of illness" criteria of being well (see Ryff, 1989a, for a review). These perspectives converge in their emphasis on six key aspects of positive functioning: self-acceptance, positive relations with others, autonomy, purpose in life, personal growth, and environmental mastery. Our research program includes empirical indicators of these constructs as well as other frequently employed operational definitions of subjective well-being and mental health (e.g., life satisfaction, happiness, depression, anxiety).

The central question is, what social-psychological processes might account for older persons' capacities to interpret events in ways that seemingly maintain or enhance their psychological well-being? Our work has focused on the role of the self in explanations of psychological well-being in old age. In this chapter, we will first describe the theoretical frameworks guiding the research program. Second, the empirical research that we and our colleagues have conducted will be presented. These studies attempt to determine the kinds of self-perceptions and interpretive processes individuals use to cope with age-related changes in physical health and functioning. A final section elaborates future directions in the study of the self and psychological well-being, giving particular attention to expansion of the *contexts* in which self mechanisms are played out, other critical *self-cognitions* that function to maintain and enhance the self, and major *social structural influences* on well-being.

THE SELF AND PSYCHOLOGICAL WELL-BEING: A SELF-SYSTEM MODEL

How individuals interpret or give meaning to their experiences is the major focus of this program of research. Figure 1 provides a graphic representation of the major concepts and relationships we have proposed.

Physical Health

"If you have your health, you have everything" is a sentiment often expressed in relation to aging. Staying healthy and avoiding illness are priorities in old age. From numerous empirical studies of the relationships among aging, health, and psychological well-being, we know that physical health is one of the best predictors of subjective well-being and life satisfaction in old age (Diener, 1984). However, we also know that both objective (e.g., physician reports, medical history) and subjective (perceived health, health self-rating

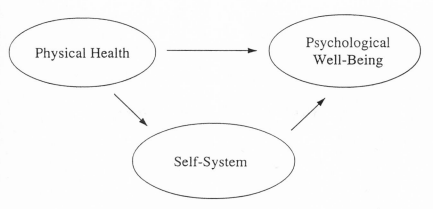

Figure 1. The Self-System Model

scales) measures of physical health explain only a small proportion of the
variance in psychological well-being (Idler and Kasl, 1991; Larson, 1978;
Markides and Lee, 1990; Okun et al., 1982). Furthermore, when subjective
health ratings are compared to objective health ratings, the subjective ratings are the most important in predicting morbidity and mortality (Idler,
1993; Kaplan, Barell, and Lusky, 1988). Asking someone to rate his or her
own health, from poor to excellent, is a better predictor of his or her own
future physical health and of mortality than are "objective" health reports.
This is true even though older adults "overestimate" their health (i.e., report they are healthier or better off than what physicians, nurses, or other
objective indices might indicate).

Most people experience changes in physical health and physical
functioning as they age. There are age-related declines in physical functioning as well as increases in diseases and chronic illnesses. Although change
in physical health may not be inevitable in old age, it is a common and
stressful experience of old age. Particularly for older women, the diseases
and illnesses of old age are accompanied by symptoms and disabilities that
are both distressing and interfere with performing day-to-day activities.
These effects, in turn, spill into other domains of life. For instance, physical health problems may interfere with one's abilities to carry out important roles or role-related activities, thereby changing one's relationships
with others, be it family or friends, and altering an individual's view of self
and the future. Because of the central importance of physical health to psychological functioning in old age, we see physical health as a major factor
that affects psychological well-being directly and indirectly through the self-
system.

The Self-System

The self-system refers to social-cognitive, interpretive mechanisms that change the relationship between a stressor (in this case, physical health) and well-being. Underlying this model is a view of the individual as a "psychological activist," as well as an adaptive organism (Thoits, 1994). We suggest that how individuals interpret, give meaning to, or make sense of their life experiences is a powerful determinant of their psychological well-being and, in fact, is more important than the experiences themselves in determining well-being. The self is central in this model because events are interpreted through and in relation to the self.

The self-system encompasses three psychosocial mechanisms derived from self-concept theory and life-span developmental theory: 1) social comparisons (the self in relation to others), 2) self-discrepancies (internal self-evaluations), and 3) social integration (the self in relation to the social structure). Each mechanism involves ways of interpreting or giving meaning to life experiences. It is these interpretations that we explore as mediators of the effects of physical health on psychological well-being in old age.

Social Comparisons

One way in which individuals judge how they are doing is by comparing themselves to others. Festinger (1954) originally suggested that individuals are motivated to evaluate their abilities and confirm their opinions. When there are no objective standards available for self-evaluation, people compare themselves with others to find out how they are doing. More recent research on the self, however, indicates that people may not be realistic, unbiased self-evaluators and that others play an important role in evaluation, maintenance, and enhancement of the self (Heidrich and Ryff, 1992; Markus and Cross, 1990; Rosenberg, 1986; Ryff and Essex, 1991; Taylor and Brown, 1988; Wills and Suls, 1991; Wood, 1989). For instance, comparisons with others can lead to positive, negative, or neutral self-evaluations that, in turn, have effects on multiple dimensions of psychological well-being (Ryff and Essex, 1992).

Social comparisons are most evident when some threat to self-esteem occurs. Both laboratory and clinical research shows that individuals engage in both upward and downward comparisons in threatening situations (Taylor and Lobel, 1989; Wills, 1981, 1991). For example, women with breast cancer typically rated their postsurgery psychological adjustments as positive and, in fact, felt they were doing even better than before they were diagnosed with cancer. These women also reported that they were doing as well as or better than other women coping with the same crisis. No matter how bad the particular woman's situation, she was able to find a comparison person who was worse off (Taylor, Wood, and Lichtman, 1983; Wood, Taylor and Lichtman, 1985). Similar effects have been found in parents of infants in neonatal intensive care units, in patients with chronic illnesses, and in couples with marital problems (Affleck and Tennen, 1991; Buunk et al., 1990; Gibbons and Gerrard, 1991).

Upward and downward social comparisons may serve different functions, but appear to be related to psychological well-being in the same way (Gibbons and Gerrard, 1991; Heidrich and Ryff, 1993b). Taylor (Taylor and Lobel, 1989) found that women with cancer actively chose real or hypothetical others for comparisons in a number of different domains that were important to their self-esteem. For example, women sought a comparison person who was worse off physically—a downward comparison— for purposes of self-evaluation and self-enhancement. However, they also sought affiliation with comparison persons who were better off—an upward comparison—as sources of motivation and inspiration or as models for learning problem-solving strategies (Wood, 1989).

Social comparisons have been infrequently studied in aging, although life-span developmental theory points to social comparisons as a mechanism in psychological well-being. Important psychological strategies in old age may include changing one's standards for success or failure in order to maintain a sense of self that is invulnerable to age-related losses (Baltes and Baltes, 1990), or modifying goals or aspirations to those that are more attainable (Birren and Renner, 1980). How might social comparison processes operate to influence well-being in the elderly? Declines in physical health or physical functioning might lead to depression, anxiety, or a loss of autonomy or purpose in life *unless* perceptions of loss and decline are offset by the perception that one compares favorably with others. If, in spite of health limitations, an older person judges that he or she is better off than some other actual or hypothetical person, the end result can be feeling good about oneself. In more theoretical terms, it may be that the favorable reports of self-esteem and life satisfaction by the elderly are, in part, explained by changes in reference groups to older individuals who are doing worse. That is, elderly persons can alter their standards or expectations for failure or success, thereby creating new frames of reference for self-evaluation as well as self-enhancement.

SELF-DISCREPANCY

A second way in which the self acts to mediate the effects of health problems is by the use of internal self-evaluations. Rosenberg's conceptualization of the self-concept as dynamic and multidimensional provides the basis for self-discrepancy theory (Rosenberg, 1986). According to Rosenberg, there are multiple aspects of the self that develop through both internal self-evaluations and interpersonal experiences. The self is dynamic because, in response to external events, different aspects of the self may be changed or modified. The self is also multidimensional; two of those dimensions are the ideal self and the actual self. Ideal self refers to the person one aspires to be and includes possible and potential selves; actual self refers to conceptions of who one really is. Individuals are motivated to achieve a match between the ideal self and the actual self because a mismatch or discrepancy results in psychological discomfort, such as depression or anxiety (Higgins, 1987; Higgins et al., 1986).

When external events, such as a change in physical health, threaten an individual's sense of self, different aspects of the self-concept are altered in an attempt to maintain an actual-ideal self match and reduce psychological distress. In this sense, achieving a match among different aspects of the self is a process of psychological adjustment that results in psychological well-being.

How might self-discrepancy operate in old age? Self-discrepancy theory was formulated to explain anxiety and depression (Strauman and Higgins, 1987). A life-span developmental view, however, is that successful aging depends on reducing the discrepancy between the actual and ideal selves and that older adults compensate for losses in some areas, such as physical health, by optimizing other important aspects of the self, such as being active in the community (Baltes and Baltes, 1990; Birren and Renner, 1980). High levels of subjective well-being in the elderly, in spite of physical health problems, may be explained in part as a decrease in actual-ideal self-discrepancy in the elderly.

SOCIAL INTEGRATION

The third aspect of the self-system involves the self in relation to the social structure, or social integration. Social breakdown theory was developed in the early 1970s to explain mental health problems occurring in old age, particularly loneliness and depression (Kuypers and Bengston, 1973). Three social system changes occurring in old age were identified that lead to negative self-attitudes and an internalized sense of reduced competence in the elderly. These were 1) a loss of normative guidelines (the absence of clear, positive behavioral expectations in old age or negative perceptions regarding age-related behavior), 2) shrinkage of roles (many former roles are terminated in old age, few meaningful alternative roles are developed, and the quantity and quality of social contacts decrease), and 3) lack of appropriate reference groups (a lack of shared, positive attitudes or values about the aged as a social group). More recent work by Riley (1994) alludes to the lack of social structural supports that facilitate maintenance or attainment of meaningful roles in old age.

Kuypers and Bengston (1973) also suggested that the individual's sense of social competence is related to his or her perceived integration in the social structure. Thus, the elderly person who perceives a high degree of normative guidance in the social world, who engages in valued roles, or who has positive perceptions of being identified as a "senior citizen" would also have more purpose in life or more positive relations with others. In other words, an older individual who feels integrated into the social structure is protected from perceiving the self as incompetent and will therefore enjoy better mental health.

Social integration has been more widely studied as a dimension of "social support." Both quality of support (feeling loved, feeling that one can count on others, having a confidante) and quantity of support (having a network available to provide aid in times of need) are associated with better health, both physical and emotional, in old age (Cohen and Wills, 1985; Cutrona, Russell, and Rose, 1986; Sarason et al., 1987; Spiegel et al., 1989; Thompson and Heller, 1990; for reviews, see George, 1989; House, Landis, and Umberson, 1988). Even when faced with declines in physical health, then, having a sense of social integration allows the older person to protect the self from feelings of reduced competence in the world and indicates that others are available for emotional and tangible support, thereby maintaining or enhancing psychological well-being.

Psychological Well-Being

The outcome in this model is psychological well-being. Ryff (1989a, 1995; Ryff and Keyes, 1995) has described six dimensions of psychological well-being in adulthood that were derived from theories of life-span development, personality development (Erikson), and positive functioning or mental health (Jahoda, Rogers), among others. From a life-span developmental perspective, well-being is not just the absence of distress or the presence of happiness. Rather, psychological well-being in adulthood is based on successfully negotiating the tasks of adult life, such as achieving intimacy and generativity, and includes a realization of one's potential and continued growth. The key dimensions of well-being are autonomy, environmental mastery, personal growth, positive relations with others, purpose in life, and self-acceptance.

Ryff and Keyes (1995) describe how some dimensions of psychological well-being change with age and sex, while others do not. For instance, based on cross-sectional data of both community and national samples, environmental mastery and autonomy appear to increase from young to middle adulthood; personal growth and purpose in life seem to decline from mid-life to old age; and positive relations and self-acceptance appear stable throughout adulthood. Women rate themselves higher on positive relations with others and personal growth than do men, but the other dimensions of well-being do not differ for men and women.

An emphasis on psychological well-being shifts the focus from explaining pathology or illness in old age to explaining successful or adaptive aging. This approach encourages us to examine the sources of strength in individuals' lives that may serve them well in times of adversity.

OLDER WOMEN AND PSYCHOLOGICAL WELL-BEING

The lives of elderly women offer a rich context in which to explore the relationship between physical health and psychological well-being. On the positive side, elderly women report doing well when it comes to their health. The majority rate their health as good or better, report that they are active and not limited in their usual activities by health problems, and say they are doing a good or excellent job of taking care of their own health (National Center for Health Statistics, 1986). On the other hand, more objective indicators of the physical health status of older women paint a different picture (Strickland, 1988; Verbrugge, 1985). Older women are likely to live alone, be widowed, be poor, and suffer from a number of chronic health conditions that negatively affect their daily lives (Bureau of the Census, 1986). Thirty-five percent say they are limited in their major activity (housework or job) by a chronic condition (Verbrugge, 1985). Older women, compared to older men, experience more acute illnesses and injuries, more disability per illness, and are more likely to suffer from depression (Nolen-Hoeksema, 1987). Because of gender differences in longevity, morbidity, and mortality, elderly women live longer than men and, in addition, live longer with chronic health problems, widowhood, and financial constraints, all of which have an impact on psychological well-being. Thus, in elderly women's lives, we can see the relationship between subjective well-being and objective distress being played out.

Testing the Self-System Model

The purpose of our first empirical study was to test whether the three aspects of the self-system—social comparisons, self-discrepancy, and social integration—mediated the relationship between physical health status and psychological well-being in older women (Heidrich and Ryff, 1993a). This study was carried out with 243 community-dwelling older women (mean age = 73.3) who reported an average of 3.3 chronic health problems (generally, arthritis, high blood pressure, or heart disease). Half of the women were widowed and lived alone.

We developed multiple paper-and-pencil measures for each of the self-system constructs and also used self-report measures of physical health and psychological well-being. Our measures of social comparisons included assessments of the frequency and consequences of both upward and downward comparisons. Our measures of self-discrepancy were based on differences scores obtained by subtracting actual self-evaluations from ideal self-evaluations. Our measures of social integration consisted of three scales to capture normative guidelines, reference groups, and positive roles.

We analyzed the relationships among these constructs using model-testing procedures. Three models were tested: a model predicting psychological distress (depression and anxiety), a model predicting psychological well-being using a subset of Ryff's measures (autonomy, personal growth, positive relations, and purpose in life), and a model predicting well-being using nondevelopmental measures (life satisfaction, happiness). In each case we tested the strength of the relationships between physical health, the self-system, and psychological well-being or distress.

In all three models, physical health was related to psychological outcomes. The higher the women's ratings of their physical health and functioning, the higher their levels of psychological well-being and the lower their levels of psychological distress. These findings converged with previous research. More important to our theoretical model, however, was the finding that physical health was directly related to social comparisons and social integration. Women in better health made more positive, although less frequent, social comparisons with others and reported higher levels of social integration. In turn, both social comparisons and social integration were related to psychological well-being. Women who made more positive social comparisons and had higher levels of social integration had higher levels of psychological well-being and lower levels of psychological distress, regardless of their physical health status.

There were some important differences in how the self-system was related to psychological well-being versus psychological distress. When well-being was the outcome, the only relationship between physical health and well-being occurred *through* the self-system. That is, physical health, per se, did not directly affect psychological well-being once the self-system interpretive mechanisms were brought into play. How women fared in comparison with others and how positively they felt about their social roles and responsibilities was more important than their physical health in explaining their psychological health. In contrast, the self-system did not totally override the effects of poor health in relation to depression and anxiety. Even when women engaged in social comparisons and felt integrated into the social structure, poor physical health continued to contribute to feelings of depression and anxiety. These relationships are depicted in Figure 2. It must be noted, however, that the presence of depression or anxiety did not necessarily rule out the presence of psychological well-being. Although 21 percent of these women had depression scores that indicated symptoms of significant clinical depression, they also had high scores on multiple dimensions of well-being, positive social comparisons, high levels of social integration, and little self-discrepancy.

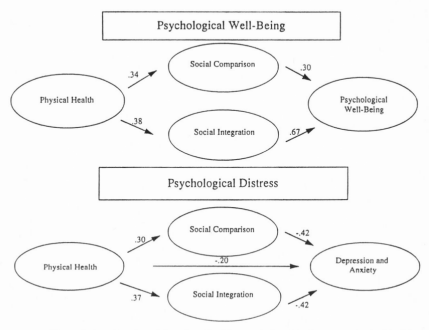

Figure 2. Results of model testing. Significant relationships between physical health, the self-system, psychological well-being, and distress.

We also found that these older women had very low levels of discrepancy between their actual and ideal self-perceptions. Since they also generally had high levels of psychological well-being, this result seemed consistent with life-span development theory regarding the match between actual and ideal selves that should occur in old age. However, we found little support in this study for the role of self-discrepancy in well-being. Physical health was not related to self-discrepancy, nor was there a relationship between self-discrepancy and well-being. In subsequent studies (described later), however, we did find important relationships between self-discrepancy and psychological well-being.

Following testing of the overall self-system model, we directed our research toward examining each aspect of the self-system individually and in more detail. A number of studies aimed to further elaborate the role of social comparisons and self-discrepancies as interpretive mechanisms will now be described.

The Intricacies of Social Comparisons

Although our model-testing approach lent substantial support to our theoretical notions of the self-system, many questions were left unanswered. For instance, what domains of women's lives elicited social comparisons, and were upward and downward comparisons related to psychological well-being in the same way? Most importantly, we wished to know if social comparisons were the most effective for women who needed them most; that is, those in the poorest health. These questions were examined using the sample of women described above, who were also followed for two years to assess changes in health, the self-system, and well-being (Heidrich, 1994; Heidrich and Ryff, 1993b).

Our assessment of social comparisons consisted of asking women to tell us how often they made social comparisons and how they felt about themselves when they made these comparisons. We asked women about upward social comparisons and downward social comparisons in twelve life domains. These domains, which are listed in Table 1, were chosen based on theory and research concerning stressful life events, coping, and normative life events, as well as on interviews with older women about coping with aging (Heidrich and Ryff, 1992).

Table 1. Social Comparison Assessments

Domains

Coping with aging	Physical health	Problem solving
Coping with change	Managing health care	Friendships
Life satisfaction	Learning new things	Physical appearance
Coping with emotions	Desired activity level	Family relationships

Because little was known about social comparisons in aging, we began by describing the kinds of social comparisons made by older women (i.e., whether upward or downward), the domains in which social comparisons took place, and how older women felt about themselves when they made social comparisons (the consequence of comparisons). In two cross-sectional studies (Heidrich and Ryff, 1993b), we found that the majority of older women engaged in social comparisons from occasionally to often. Overall, they indicated they were doing well in comparison with others and that social comparisons made them feel good about themselves. This was true for both upward and downward comparisons, although downward comparisons were more frequent and more positive than upward comparisons. Most importantly, these women reported feeling good about themselves in comparison with others whether they compared themselves with someone they perceived as doing better than they (upward comparisons) or doing worse than they (downward comparisons). These results support the self-enhancing function of social comparisons. That is, we engage in social comparisons precisely to feel better about ourselves or to enhance our self-esteem.

Different life domains engendered more frequent social comparisons, suggesting that some domains are more salient in older women's lives, perhaps in importance, difficulty, or uncertainty. These domains were physical health, activity level, coping with aging, and physical appearance, all of which are domains in which losses or decrements are expected or considered normative in old age. In these domains, downward comparisons were more frequent than upward. There were two domains in which upward comparisons predominated: physical appearance and the ability to learn new things. These may be domains in which women are motivated by a desire for self-improvement and seek role models or sources of inspiration (Taylor and Lobel, 1989; Wood, 1989).

Although physical health was the domain in which women made the most social comparisons, it was also the domain in which women had the highest ratings for feeling good about themselves. That is, women felt the best about themselves when they made downward comparisons with others about their physical health. Thus we see that although losses might be expected in old age, in this case, women's interpretive processes resulted in positive self-perceptions.

Over time (two years), there was little change in the physical health status and little change in the domains that were associated with the frequency of comparisons. Physical health continued to be the most salient domain (i.e., to elicit the most social comparisons) with the most positive consequences (Heidrich, 1992).

The second aim of our examination of social comparisons was to understand how social comparisons are related to different aspects of psychological well-being and to test the hypothesis that social comparisons would be most effective for women in the worst physical health. We predicted that women with more health problems in later life would use social comparisons more frequently because they would be motivated to protect or enhance their sense of self. We also predicted, based on the self-system model, that social comparisons would be more important than physical health to women's psychological well-being. We examined these predictions using multiple regression procedures.

Women with more physical health problems reported using upward and downward comparisons more frequently than did women in good health, and these effects were consistent over two years. Women who were in poorer health at the beginning of the study used social comparisons more frequently and continued to use more frequent social comparisons two years later. In addition, the consequences of their comparisons were less positive both concurrently and over time. However, it is important to note that all of these women reported positive consequences of social comparisons; their mean scores were above the midpoint of the scale, indicating that they felt good about themselves in comparison with others. Their ratings were, however, somewhat less positive than those of women in good health.

Psychological well-being for women, regardless of their health status, was related to the consequences of social comparisons, but not the frequency. Positive comparisons with others were associated with higher levels of autonomy, positive relations with others, and personal growth, and lower levels of depression and anxiety. The effects of social comparisons were more important than the effects of physical health problems in relation to psychological well-being in cross-sectional analyses. Across two years, after controlling for psychological well-being and physical health as of the first assessment, positive concurrent social comparisons were related to declines in depression at the second assessment.

The final hypothesis was that the effects of social comparisons would be strongest for women in the worst health. Moderating effects of social comparisons were examined by testing the interaction of the consequences of comparison and physical health separately for upward and downward consequences. As expected, the effect of social comparisons was different for women in poor health compared to women in good health. For women in good health, social comparisons made little difference in their psychological well-being. However, for women in poor health, how they felt about themselves in comparison with others was strongly related to their feelings of personal growth, positive relations with others, and depression. Women in poor health whose comparisons with others were more positive had profiles of psychological well-being similar to those of women in good health. Women in poor health whose comparisons with others were less positive had significantly higher levels of depression and lower levels of well-being. Some of these effects are illustrated in Figure 3.

Similar results were found in the longitudinal data. Social comparisons continued to be particularly important for women in poor health. For women in the poorest health at the first assessment, those who engaged in positive upward or downward comparisons showed higher levels of psychological well-being and lower levels of psychological distress at the second assessment. For women in good health at the first assessment, second-assessment levels of well-being did not systematically vary as a function of social comparison processes.

Although the self-system model proposes that prior health status sets the stage for social comparison processes, which then interact with health profiles in accounting for change in psychological well-being, there are other possible relationships to consider. For instance, it may be that psychological health causes changes in physical health. We also examined this alternative explanation in our longitudinal data by testing a series of regression models in which each initial psychological well-being measure was used to predict each subsequent physical health measure. Thus, these analyses addressed whether prior psychological functioning is related to change in physical health over time. Little support for this alternative model was found, except that depression at the first assessment predicted an increase in health symptoms at the second assessment.

In summary, the above findings supported our notion that social comparisons are interpretive processes used to maintain or enhance psychological well-being in the face of threats to physical health in old age. Poorer health was associated with the more frequent use of social comparisons, and positive social comparisons mediated the relationship between physical health and psychological well-being. Finally, for women in the poorest health, positive social comparisons allowed them to maintain levels of psychological well-being no different from those of women in good health.

Self-Discrepancy Research

Our initial model-testing research offered little support for the notion that self-discrepancies function to maintain psychological well-being in older women. However, the lack of significant effects in our first study may have had methodological, as well as conceptual, reasons. For example, our mea-

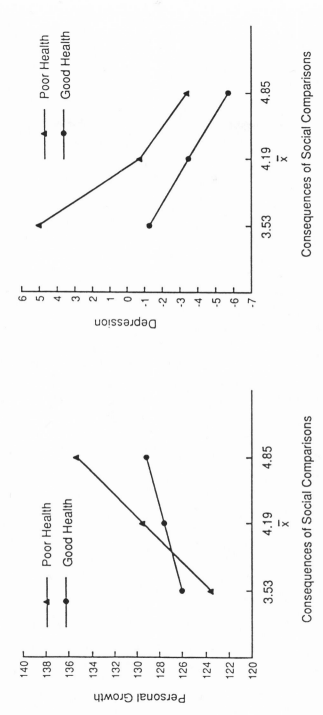

Figure 3. *Significant interactions. Data refer to scores on each assessment from low to high.*

sure of self-discrepancy was problematic, as it was based on difference scores. Further, physical health may have had negligible effects on self-discrepancies because ideal-actual self-conceptions may be firmly established by old age and, thus, invulnerable to other influences.

It is also possible that self-discrepancies were measured in the wrong realm (i.e., psychological functioning). Had actual-ideal self-discrepancies been measured in the same life domains in which social comparisons were assessed (e.g., physical health, coping with aging, desired activity level), we may have found both a greater level of self-discrepancy and more powerful relationships among physical health, self-discrepancies, and mental health outcomes. We also had evidence of differences in self-discrepancies from young adulthood to old age that encouraged us to continue exploring the role of self-discrepancy.

EVIDENCE FOR SHIFTS IN SELF-DISCREPANCY WITH AGE

Ryff (1991) asked young, middle-aged and elderly adults to evaluate themselves on the six dimensions of psychological well-being according to present, past, future, and ideal self-assessments. The comparison of present and ideal self-ratings indicated that, with age, there was greater congruence between aspects of the ideal and actual selves. The decrease in actual-ideal discrepancy in old age was due to lowered ratings for ideal self-assessments by the older adults. That is, older adults had lower ideal ratings, but generally similar ratings of actual self when compared with young and middle-aged adults.

This study was cross-sectional, but in longitudinal work, we also gathered data on actual and ideal self-assessments of older women across two years (Heidrich, 1993). Over this time period, there were no significant changes in ideal ratings of positive relations or autonomy, but significant declines were obtained in ideal ratings of personal growth and purpose in life. These declines were not related to physical health problems. Two years is a relatively short period and in general there was little change in either physical or mental health. That changes occurred in two aspects of ideal self did, however, converge with prior cross-sectional evidence of decline in self-discrepancy in some aspects of the self in old age.

SELF-DISCREPANCY AND MAJOR HEALTH THREATS

A second study was conducted to address two major shortcomings of earlier research in this area (Heidrich, Forsthoff, and Ward, 1994). First, we sought to measure self-discrepancies in domains other than psychological well-being so that we could determine whether domain-specific self-discrepancies were related to well-being. Second, we wished to examine whether self-discrepancy was related to psychological well-being for individuals faced with a major threat to the self; in this case, a diagnosis of cancer.

The diagnosis of cancer can be particularly threatening to the self because it is associated with fear of pain and death due to the disease and fear of painful, debilitating, or disfiguring treatment (Levin, Cleeland, and Dar, 1985; Ward, Heidrich, and Wolberg, 1989; Weisman, 1979). Therefore, the diagnosis of cancer may be a particularly potent motivation for changing assessments of both the actual and the ideal self (Curbow et al., 1990). In fact, similar to the paradox of successful aging, a similar finding concerning adjustment to cancer exists. Although persons with cancer initially experience high levels of distress, over time they are as well adjusted as others, and, in fact, may perceive themselves as being better adjusted than they were before the illness (Wood, Taylor, and Lichtman, 1985; Zenmore et al., 1989).

Taylor argues, based on studies of women with cancer, that one way individuals adjust to threatening events is by altering the view of the self in such a way that self-esteem is enhanced (Taylor, 1983). Heidrich and Ward (1992) found that elderly women with cancer had lower actual and ideal self-ratings than women without cancer, but were no different in self-discrepancies or adjustment. They suggested that women with cancer may be lowering their expectations concerning their ideal selves in order to more closely align their ideal self-assessments with their now lower actual self-assessments. This increased congruence between their ideal and actual self-conceptions may serve to reduce psychological distress.

To examine the role of self-discrepancies more systematically, adults (n = 108) with cancer completed a series of self-report instruments about their illness and health status, psychological well-being, and self-discrepancies. In terms of the diagnosis of cancer, the most frequently reported were breast cancer (27 percent), colorectal cancer (20 percent), lung cancer (13 percent), and lymphoma (12 percent). The sample was somewhat evenly divided among those who described their cancer as local (45 percent) versus metastatic (36 percent), and acute (51 percent) versus chronic (43 percent). Individuals' self-reports of their disease status (local vs. metastatic, an indication of the severity of the illness) corresponded in a meaningful way with their perceptions regarding the time line of the illness (acute versus chronic). Current treatment included chemotherapy (61 percent) and radiotherapy (10 percent). The average number of years since diagnosis was 3.4 $(SD = 4.6)$.

A twenty-item self-discrepancy scale was developed for this study. Before completing the scale, participants read a description and example of actual self, ideal self, and a match between actual and ideal selves and then were asked to take a few minutes to think about their personal qualities, goals, and dreams about themselves. They then were asked to indicate the extent of their agreement ("strongly agree" to "strongly disagree" on a six-point scale) with the statement "My actual self and ideal self are a very close match" in each of twenty life domains. Examples of domains include, "my physical health," "coping with change," and "pursuing my leisure interests and hobbies." Higher scores indicate higher levels of self-discrepancy (i.e., little match between actual and ideal self).

Multiple regression analyses were performed to examine how self-discrepancies mediated the relationship between physical health (in this case, severity of illness, symptoms, functional status) and psychological well-being. Regardless of the level of symptoms, functional status, or perceptions of cancer as a chronic illness, individuals with less self-discrepancy had higher levels of purpose in life and positive relations with others and lower levels of depression. Conversely, individuals with more self-discrepancy had higher levels of depression and lower levels of psychological well-being.

As predicted in the self-system model, physical health had direct effects on psychological well-being for these individuals with cancer. The more severe the illness (in terms of symptoms or perceived chronicity) the higher the level of self-discrepancy and the lower the level of psychological well-being. However, self-discrepancy was more important than illness-related variables in explaining psychological well-being. The greater the match between actual and ideal self, the higher the level of psychological well-being and the lower the level of depression.

This study also indicated that self-discrepancy may have differential relationships with different aspects of psychological well-being. For instance, purpose in life may be an especially meaningful aspect of adjustment for those facing a life-threatening illness. Self-discrepancy was more important than physical health status in participants' senses of having meaning or purpose in life. Individuals whose ideal and actual selves were more closely aligned had higher levels of purpose in life, regardless of the severity of their diseases.

The category of positive relations with others taps the perception that one has warm, satisfying, trusting relationships with others, that one is capable of strong empathy and affection, and understands the give-and-take of human relationships (Ryff, 1989b). Unlike purpose in life and depression, there was no direct effect of physical health on positive relations with others. However, self-discrepancies did predict positive relations. Thus, self-discrepancy was more important than physical health in patients' perceptions of their relations with others.

A somewhat different pattern emerged in relation to psychological distress or depression similar to findings regarding the self-system model described earlier (Heidrich and Ryff, 1993a). That is, physical health continued to be related to depression even after self-discrepancies were taken into account. It may be that self-discrepancies are more powerful in determining well-being than depression, or, alternatively, perceptions about physical health may have a greater impact on psychological distress than on psychological well-being.

In summary, evidence from both cross-sectional and longitudinal data points to declines in ideal self-assessments in old age, at least for select aspects of the self. We consider this partial support for the notion that self-discrepancies are reduced with age, but further research is needed to test the hypothesis directly. We also have evidence that self-discrepancy is related to physical health status in our study of cancer patients and, more importantly, that self-discrepancy is related to psychological functioning. In adults with cancer, self-discrepancy was more powerful than illness-related factors in predicting psychological well-being and, to a lesser extent, depression.

FUTURE DIRECTIONS

The previous sections summarize a number of studies built around a model of the self-system and psychological well-being. These studies offer substantial support for the notion that interpretive mechanisms related to the self help explain positive psychological outcomes in old age. The model is important because it provides a framework for conceptualizing *dynamic* processes of aging. There are numerous directions for broadening the scope of inquiry regarding the role of the self in psychological well-being. Each aspect of the self-system model provides a springboard for these inquiries. The following section highlights a number of these directions, including other life transitions, other self-related mechanisms, and the role of social-structural variables.

Life Transitions, the Self, and Well-Being

In our original conceptualization of the self-system model, we focused on physical health as the age-related stressor that influences both the self-system and psychological well-being. Our rationale for this approach included the importance of physical health and functioning to quality of life in older adulthood, the personal and social costs of illness and disability in old age, and the lay belief that declines in physical health are to some extent inevitable in old age. All of these factors underscore the salience of physical health in the lives of older adults. The research to date supports this conceptualization of physical health status as an important factor in relation to both the self and well-being. Yet both life-span theory and some of our own descriptive data indicate that other life events may provide important contexts for examining the role of the self.

Life-span developmental theory points to the importance of the type and the timing of life events in relation to psychological adjustment. Certain life events are considered normative in old age—retirement and widowhood, for example—and are expected or considered "on time" when they occur in old age. Although these events, whether positive or negative, may be stressful, some degree of anticipatory socialization probably takes place because they are expected. A period of adjustment to the event is allowed, during which some efforts at coping with the event take place, but generally individuals are expected to, and typically do, make these transitions successfully. Other life events are considered nonnormative because they are unexpected or atypical (e.g., a natural disaster, placing a spouse in a nursing home) or because they occur at the wrong time (e.g., widowhood at a young age). These events are considered highly stressful, requiring substantial coping efforts and personal and social resources in order for individuals to protect and maintain their mental health (Ryff and Heidrich, 1994).

Since both types of events are considered stressful, both theoretically require the individual to adapt to maintain or enhance his or her psychological well-being. There are a number of descriptive questions to be answered regarding the influence of life events on the self-system. A very general question is whether the self-system model holds for other age-related stressful events, such as adaptation to retirement or widowhood, or the taking on of new roles in old age (e.g., late-life marriage, major volunteer work commitments). For example, interpretive processes related to the self have been investigated in research on the effects of community relocation on the physical and psychological health of older women (Smider, Essex, and Ryff, 1994; Ryff and Essex, 1992). Self-assessments based on social comparisons and reflected appraisals mediated the impact of the stress of relocation on well-being. Another study of midlife adults (Ryff, Lee, Essex, and Schmutte, 1994) examined the transition of launching children into adulthood and its relation to psychological well-being. For mid-life parents, psychological well-being was related to their assessments of their children's success and their own feelings of responsibility for how their children turned out. These approaches test the limits of the self-system model as a general model of adaptation in old age.

The model could be further explicated by a comparative approach to the study of age-related life transitions. For example, we have evidence that more severe health threats motivate individuals to engage in social comparisons more frequently in an attempt to buffer those threats, and, under conditions of severe threat, social comparisons protect the self and maintain psychological well-being. A further test of the buffering effect of social comparisons could consider the relative influence of life transitions considered more or less stressful on the self and well-being. Do normative versus nonnormative transitions have a differential impact on the self-system? Do positive and negative events affect the self in different ways? Do they affect different aspects of the self-system? For example, negative life events may lead one to lower one's ideal-self standards to match more closely the realities of the situation, or may motivate an individual to learn new ways of coping from others who have adapted well. Do positive life events have a similar impact on the self-system? If positive life events increase psychological well-being, is this a direct effect or due to adaptive changes in different aspects of the self-system? An example of the latter might be the influence of positive events on self-discrepancy. A positive life experience may raise one's actual self-assessments, thereby increasing the congruence between actual and ideal selves resulting in higher levels of psychological well-being.

Our descriptive data further suggest that there may be domains of life, perhaps age-related, that deserve scrutiny. Our research on social comparisons suggests particular domains of life require attention: coping with aging, maintaining a desired activity level, and being able to learn new things. How individuals manage change in abilities or perceptions in these domains gives insight into how mental health is maintained. These and other salient later-life domains need elaboration to understand fully the complexity of the self in relation to well-being.

In summary, the model of the self-system can be extended to examine the processes of adaptation during numerous life transitions and in salient life domains. Different ways of organizing and describing critical aspects of life transitions offer opportunities to examine the conditions under which self-system mechanisms are brought into play and maintain or enhance psychological well-being.

Additional Critical Self-Cognitions

The self-system model proposes three aspects of the self that encompass interpersonal, intrapersonal, and social structural processes involved in the formation of the self-concept. Although this formulation is meant to offer a comprehensive and multidimensional view of the self, research and theory on the self suggest other critical self-cognitions that function to maintain and enhance the individual's sense of self. Attention to these mechanisms offers opportunities for further explicating the role of the self in psychological well-being. Rosenberg's (1986) self-concept theory offers additional ways of examining the role of the self. The self is not only multidimensional (e.g., the actual and ideal selves), but aspects of the self are organized in a hierarchical manner such that some aspects of the self are more important or central to one's self-concept and, ultimately, self-esteem. These central aspects of the self should be more powerful determinants of psychological well-being than less central aspects of the self. Rosenberg also describes the self as dynamic, and we have shown that assessments of the actual and ideal selves do change over time. What also may change, however, is the relative importance or centrality of any self-aspect. An adaptive mechanism related to the centrality of an aspect is a possible shift in the hierarchical organization of aspects of the self in response to life transitions. For instance, physical health may be a central aspect of the self in old age *until* declines in physical health become so great that adaptive responses on the part of the self are required. A shift in centrality may occur in which physical health is replaced by another, perhaps still positive, aspect of the self. This shift in centrality serves a self-enhancing function because self-esteem is protected.

Evidence for the importance of psychological centrality in well-being has been demonstrated in research on older women's relocation (Ryff and Essex, 1992; Kling, Ryff, and Essex, 1994). For instance, women who reported that family (as compared to health, for example) was central to their lives and who reported positive self-assessments (e.g., social comparisons) or self-perceptions about family had higher levels of psychological well-being. Conversely, women for whom family was central but who reported less positive self-assessments had more negative psychological outcomes. Further, self-assessments were not related to well-being as strongly in domains that were not central to women's lives.

Because the self is dynamic, the impact of a change in self-evaluations on psychological well-being could be mitigated by lowering the importance of the domain in which the assessment occurs. The relocation research indicated that shifts occur from pre- to post-move in the centrality of health and friendships in women's lives (Kling, Ryff and Essex, 1994). For instance, for some women, self-evaluations regarding their health declined over time. If they also had a corresponding decrease in the centrality of health, well-being was higher than if they had a corresponding increase in the centrality of health.

Psychological centrality appears to be another important interpretive mechanism related to the self that sheds light on how psychological well-being in old age is maintained. Other lines of research also offer further direction in the understanding of the self, including research on possible selves (Markus and Wurf, 1987), social goals (Brandtstaedter and Rothermund, 1994), and socioemotional selectivity (Lang and Carstensen, 1994).

Social-Structural Influences on the Self

In studying the self and well-being, we have concentrated on explaining individual differences in psychological outcomes, working primarily at the level of the individual. There are, however, broad social-structural variables that potentially influence each piece of the self-system model and add to the explanation of psychological well-being. Two of these are gender and social class.

GENDER AND WELL-BEING

The relationship between physical health, the self, and psychological well-being in old age needs to be examined for gender differences because gender potentially influences the self-system model at three points: 1) through gender differences in physical health in old age, 2) through gender differences in the self-system, and 3) through gender differences in the physical and psychological well-being outcomes that are influenced.

Explanations of psychological well-being may be strengthened by understanding gender differences. Further, gender differences may be better explained in the context of the self-system model. For instance, there are gender differences in physical health in old age. Men have a lower life expectancy and higher mortality rates at all ages and for most leading causes of death, but women have higher morbidity rates (Strickland, 1988). Women are more likely than men to suffer from acute illness and chronic conditions, especially hypertension, diabetes, and arthritis in old age (Verbrugge, 1985), restrict their activities due to health problems (Jette and Branch, 1981; Van Nostrand, Furner, and Suzman, 1993), and seek and receive medical care (Branch and Jette, 1981; Strickland, 1988; Verbrugge, 1985, 1989).

Second, gender is related to psychological well-being. Women report higher levels of stress and more depression than men (McGrath et al., 1990), and, as noted earlier, there are age-related gender differences in Ryff's well-being measures. Biological, health behavior, and social role theories to account for these differences have met with only partial success.

Most importantly, there may be gender differences in self-system mechanisms. Although it is not clear whether such differences may be due to self-system differences or to gender differences in life events, domains, or related contextual factors, numerous hypotheses can be generated and examined in the context of the model. For instance, women report higher levels of social support than men, which may explain higher levels of some aspects of psychological well-being (Berkman and Smye, 1979; George, 1989; House, Landis, and Umberson, 1988; Kaplan, Cassel, and Gore, 1977). However, women also report higher levels of stress and depression than men, in spite of the buffering effects of social support. Attention to self-system mechanisms may provide explanations for these seeming contradictions. Women may be more likely than men to engage in social comparisons because they are more likely to experience functional difficulties, be widowed, live alone, or be poor. Thus, the level of threat to the self may be higher for women than men. On the other hand, because older women are likely to have more extensive social networks, they may have more opportunity for self-enhancing social comparisons to occur, thus protecting their mental health. Likewise, gender may influence the domains of actual or ideal self in which discrepancies are more likely to occur; for example, the domain of interpersonal relationships for women and autonomy/individuality for men (Jordan et al., 1991; Josephs, Markus, and Tafarodi, 1992; Markus and Cross, 1990). Yet the overall level of self-discrepancy may not differ between men and women.

In summary, attention to the role of gender in the relationship between self and well-being may provide explanations for some of the well-documented gender differences in morbidity, mortality, and mental health. Such knowledge would provide a basis for research concerning clinical interventions to maintain mental health in older men and women.

SOCIAL CLASS AND WELL-BEING

Social class may also be a major influence on the relationship between health, the self, and well-being. There is overwhelming evidence that poverty is linked to poor physical and mental health and to higher mortality rates. There is also evidence that there is a linear relationship between socioeconomic status (income or education in the United States) and health, and that the relationship between social class and health holds across all social strata (Adler et al., 1994). These effects have been demonstrated using large-scale longitudinal data sets in the United States and in Britain (Marmot et al., in review). The results from Great Britain are notable because the national health care system in Britain assures equal access to care for all, so that poverty should not prevent or deter access to care. Data from the United States also show that this relationship holds for psychological well-being: that psychological well-being increases in a linear fashion with education and income (Marmot et al., in review). One explanation for these effects is that health and well-being outcomes are determined by experiences early in life that shape the kinds of lives people lead (e.g., health behaviors) and the environments in which they live.

If so, then social class also should add to the explanation of the relationships between self and well-being. Social class appears directly to influence physical health status (and perhaps other salient life domains, such as activities in old age) and psychological well-being, and these effects need to be taken into account. More importantly, the self-system may offer explanations of the effect of social class, particularly on psychological well-being. For instance, the complexity and hierarchy of self-aspects can be shaped by childhood experiences in the formation of what is possible, expected, desired, feared, or ideal in terms of the self. Or, one's sense of integration in the social structure—whether an individual perceives a group identity that is desired or worthwhile—may be a function of social class. Socioeconomic status (indexed by level of education, income, or occupational status) may also play powerfully into the nature and consequences of the social comparisons in which one engages.

Concluding Thoughts on Psychological Well-Being

The self-system model focuses on explanations of psychological well-being. This is a departure from an abundant literature in which health, whether physical or mental, is operationalized as the absence of distress or illness. Life-span theory, theories of mental health, and lay descriptions of health indicate that well-being is *not* merely the absence of distress or the presence of positive mood, but is a complex and multidimensional phenomenon. Dimensions of well-being include having a sense of purpose or meaning in life; feeling that one is continuing to grow and develop as a person; having warm, positive, intimate relations with others; autonomy, or self-confidence and control; accepting oneself; and developing a sense of mastery about negotiating one's daily life. We have shown age, gender, and social class differences in these dimensions of psychological well-being (Ryff, 1995) and that different facets of well-being have unique relationships with physical health and functioning as well as with different dimensions of the self-system. Understanding successful adaptation in old age thus requires attention to the myriad ways in which well-being is both expressed and maintained. Further attention to these differences also affords a way to identify different patterns or typologies of psychological well-being and the ways in which individuals experience them over time. In this way, conceptions of mental health can be broadened to encompass more than the absence of distress or illness by focusing on the maintenance and development of multiple dimensions of well-being.

In summary, we have described a model of the self-system developed to explain the relationship between physical health, the self, and psychological well-being in old age. We have reviewed empirical research that has directly examined this model, as well as studies that support our conceptualizations of social comparisons, self-discrepancies, and psychological well-being. Finally, we offered thoughts on promising directions for research that would shed light on each aspect of the model and the relationships among them. Although we have focused on theoretical explanations and empirical evidence, there are numerous and important avenues for clinical investigations and interventions suggested by our approach. As a huge cohort of adults moves closer to old age, opportunities to discover paths to physical and mental health are indeed rich. This program of research seeks to illuminate that pathway leading through the self.

REFERENCES

Adler, N.E., Boyce, T., Chesney, M.A., et al. (1994). Socioeconomic status and health: The challenge of the gradient. *American Psychologist*, 49:15–24.

Affleck, G., and Tennen, H. (1991). Social comparison and coping with major medical problems. In J. Suls and T.A. Wills (eds.), *Social comparison: Contemporary theory and research*, 369–394. Hillsdale, NJ: Lawrence Erlbaum.

Baltes, P.B. and Baltes, M.M. (1990). Psychological perspectives on successful aging: A model of selective optimization with compensation. In P.B. Baltes and M. M. Baltes (eds.), *Successful aging: Perspectives from the behavioral sciences*, 1–34. New York: Cambridge University Press.

Berkman, L.F., and Smye, S.L. (1979). Social networks, host resistance, and mortality: A nine-year follow-up of Alameda County residents. *American Journal of Epidemiology*, 109:186–204.

Birren, J. E., and Renner, V.J. (1980). Concepts and issues of mental health and aging. In J. E. Birren and R. B. Sloane (eds.), *Handbook of mental health and aging*, 3–33. Englewood Cliffs, NJ: Prentice-Hall.

Branch, L.G., and Jette, A.M., (1981). The Framingham Disability Study: I. Social disability among the aging. *American Journal of Public Health*, 71:1202–1210.

Brandtstaedter, J., and Rothermund, K. (1994). Self-percepts of control in middle and later adulthood: Buffering losses by rescaling goals. *Psychology and Aging*, 9:265–273.

Bureau of the Census. (1986). *Age structure of the U.S. population in the 21st century*. (U.S. Dept. of Commerce, SB-1-86). Washington, DC: U.S. Government Printing Office.

Buunk, B. P., Collins, R.L., Taylor, S. E., et al. (1990). The affective consequences of social comparison: Either direction has its ups and downs. *Journal of Personality and Social Psychology*, 59:1238–1249.

Cohen, S., and Wills, T.A. (1985). Stress, social support, and the buffering hypothesis. *Psychological Bulletin*, 98:310–357.

Curbow, B., Somerfield, M., Legro, M., and Sonnega, J. (1990). Self-concept and cancer in adults: Theoretical and methodological issues. *Social Science and Medicine*, 31:115–128.

Cutrona, C., Russell, D., and Rose, J. (1986). Social support and adaptation to stress by the elderly. *Journal of Psychology and Aging*, 1:47–54.

Diener, E. (1984). Subjective well-being. *Psychological Bulletin*, 95:542–575.

Festinger, L. (1954). A theory of social comparison processes. *Human Relations*, 7:117–140.

George, L.K. (1989). Stress, social support, and depression over the life course. In M.S. Markides and C.L. Cooper (eds.), *Aging, stress, and health*, 241–267. New York: Wiley.

Gibbons, F.X., and Gerrard, M. (1991). Downward comparisons and coping with threat. In J. Suls and T.A. Wills (eds.), *Social comparison: Contemporary theory and research*, 317–346. Hillsdale, NJ: Lawrence Erlbaum.

Heidrich, S. M. (1992). Social comparison processes over time: Influences on well-being. Poster presented at the 45th Annual Scientific Meeting of the Gerontological Society of America, Washington, DC.

———. (1993). The relationship between physical health and psychological well-being in elderly women: A developmental perspective. *Research in Nursing and Health*, 16:123–130.

———. (1994). The self, physical health, and depression in elderly women. *Western Journal of Nursing Research*, 16:544–555.

Heidrich, S.M., Forsthoff, C.A., and Ward, S.E. (1994). Adjustment to cancer: The self as mediator. *Health Psychology*, 13:346–353.

Heidrich, S.M., and Ryff, C.D. (1992). How elderly women cope: Concerns and strategies. *Public Health Nursing*, 9:200–208.

———. (1993a). Physical and mental health in later life: The self-system as mediator. *Psychology and Aging*, 8:327–338.

———. (1993b). The role of social comparison processes in the psychological adaptation of the elderly. *Journal of Gerontology: Psychological Sciences*, 48:127–131.

Heidrich, S.M., and Ward, S.E. (1992). The role of the self in adjustment to cancer in elderly women. *Oncology Nursing Forum*, 9:1491–1496.

Higgins, E.T. (1987). Self-discrepancy: A theory relating self and affect. *Psychological Review*, 94:319–340.

Higgins, E.T., Bond, R.N., Klein, R., and Strauman, T. (1986). Self-discrepancies and emotional vulnerability: How magnitude, accessibility, and type of discrepancy influence affect. *Journal of Personality and Social Psychology*, 51:5–15.

House, J.S., Landis, K.R., and Umberson, D. (1988). Social relationships and health. *Science*, 241: 540–545.

Idler, E.L. (1993). Age differences in self-assessments of health: Age changes, cohort differences, or survivorship? *Journal of Gerontology*, 48:S289–300.

Idler, E.L., and Kasl, S. (1991). Health perceptions and survival: Do global evaluations of health status really predict mortality? *Journal of Gerontology: Social Sciences*, 46:S55–65.

Jette, A.M., and Branch, L.G. (1981). The Framingham Disability Study: II. Physical disability among the aging. *American Journal of Public Health*, 71:1211–1216.

Jordan, J.V., Kaplan, A.G., Miller, J.B., et al. (1991). *Women's growth in connection: Writings from the Stone Center*. New York: Guilford.

Josephs, R.A., Markus, H.R., and Tafarodi, R.W. (1992). Gender and self-esteem. *Journal of Personality and Social Psychology*, 63:391–402.

Kaplan, B.H., Cassel, J.C., and Gore, S. (1977). Social support and health. *Medical Care*, 15:47–58.

Kaplan, G., Barell, V., & Lusky, A. (1988). Subjective state of health and survival among elderly adults. *Journal of Gerontology: Social Sciences*, 43:S114–120.

Kling, K.C., Ryff, C.D., and Essex, M.E. (1994). Adaptive changes in the self concept during a life transition. Paper presented at a symposium on *Common themes in diverse transitions of aging*, 47th Annual Meeting of the Gerontological Society of America, Atlanta, GA.

Kuypers, J. A., and Bengston, V.L. (1973). Social breakdown and competence. *Human Development*, 16:181–201.

Lang, F.R., and Carstensen, L.L. (1994). Close emotional relationships in late life: Further support for proactive aging in the social domain. *Psychology and Aging*, 9:315–324.

Larson, R. (1978). Thirty years of research on the subjective well-being of older Americans. *Journal of Gerontology*, 33:109–125.

Levin, D., Cleeland, C., and Dar, R. (1985). Public attitudes toward cancer pain. *Cancer*, 56:2337–2339.

Markides, K.S., and Lee, D.J. (1990). Predictors of well-being and functioning in older Mexican-Americans and Anglos: An eight-year follow-up. *Journal of Gerontology: Social Sciences*, 45:S69–73.

Markus, H., and Cross, S. (1990). The interpersonal self. In L.A. Pervin (ed.), *Handbook of personality: Theory and research*, 576–608. New York: Guilford.

Markus, H., and Wurf, E. (1987). The dynamic self-concept: A social-psychological perspective. *Annual Review of Psychology*, 38:299–337.

Marmot, M., Ryff, C.D., Bumpass, L.L., et al. (in review). Social inequalities in health: A major public health problem.

McGrath, E., Keita, G.P., Strickland, B.R., and Russo, N.F. (eds.). (1990). *Women and depression: Risk factors and treatment issues*. Washington, DC: American Psychological Association.

National Center for Health Statistics, and Kovar, M.G. (1986). Aging in the eighties, age 65 and over and living alone, contacts with families, friends, and neighbors. In *Advance data from vital and health statistics, vol. 116* (DHHS Pub. No. 86-1250). Hyattsville, MD: Public Health Service.

Nolen-Hoeksema, S. (1987). Sex differences in unipolar depression: Evidence and theory. *Psychological Bulletin*, 101:259–282.

Okun, M.A., Stock, W.A., Haring, M.J., and Witter, R.A. (1984). Health and subjective well-being: A meta-analysis. *International Journal of Aging and Human Development*, 19:111–132.

Riley, M.W. (1994). Aging and society: Past, present, and future. *The Gerontologist*, 34:436–446.

Rosenberg, M. (1986). *Conceiving the self*. New York: Basic Books.

Ryff, C.D. (1989a). Beyond Ponce de Leon and life satisfaction: New directions in quest of successful aging. *International Journal of Behavioral Development*, 12:35–55.

———. (1989b). Happiness is everything, or is it? Explorations on the meaning of psychological well-being. *Journal of Personality and Social Psychology*, 57:1069–1081.

———. (1991). Possible selves in adulthood and old age: A tale of shifting horizons. *Psychology and Aging*, 6:286–295.

———. (1995). Psychological well-being in adult life. *Current Directions in Psychological Science*, 4:99–104.

Ryff, C.D., and Essex, M.J. (1991). Psychological well-being in adulthood and old age: Descriptive markers and explanatory processes. In K.W. Schaie and M. Powell Lawton (eds.), *Annual review of gerontology and geriatrics*, 144–171. Vol. 11, 144–171. New York: Springer.

———. (1992). The interpretation of life experience and well-being: The sample case of relocation. *Psychology and Aging*, 7:507–517.

Ryff, C.D., and Heidrich, S.M. (1994). Past life experiences and perceived changes in psychological well-being. Paper presented at a symposium on *Causes and consequences of perceived personality change*, at the 102nd Annual Convention of the American Psychological Association, Los Angeles, CA.

Ryff, C.D., and Keyes, C.L.M. (1995). The structure of psychological well-being revisited. *Journal of Personality and Social Psychology*, 69:719–727.

Ryff, C.D., Lee, Y.H., Essex, M.J., and Schmutte, P.S. (1994). My children and me: Midlife evaluations of grown children and of self. *Psychology and Aging*, 9:195–205.

Sarason, B.R., Shearin, E.N., Pierce, G.R., and Sarason, I.G. (1987). Interrelations of social support measures: Theoretical and practical implications. *Journal of Personality and Social Psychology*, 52:813–832.

Smider, N.A., Essex, M.J., and Ryff, C.D. (1994). Adaptation to relocation: The interactive influences of psychological resources and contextual factors. Paper presented at the 47th Annual Scientific Meeting of the Gerontological Society of America, Atlanta, GA.

Spiegel, D., Bloom, J.R., Kraemer, H.C., and Gottheil, E. (1989). Effect of psychosocial treatment on survival of patients with metastatic breast cancer. *The Lancet*, 2:888–891.

Strauman, T.J., and Higgins, E.T. (1987). Automatic activation of self-discrepancies and emotional syndromes: When cognitive structures influence affect. *Journal of Personality and Social Psychology*, 53:1004–1014.

Strickland, B.R. (1988). Sex-related differences in health and illness. *Psychology of Women Quarterly*, 12:381–399.

Taylor, S.E. (1983). Adjustment to threatening events: A theory of cognitive adaptation. *American Psychologist*, 38:1161–1173.

Taylor, S.E. and Brown, J.D. (1988). Illusion and well-being: A social psychological perspective on mental health. *Psychological Bulletin*, 103:193–210.

Taylor, S.E., and Lobel, M. (1989). Social comparison activity under threat: Downward evaluation and upward contacts. *Psychological Review*, 96:569–575.

Taylor, S.E., Wood, J.V., and Lichtman, R.R. (1983). It could be worse: Selective evaluation as a response to victimization. *Journal of Social Issues*, 39:19–40.

Thompson, M.G., and Heller, K. (1990). Facets of support related to well-being: Quantitative social isolation and perceived family support in a sample of elderly women. *Psychology and Aging*, 5:535–544.

Thoits, P.A. (1994). Stressor and problem-solving: The individual as psychological activist. *Journal of Health and Social Behavior*, 35:143–159.

Van Nostrand, J.F., Furner, S.E., and Suzman, R., (eds.). (1993). *Health data on older Americans: United States, 1992*. Vital Health Stat 3(27). Hyattsville, MD: National Center for Health Statistics.

Verbrugge, L.M. (1985). An epidemiological profile of older women. In M.R. Haug, A.B. Ford, and M. Sheafor (eds.), *The physical and mental health of aged women*. New York: Springer.

———. (1989). The twain meet: Empirical explanations of sex differences in health and mortality. *Journal of Health and Social Behavior*, 30:282–304.

Ward, S.E., Heidrich, S.M., and Wolberg, W.H. (1989). Factors women take into account when deciding upon type of surgery for breast cancer. *Cancer Nursing*, 12:344–351.

Weisman, A. (1979). *Coping with cancer*. New York: McGraw-Hill.

Wills, T.A. (1981). Downward comparison principles in social psychology. *Psychological Bulletin*, 90:245–271.

———. (1991). Similarity and self-esteem in downward comparison. In J. Suls and T.A. Wills (eds.), *Social comparison: Contemporary theory and research*, 51–78. Hillsdale, NJ: Lawrence Erlbaum.

Wills, T.A., and Suls, J. (1991). Commentary: Neo-social comparison theory and beyond. In J. Suls and T.A. Wills (eds.), *Social comparison: Contemporary theory and research*, 395–411. Hillsdale, NJ: Lawrence Erlbaum.

Wood, J.V. (1989). Theory and research concerning social comparisons of personal attributes. *Psychological Bulletin*, 106:231–248.

Wood, J.V., Taylor, S.E., and Lichtman, R.R. (1985). Social comparison in adjustment to breast cancer. *Journal of Personality and Social Psychology*, 49:1169–1183.

Zenmore, R., Rinholm, J., Shepel, L., and Richards, M. (1989). Some social and emotional consequences of breast cancer and mastectomy: A content analysis of 87 interviews. *Journal of Psychosocial Oncology,* 7:33–45.

The Experience of Retirement for Active Older Adults

Len Sperry
Pamela Wolfe

Over the past three decades, retirement age was for all practical purposes synonymous with eligibility for full Social Security benefits. The United States' Social Security system was instituted in 1935 in part to reduce widespread unemployment by shifting jobs held by older workers (who would retire) to younger workers. While sixty-five had been established as the eligibility age, it is now anticipated that the age will be increased to sixty-six in 2009 and sixty-seven by 2027. Besides changes in the Social Security system, changes in society, as well as changes in the work force, are greatly influencing the experience of retirement and may result in a new conception of retirement in the twenty-first century.

For the past several decades, retirement was viewed and experienced as a reward and respite: a reward for years of dedicated labor, and a respite on life's journey to leisurely review one's past accomplishments and contemplate the future. Now it appears that because of increasing life expectancy, predicted shortfalls in the Social Security system, and the anticipated labor force shortage by the year 2000, many "baby boomers" who will reach their sixty-seventh year around the turn of the century will experience retirement quite differently than retirees yesterday or even today.

While rapid social change makes it difficult to predict with certitude how retirement will be experienced a decade from now, this chapter will attempt to portray the phenomenon of retirement as is it currently being experienced by healthy older adults at the end of the twentieth century. The chapter will first describe the process of retirement, particularly from the perspective of healthy, high-functioning older persons. Then it will explore four sets of factors that influence retirement experiences: health, marital support, social support, and quality of life. Finally, it will describe the results of a study involving health, social support, and psychological well-being in retired executives and their spouses.

THE PROCESS OF RETIREMENT

Retirement involves a major life transition for most individuals. This section describes this process of transition, including people's type of retirement, gender, occupational status, and reemployment.

Type of Retirement: Voluntary or Involuntary

Retirement represents a life change that is subject to widely varying degrees of individual control. Life change events, such as retirement, are more likely to be judged as threats when they are perceived to be out of the individual's control (Taylor, 1983). Thus retirement that is perceived as voluntary and controllable would be expected to be perceived as less threatening than retirement perceived as involuntary.

Floyd et al. (1992) studied 369 retirees completing questionnaires developed to measure retirement as a life transition. It found that analysis of items concerning reasons for retirement documented four primary reasons and that 86 percent of respondents rated one or another of these as being clearly more important than the other three. The four primary reasons were escape from job stress, desire to pursue one's own interests, response to employer's pressure to retire, and presence of circumstances, such as health problems, mandating retirement. The results indicated that those who reported being pressured into retirement experienced the most negative initial crisis period immediately following retirement, which differed significantly from the ratings of initial crisis of the retirees who desired to pursue their own interests. The pressured group also reported significantly less positive long-term changes from pre- to postretirement as compared with both the "own interests" and "job stress" groups.

Braithwaite, Gibson, and Bosly-Craft (1986) interviewed 487 Australian retirees, few of whom had the option of working past retirement age. They found that although 68 percent of respondents claimed to encounter no problems with retirement, reluctance to retire was correlated with a difficult transition period. They did not find, however, a correlation with long-term or wide-ranging negative effects on life style. They felt that with adequate time, reluctant retirees manage to restructure their lives and restore their equilibrium.

Perhaps with more time the group pressured to retire in the Floyd et al. sample would also have developed more satisfaction with life in retirement. Both the men and women in that sample had been retired a mean of less than 4.5 years, while the Australian sample had been retired a mean of 7.4 years for men and 11.7 years for women. At any rate, allowing individuals to remain in the work force until they are ready to retire may help to reduce the difficulties they face in this life transition.

Gender

Until recent years, there has been little research into the retirement experiences of women. Many assumed that women's primary orientation was to home and family, so the cessation of outside employment would pose little problem for them. Recent studies do not support this premise. It is noteworthy that women, especially those whose work life began some years ago, continue to be in lower-paying jobs with fewer pension and medical benefits compared to men (Cohen, 1984). Many retired women are completely dependent on Social Security income, which can decline 33 to 50 percent if they are widowed. Divorced women are also more vulnerable to inadequate Social Security and pension benefits. Inflation can reduce income and assets of women years after retirement. It is not surprising that women are reported to account for 71 percent of the elderly poor (Breeze, 1986).

Women considering retirement perceive financial security to be a major concern. Keddy and Singleton (1991) examined the perceptions of life after retirement of 111 women employees, of varying age and socioeconomic status, of a large Canadian university. They found that although concerns about attitude toward retirement and leisure issues were significant, the most significant concern was financial well-being.

Many studies have shown positive correlations between income and retirement satisfaction. Seccombe and Lee (1986) examined the effect of gender on this relationship, examining the differences between 859 men and 671 women residents of Washington state in levels of self-reported satisfaction with retirement. The results of this study showed a small but significantly lower level of retirement satisfaction for retired women compared to men at the $p < .01$ level. Women had significantly lower incomes than men and were much less likely to be currently married, but did not differ in terms of self-rated health. Regardless of gender, those in better health and with higher incomes were most likely to be satisfied with retirement. Married people also expressed higher levels of retirement satisfaction than did unmarried people. This effect was quite small, however, and did not reach statistical significance for women.

It was concluded that retirement satisfaction is responsive to the same causal processes regardless of gender. Women report lower levels of retirement satisfaction than men, because women have lower income in retirement and to a lesser degree because women are less likely to be married.

Floyd et al. (1992) assessed retirement satisfaction of 243 female and 159 male retirees, using a fifty-one-item retirement satisfaction questionnaire.

Five significant gender differences were found. Women anticipated less satisfaction and experienced more immediate stress following retirement than did men. However, women also rated social activities and reduced stress and responsibilities as more important sources of enjoyment in retirement than did men. They additionally reported spending more time in leisure activities with their friends.

The idea that women find retirement less stressful than men because of their multiplicity of social roles is not supported by these studies. The few gender effects noted are consistent with a slightly more difficult adjustment for women, and support the importance of social contacts for women.

Occupational Status

Recent studies have shown contradictory findings regarding the effect of occupational status on retirement. Richardson and Kilty (1991) evaluated 222 workers in the central Ohio area at the time of retirement and at six- and twelve-month follow-ups. The subjects were derived from a wide range of occupations. Lower occupational status was found to be an important predictor of decline in well-being after retirement, more important than either income or education. Those with lower prestige were hypothesized to experience more discontinuity in retirement, whereas those with higher status often maintained continuity by retaining professional contacts and involvements.

The Seccombe and Lee (1986) study described in the previous section, examining satisfaction with retirement, found no independent correlation between occupational status and satisfaction when health and income were controlled. They believed that higher-status workers are more satisfied with retirement simply because they have higher incomes and better health.

Floyd et al. (1992) found higher scores for enjoyment of certain aspects of retirement in those with less education and income. Thus it seems that a clear relationship between retirement and socioeconomic status has not emerged yet.

Sonnenfeld (1988) extensively studied those at the highest status levels of American society, the chief executive officers (CEOs) of major corporations. In his book, *The Hero's Farewell: What Happens When CEOs Retire,* Sonnenfeld hypothesized that some chief executives have difficulties in traversing the Eriksonian late-life stage of "integrity vs. despair" because they have especially high standards of accomplishment and because their personal identities tend to be fused with their corporate identities. Sonnenfeld found that degree of satisfaction with retirement was a function of the level of mastery the CEO had achieved in forging a personal identity that was distinct from corporate identity, coming to terms with mortality, and realistically defining a lasting contribution. Based on extensive interview research with over 100 retired CEOs, Sonnenfeld concluded that "heroic stature" is a basic motivation for individuals to rise to the rank of CEO; they are in search of extraordinary achievement, which will guarantee that their heroic reputation will live on long after they have left the corporation. While some retired CEOs were found to be quite dissatisfied and frustrated with retirement because they did not believe they had achieved greatness yet—and so went on to found other corporations or maneuvered to regain their power with the "old" corporation—others were quite satisfied and went on to enjoy their families, hobbies, and life in general. Typically, level of psychological maturity, marital satisfaction, and overall psychological well-being correlated with a CEO's capacity to relinquish "heroic stature." Sonnenfeld used a number of data sources to derive profiles of four CEO departure styles. The four styles range from "less satisfied with retirement" and "psychologically healthy" to "more satisfied" and "more healthy."

The "monarch" departure style characterizes those leaders most attached to their roles as chief executives. Often they do not leave office by their own choice, but lead their corporations until removed from office forcibly. Monarchs become enamored by "heroic stature" and are greatly frustrated by not achieving the identity of "immortality" that they believe they must. Consequently, they intend to stay with a job until this stature is achieved. Not surprisingly, they usually have no succession plans, and are quite angry to be forced into retirement. Their career identities and personal identities were found to be virtually synonymous.

"Generals" also leave office reluctantly, but with the initial belief that they have left the firm behind. Mourning their losses in retirement, they question the competence of their successors, and seek return to office to rescue their firms. Often they continue on as corporate directors and plot to undermine their successors so they can return in the "savior" role. Needless to say, the savior role is a variant of heroic stature. They may establish succession plans, but still find retirement difficult.

Lee Iacocca's 1995 involvement in an attempted hostile takeover of Chrysler Corporation illustrates the general's style. He is reported to have reluctantly retired from Chrysler in 1992, and recently conceded that reading or playing golf for twenty years was something he just could not do. Attempting to return to the helm of Chrysler was consistent with the general's pattern.

Unlike the monarchs and generals, the "ambassadors" are not threatened by their firms' ability to carry on without them. They expressed the greatest feelings of contentment on retiring and leave their firms with feelings of pride and pleasure, achieving a high degree of what Erikson called "ego integrity." Their personal identities are really quite distinct from their career identities. Thus, they show only some degree of heroic stature. Nevertheless, they are concerned about the permanent impact that the corporation—rather than they themselves—make on the community. They tend to take pride and pleasure in both their accomplishments and retirement. Ambassadors might continue on as directors, but do not attempt to sabotage the new CEOs. Instead, they turn their leadership talents to civic causes. Like Jimmy Carter in his postpresidency period, ambassadors tend to assume elder-statesman status.

For the last group of departing leaders, the "governors," retirement means a career switch, commonly into top government posts, new start-up ventures, or turnaround challenges. They experience the least attachment to a leadership role in a given firm, but still long for the opportunity to have an impact. They exhibit some degree of heroic stature but often are not fully satisfied that they have left sufficient legacies. Therefore, they attempt another career or careers to come a little closer to achieving their dreams. Governors tend to exit their jobs gracefully and usually have no contact with the corporation's board, unlike generals.

Reemployment

Society's attitudes and policies concerning the employment of older workers vary with changing demographic and economic conditions. Currently, declining birth and increasing life-expectancy rates have resulted in an escalating number of nonworkers compared to workers in American society. Thus, the economic burdens of retirement have expanded and public policy measures are sought to deal with this problem. Partial or full reemployment after conventional retirement age is one suggested strategy. Data from the National Longitudinal Survey of Older Men (Parnes, 1981), a survey done from 1969 to 1983 with over 5,000 males in the original sample, were examined by Beck (1983) regarding the problem of reemployment. He found that 67 percent of subjects were fully retired and did not work at all after retirement. The people most likely to return to work were those with high job autonomy and high job demand before retirement. Work attitudes and health were also found to have important predictive value. In regard to income, Beck concluded that financial motivation to work only occurs at or below the poverty line. Laborers were not likely to work despite financial limitations and those in higher income ranges were not affected by actual benefit rates as much as by other factors.

Morrow-Howell and Leon (1988), using an ongoing panel study of United States households, produced a predictive model of continued work after retirement. Independent indicators of continued work included type of employment in the last year after retirement, good health, nonurban residence, higher preretirement income, and self-employment. Good health was the most important predictor.

Toughill et al. (1993) conducted a questionnaire study of 216 predominantly white middle-class female subjects involved in organizations for seniors in New Jersey. Only slightly less than 12 percent of this sample was working for pay. When asked if they would be interested in part-time employment currently or in the future, 65 percent said no and 15 percent did not answer. Seventy-five percent, however, said they would be willing to work if the nation needed them during a time of severe labor shortage. The better the health status, the more likely the subject was to be interested in part-time employment, to be willing to work full-time in a period of national need, and to see him- or herself as a potentially useful worker. Interest in employment was not related to current income status.

Thus, the majority of the retired have not returned to work. Whether reemployment will occur seems clearly related to health status. Financial situation, however, has not been clearly related to reemployment. Further study of older persons' attitudes toward employment and prior work habits may be helpful in predicting those who could be targeted for postretirement employment and how recruitment efforts could be designed.

HEALTH AND WELL-BEING

Health, both physical and mental, has a great impact on the experience of retirement. This section reviews data on health and well-being in retirement.

For most people, retirement seems to be a more or less normal and anticipated event without major difficulties. However, relationships between retirement and psychosocial adaptation and physical health have been documented. In the Seccombe and Lee (1986) sample discussed above, the strongest correlate of satisfaction with retirement was self-rated health status. The Braithwaite, Gibson, and Bosly-Craft (1986) data, also described above, showed that those retiring for health reasons were somewhat more likely to experience a difficult adjustment, and additionally reported lower levels of morale and activity after retirement presumably related to continued poor health.

If preretirement health status is taken into account, research has shown little effect of retirement itself on subsequent physical health (Palmore, Fillenbaum, and George, 1984). Salokangas and Joukamaa (1991) found no deterioration in physical health resulting from retirement. They examined data from a long-term prospective study of older adults in the Turku, Finland, area. The subjects were initially evaluated at age sixty-two in 1982, and reevaluated in 1986. One hundred fifty-two subjects for whom followup was available were working in 1982, while sixty-eight had already retired for non-health reasons; by 1986, all subjects had retired. The number of physical illnesses documented by data from the Social Insurance Institution increased in 9 percent, decreased in 2 percent and remained the same in 89 percent of the sample without significant differences between those with prior or recent retirement. Subjective evaluation of physical health also remained chiefly the same in the group retiring during the follow-up.

Retirement studies have rarely used standardized measures of psychological distress or mental health and instead have relied on measures of happiness, self-esteem, morale, or life satisfaction (Bosse et al., 1987). Bosse et al. (1987) used a standard instrument designed to assess symptoms of mental illness, the SCL–90–R. They evaluated 1,513 older men, participants in the Normative Aging Study (Bell, Rose, and Damon, 1972), who averaged 60.4 years in age. Analysis indicated that retirees reported more psychological symptoms than did workers, even after controlling for physical health status. Retirees showed greater symptom levels on the somatization and obsessive-compulsive subscales that were significant at the $p <. 001$ level. It was hypothesized that lack of a structured work role may allow individuals so predisposed to spend more time obsessing about relatively trivial concerns, including minor, nonspecific aches and pains. Less significant differences were also found for the depression and phobic anxiety subscales.

It was noted that the cross-sectional nature of the data made it difficult to determine the direction of the association. Poor mental health, like poor physical health, may lead to retirement, rather than retirement adversely affecting mental health. Further longitudinal studies will be needed to address issues of causality.

The Impact of Retirement on Marriage

An emerging finding in a number of studies on marital factors in retirement is the centrality of marriage for most retirees. In the National Longitudinal Study of Men (Parnes, 1981) 86.7 percent of men who retired between 1966 and 1977 were married and living with their spouses. Similarly, Atchley and Miller (1983) found the figure to be 65 percent in those retiring between 1975 and 1981. As mortality rates decline and earlier retirement increases, the percentage of individuals retiring as part of a married couple will continue to increase. In short, marriage is the context in which most retirees find themselves. Thus, research on retirement issues, ranging from decisions about retirement to life satisfaction and adjustment to retirement, should account for marital status. Unfortunately, many studies of retirement have not considered marriage as a central or moderating variable (Atchley, (1992).

It is commonly believed that retirement is a stressful life transition that negatively affects the marriage relationship for one or both spouses. Bernard (1972) termed this negative impact of the husband's retirement on the wife's well-being "the female disadvantage." Actually, research on the quality of marriage and marital satisfaction shows little, if any, threat to the marital relationship. In fact, the opposite has been noted: Marital and life satisfaction tend to increase in the retirement years. This section reviews research on such topics as adjustment to retirement, marital satisfaction, division of household work, friends, and quality of life or life satisfaction. Much of the cited research concerns traditional couples in which only the husband works outside the home. This is not surprising, as a majority of retired couples studied in the 1960s through the early 1980s were traditional couples. More recently published research also includes dual wage-earner couples and their experience of retirement.

Adjustment to Retirement and Retirement Satisfaction

Adjustment to retirement appears to be a function of several factors, including health, expectations, goal-directedness, perceived control, gender, and occupational status. Unfortunately, measurement of retirement adjustment and satisfaction has been quite primitive. Fortunately, Floyd et al. (1992) have developed a fifty-one-item Retirement Satisfaction Inventory with acceptable reliability and validity properties that has been used both for research purposes and in counseling settings as a brief screening device for identifying problem areas and issues for intervention. Rather than providing merely a global rating of satisfaction with retirement, the Retirement Satisfaction Inventory also assesses specific sources of satisfaction and dissatisfaction involving retirement.

Braithwaite, Gibson, and Bosly-Craft (1986) set out to study retirees who reported difficulty in making the transition to retirement. They found two predictors of poor adjustment that had quite different consequences for the retirees experiencing them. Retirement that was health-related and negative feelings about retirement were linked with low physical and social activity and involvement, as well as poor physical and mental health and inadequate income in the years following retirement.

Expectation about the experience of retirement appears to have a bearing on adjustment to retirement. Often, a busy spouse who has been overly focused on career to the detriment of the marital relationship promises to focus more on spouse and family after retirement. In their cross-sectional interview study of 217 husband-working couples and husband-retired couples, Vinick and Ekerdt (1992) found that while couples planning for retirement hoped to make changes in their activities, few of these expectations were realized. Studied were joint social activities, couple-only social activities, the husband's personal pursuits, the wife's personal pursuits, and the husband's and wife's household tasks. The researchers found that with the exception of the husband's household tasks, at least half of the men and women in husband-retired couples described no changes in activities from pre- to postretirement. While 80 percent of couples expected to spend more time together in couple-only activities, only 52 percent and 47 percent of men and women, respectively, reported such an increase. In wife-working couples, 80 percent expected an increase in couple-only activities, but less than 33 percent reported such an increase. Similarly, while over fifty percent of the men queried expected to spend more time on hobbies and other leisure pursuits, only thirty-three percent reported such increases. It is important to note that the majority of retired couples in this study reported a continuity in level of participation in activities from before retirement until after.

What are the implications of this study? The researchers suggest that a lack of couple consensus on expectations may be detrimental to retirement adjustment. They suggest that preretired couples be encouraged to share their expectations about activities in retirement and base their projections on a realistic assessment of the present situation. If activity changes after retirement are desired to resuscitate a troubled marriage, considerable joint efforts—like counseling—may be necessary to achieve adequate levels of retirement satisfaction and adjustment.

An important predictor of adjustment to retirement is goal-directedness, that is, the ability to maintain a sense of purpose and direction. Researchers found that highly goal-directed retirees were more outgoing and socially involved than poorly goal-directed retirees. Poorly goal-directed retirees tended to be self-critical, dissatisfied, and solicitous of emotional support (Payne, Robbins, and Dougherty, 1991). Ability to be goal-directed reflects one's perception of control over life circumstances. Abel and Hayslip (1986) report that perceived control—locus of control—was related to measures of adjustment on the job and in retirement among older adults.

Marital Satisfaction and Retirement
While some early studies (Luckey, 1966; Glass and Wright, 1977) reported

declines in marital satisfaction in the retirement years, other studies (Glen, 1975) found marital satisfaction to increase throughout the family life cycle. More recent research is likely to report a curvilinear relationship between marital satisfaction and the various stages of the family life cycle (Anderson et al., 1983). Current research hypothesizes that elderly couples tend to have more positive interactions and less negative sentiments than younger couples. Condie (1989) studied fifty-eight couples married for at least fifty years with a self-report questionnaire and a two-hour tape-recorded interview. He found that marital satisfaction declined during the child-rearing years of relationships and increased in the later years, especially in retirement.

Gilford and Bengston (1979) found there to be two components to marital satisfaction: a positive one that included interactions such as discussing, working, and laughing together; and a negative one that included disagreement, anger, and criticism. Results of their longitudinal research showed that the negative component declined steadily over time, while the positive component followed the U-shaped or curvilinear pattern noted in other studies of marital satisfaction. Since offspring tend to leave the family context at a time when the couple is approaching the later part of mid-life, marital satisfaction tends to increase steadily among the elderly. Thus, retirement is usually situated in the context of rising marital satisfaction.

Results from the Ohio Longitudinal Study of Aging and Adaptation (Atchley and Miller, 1983), involving 399 couples, indicate that marital dissatisfaction was reported by only 1.8 percent of respondents, while 68.1 percent reported they were extremely satisfied with their marriages. Related findings were that retired husbands were more likely to say they were extremely satisfied when compared to working husbands, and that there were no significant gender differences. Older husbands tended to report the highest levels of satisfaction. For wives, recent disability was the only significant predictor, with those experiencing recent disability reporting they were extremely satisfied rather than just satisfied with their marriage. This finding was surprising in that health problems are expected to create a strain on relationships. However, in the in-depth interview phase of the study, it was learned that caregiving provided the caregiver a sense of security and purpose, while care receiving provided the recipient a sense of security and being cared about. Accordingly, both caregiver and care receiver reported increased marital satisfaction (Atchley, 1982; 1992).

The quality of marriage and, subsequently, marital satisfaction is likely to be a function of one or more personal and interpersonal factors. Results from the Scandinavian study of aging, the TURVA project, suggest that empathy is an important factor in marital satisfaction. It was found that couples who experienced a close marital relationship in which the spouse was described as empathic were less likely to report depressive or other psychological symptoms. On the other hand, psychological symptoms were most common in those who reported that their relationship to their spouse was distant (Salokangas, Mattila, and Joukamaa, 1988). In a cross-sectional study of 229 older couples, decreased financial resources and clinical depression significantly lowered the quality of the marital relationship (Wright, 1990).

In an important study of older dual wage-earner couples, Anderson (1992) reports data from the Aging Couples Study regarding marital support and quality. She studied the impact of the timing of retirement on conjugal support. Anderson anticipated that if both working spouses retired at the same time, there would be no difference in degree of conjugal support, whereas it would increase or decrease when one spouse retired before the other. No such differences were found in the 298 couples studied. Husband and wives were not more supportive of each other during the transition into retirement as had been predicted. Accordingly, Anderson concluded that the kind and type of support exchange after retirement is influenced by the couple's exchange of such support during preretirement years.

Division of Household Work

Division of household work is probably the most commonly studied factor in the impact of retirement on marriage literature. Current research consistently shows that sharing of household tasks and activities tends to increase in retirement. Condie (1989) reported on fifty-eight couples married fifty years or more. He found that as men retire, they become more involved in housework and household duties. It has been hypothesized that increasing household duties may ease the husband's transition from work to retirement and provide a boost in self-esteem. Nevertheless, women continue to have primary responsibility for housework. Condie found that among golden-anniversary couples, duties were divided up largely on traditional gender lines: the husband cutting the grass and doing repairs, the wife cooking and washing dishes. However, Condie found that finances and grocery shopping tended to be handled by both equally. One-fourth of the couples shared equally in preparing breakfast and doing the evening dishes.

Atchley (1976) speculated that major changes in household activity patterns occurred only with a significant restructuring of life goals. Szinovacz's (1989) research supported Atchley's view. She found that retirees either maintained or slightly expanded their preretirement household work time and duties, and that wives were more likely than their husbands to report increased household work time and duties. In her cross-sectional study of 611 retirees, Szinovacz found that health and retirement timing were the key couple characteristics that predicted role behavior in household tasks after retirement. Specifically, illness of the wife, but not of the husband, appeared to bring about a redistribution of household responsibilities. Timing of a spouse's retirement was clearly predictive of increased involvement when the other spouse was still employed. Dorfman (1992) studied household tasks in a rural sample of 149 retired couples and found a greater degree of equalitarianism after retirement in household work. Vinick and Ekerdt (1991) studied ninety-two retired couples and found that the majority of men reported they increased their participation in household tasks. Parenthetically, it is interesting to ponder the methodological concern raised by Dorfman (1992). She notes that significant differences have been found between husbands' and wives' reports on the same household activities. The implication is that husbands may be misperceiving and overreporting the amount and type of household work they do. Needless to say, such discrepancies need to be further studied to clarify their meaning.

Friends and Family Support Systems

Do married couples increase their social networks and the number of friends during the course of retirement? Do they change the nature of their relationships with their children and other relatives? Much less is known about this aspect of marriage and retirement. Generally speaking, retired couples slightly expand their social networks and spend more time with relatives (Vinick and Ekerdt, 1992). Brubaker and Ade-Ridder (1986) compared 103 older couples residing in a retirement facility with 232 older couples residing in the community; those in the retirement facility spent significantly less time with friends than couples living in the larger community. On the other hand, couples in the facility reported slightly higher levels of marital quality. There were no significant differences in the amount of time spent with family members. In an earlier study, Ade-Ridder (1985) compared couples married more than fifty years with those married less than fifty years. Those married less than fifty years spent more time socializing with friends than those married more than fifty years. Retired older adults typically report that friends provide more important and satisfying companionship than do their children. Furthermore, friends have a stronger relation to the retired elderly's well-being than family members (Antonucci, 1990). Being with friends is also reported to be more stimulating than being with children and other relatives (Larson, Mannell, and Zuzanek, 1986). It might be concluded that even though older adults count on their family for many needs, they enjoy their friendships and social contacts much more.

In addition to the research on the impact of health status and marital satisfaction on retirement, another line of research involves quality of life and life satisfaction. This section briefly overviews research findings on life satisfaction and quality of life.

Overall life satisfaction of elderly couples tends to be rather high. Sporaskowski and Hughston (1978) queried forty couples married more than fifty years about the most and least satisfying periods of their married lives. Childbearing, preschool, and aging periods were noted as most satisfying, while childbearing, launching a family, and the middle years were described as the least satisfying. That childbearing is listed in both categories indicates the strains as well as satisfaction that accompany that stage of parenthood. Research by Atchley and Miller (1983) and Brubaker (1985) suggests that life satisfaction is very high in the retired elderly, but not surprisingly, is linked to health status and marital satisfaction.

Other factors have been hypothesized to influence quality of life. These include sense of coherence, religious orientation, local environment, and relationship with grandchildren. Sagy, Antonovsky, and Adler (1990) found that a sense of coherence—the belief that life has meaning and purpose—best predicted life satisfaction in their study of 805 Israeli retirees. Subjective health status was the second most powerful predictor. Van Haitsma (1986) reported that an intrinsic religion was related to life satisfaction and quality of life in a study of 85 retirement home residents. Reitzes, Mutran, and Pope (1991) contend that geographic location greatly impacts quality of life. Retired males, aged sixty to seventy-four, living in suburbs were compared with urban dwellers on a measure of psychological well-being. A total of 1,654 males were surveyed. Those residing in suburbs had the highest well-being scores compared to those living in central cities. Poor health tended to reduce the well-being of suburbanites more than for city dwellers. It appears that suburban living indirectly influenced well-being by facilitating informal activities. Finally, in a structured interview study of 301 retired grandparents, Thomas (1990) found that a positive relationship with a grandchild was a significant predictor of morale and life satisfaction.

HEALTH AND WELL-BEING IN RETIRED SENIOR EXECUTIVES AND THEIR SPOUSES

Senior executives, particularly chief executive officers (CEOs), have been reported to experience different retirement patterns (Sonnenfeld, 1988), and usually better overall health and well-being (Sperry, 1993) than nonexecutives. In comparison to the many studies reporting on retirement patterns, health, and well-being of retired workers, very little has focused on senior executives. Accordingly, the Foley Center on Aging and Development at the Medical College of Wisconsin designed a multifaceted pilot study to examine retirement patterns, health, and well-being among senior executives.

Specifically, the study examined the influence of personality, optimism, social support, generativity, and retirement patterns on various dimensions of physical health and psychological well-being among senior executives and their spouses. Given that most retired senior executives are married and that the marriage relationship significantly affects health and well-being, this study attended closely to couple dynamics.

Accordingly, fourteen retired senior executives and their spouses were enlisted for the study. All had been retired at least two years prior to data collection. Data collection consisted of a set of self-report measures as well as individual and joint structured interviews.

Self-report questionnaires included the RAND Health Status Questionnaire (1.0), Schedule of Illness, Dyadic Adjustment Scale, the Neuroticism Scale of the NEO Inventory, Loyola Generativity Scale, Life Orientation Test, Social Network Index, Social Support and Social Undermining Scale, Psychological Well-Being Scale, the Center for Epidemiological Studies Symptom Scale of Depression (CES-D), and the anxiety scale of the Jackson Personality Inventory. The structured interview included closed-ended questions about background and health practices, and open-ended questions about the decision to retire, planning for retirement, and adaptation to retirement.

The average age of the study participants was seventy. Because there were no significant differences between retirees and spouses on any measure, analyses were conducted on the total sample of twenty-eight participants. The physical health measures showed participants to be in good health, although the average number of health problems was 2.7. The majority of study participants rated their retirement as a positive experience. Surprisingly, given their executive status and business acumen, most reported no formal retirement planning. Activities during retirement consisted of mainly leisure and recreational pursuits. Unlike the findings in Sonnenfeld's study (1988), only a few CEO participants continued to be moderately involved in the corporation from which they formally retired. One retiree reported starting a new business. Six of the fourteen senior executives indicated that they participated in internal corporate events, while only four retained a formal consultation relationship with that corporation. In short, the majority of these retired executives have actually retired. Only one reported that retirement was due to mandatory company policy.

Similar to Sonnenfeld's (1988) data, spouses found the first year of retirement much more stressful than the retiree reported it to be. Unlike those retirees studied by Sonnenfeld, the majority of these retirees found retirement to be rejuvenating, positive, and only minimally stressful. Only two of the subjects seemed to have significant difficulties with retirement.

One subject seemed an apt example of the general's retirement style as described by Sonnenfeld. He left his firm several years early due to disagreement with another top officer, and indicated, "Either he left or I left." Sonnenfeld's generals, too, were involved in internal rivalries. During their tenures in office they were often able to act as a bridge between competing factions, but in retirement they tended to undermine their successors. Sonnenfeld described these retirees as lamenting the loss of power and prestige but, nonetheless, being the only CEOs to appreciate relaxation from stress in retirement. For them, retirement meant the end of a losing battle to stay in charge. Similarly, this retiree general described initial difficulties in adjusting to the loss of executive perks and authority, as well as "being in the mainstream." Despite these losses, he, too, found the lack of stress in retirement to be rejuvenating. Sonnenfeld also noted that the generals seemed to find other roles, such as those in family life, less satisfying. Similarly this retiree, when compared to the remainder of our sample, scored a full standard deviation below the mean on the Dyadic Adjustment Scale of marital adjustment.

The other subject experiencing a difficult retirement seemed to be an example of Sonnenfeld's monarch retirement style. He was one of the founding partners of a small service corporation. He indicated that nothing about retirement was rejuvenating and he often regretted having to retire when he did. His only reason for retirement was a life-threatening health problem. He maintained that he was only partially retired and continued to keep an office at the firm. The monarchs described by Sonnenfeld also felt very frustrated by the loss of their leadership roles and did not leave their positions by choice.

The general and monarch retirees differed from the remainder of the sample in having a combination of the highest neuroticism measures along with the lowest well-being measures. These factors were significantly related to higher levels of retirement stress.

The majority of the subjects' retirement patterns best fit the ambassador style as described by Sonnenfeld. They left their firms without regret and their personal lives were relatively free of the internal turmoil and external threat characterizing the generals and monarchs. The ambassador retirees studied by Sonnenfeld often remained involved in the firms from which they retired. They served as postretirement mentors and often served on boards of directors. Seven of the study subjects maintained such contact; five of them were in the ambassador group. A good example of such a retiree is Mr. R., who gradually transferred leadership of his firm to his son, but continued to spend a few hours a month serving as chairman of the board and advising his successor when advice was solicited.

Sonnenfeld labeled his fourth retirement style that of the governor. These retirees had the least attachment to a leadership role in a given firm, but in retirement continued to long for opportunities to have an impact. For them, retirement often meant a career switch that was impatiently awaited. Two study subjects' retirement patterns seemed characteristic of the governor's style. Both retired without regrets. One went on to be occupied by full-time volunteering as the head of a local civic organization. The other "retiree" indicated he had actually "retired" three times. First he left private business to enter top-level government service, again retiring from that to head a local nonprofit concern, and finally to serve as director of a national charitable organization. The two general retirees had the highest dyadic adjustment scores of any CEOs in the sample. They also both had high scores on the personality measure of optimism.

Concluding Comments

The Foley Center Study of retired executives just described nicely summarizes much of the previously reported research on retirement for active older adults. Among the retiring executives and their spouses, significant correlations were noted between retirement-related stress and negative health change as well as neuroticism and lower levels of psychological well-being. Better health status was correlated with younger age and lower levels of depression. Higher levels of psychological well-being were associated with lower ratings of retirement stress and neuroticism.

Sonnenfeld's four retirement patterns were found to be conceptually useful in examining the data of this pilot study. This study's executives showed varieties of retirement that were reasonably similar to Sonnenfeld's four patterns. It remains to be seen whether the validity of these patterns will be confirmed by further studies.

References

Abel, B., and Hayslip, B. (1986). Locus of control and attitudes toward work and retirement. *Journal of Psychology*, 120:479–487.

Ade-Ridder, L. (1985). Quality of marriage: A comparison between golden working couples and couples married less than fifty years. *Lifestyles*, 7:224–237.

Anderson, S.A., Russell, C.S., and Schumm, W.A. (1983). Perceived marital quality and family life-cycle categories: A further analysis. *Journal of Marriage and the Family*, 45:127–39.

Anderson, T. (1992). Conjugal support among working-wife and retired-wife couples. In M. Szinovacz, D. Ekerdt, and B. Vinick (eds.), *Families and retirement*, 174–188. Newbury Park, CA: Sage.

Antonucci, T.C. (1990). Social supports and social relationships. In R.H. Binstock and L.K. George (eds.), *Handbook of aging and the social sciences*, 205–226. 3rd ed. San Diego: Academic Press.

Atchley, R.C. (1976). *The sociology of retirement*. Cambridge, MA: Schenkman.

———. (1982). The process of retirement: Comparing women and men. In M. Szinovacz (ed.), *Women's retirement: Policy implications of recent research*, 120–129. Beverly Hills: Sage.

Atchley, R.C. (1992). Retirement and marital satisfaction. In M. Szinovacz, D. Ekerdt, and B. Vinick (eds.), *Families and retirement*, 145–158. Newbury Park, CA: Sage.

Atchley, R.C., and Miller, S.J. (1983). Types of elderly couples. In T.H. Brubaker (ed.), *Family relationships in later life*, 48–67. Beverly Hills: Sage.

Beck, S. (1983). Determinants of return to work after retirement. Final report for Grant No. 1 R23 AG 03565-0 1, Kansas City, MO.

Bell, B., Rose, C.L., and Damon, A. (1972). The Normative Aging Study: An interdisciplinary study of health and aging. *Aging and Human Development*, 3:3–17.

Bernard, J. (1972). *The future of marriage*. New York: World Publishing.

Bosse, R., Aldwin, C.M., Levenson, M.R., and Ekerdt, D.J. (1987). Mental health differences among retirees and workers: Findings from the normative aging study. *Psychology and Aging* 2(4):383–389.

Braithwaite, V., Gibson, D., and Bosly-Craft, R. (1986). An exploratory study of poor adjustment styles among retirees. *Social Science and Medicine*, 23:493–499.

Breeze, N. (1986). Cronesnest: The vision. In M. Bell (ed.), *Women as elders: Images, visions, and issues*, 7–13. New York: Haworth Press.

Brubaker, T.H. (1985). Responsibility for household tasks: A look at golden anniversary couples aged 75 years and older. In W.A. Peterson and J. Quadagno (eds.), *Social bonds in later life*, 171–192. Beverly Hills: Sage.

Brubaker, T.H., and Ade-Ridder, L. (1986). Husbands' responsibility for household tasks in older marriages: Does living situation make a difference? In R.A. Lewis and R.E. Salt (eds.), *Men in families*, 121–137. Beverly Hills: Sage.

Cohen, L. (1984). *Small expectations: Society's betrayal of older women*. Toronto: McClell and Stewart.

Condie, S. (1989). Older married couples. In S. Bahr and E. Peterson (eds.), *Aging and the family*, 142–158. New York: Lexington.

Dorfman, L. (1992). Couples in retirement: Division of household work. In M. Szinovacz, D. Ekerdt, and B. Vinick (eds.), *Families in retirement*, 159–173. Newbury Park, CA: Sage.

Floyd, F., Hayes, S., Doll, R., et al. (1992). Assessing retirement satisfaction and perceptions of retirement experiences. *Psychology and Aging*, 7:609–621.

Gilford, R., and Bengston, V.L. (1979). Measuring marital satisfaction in three generations: Positive and negative dimensions. *Journal of Marriage and the Family*, 41:387–398.

Glass, S.P., and Wright, T.L. (1977). The relationship of extramarital sex, length of marriage, and sex differences on marital satisfaction and romanticism: Athanasiou's data reanalyzed. *Journal of Marriage and the Family*, 39:691–703.

Glen, N.D. (1975). Psychological well-being in the post-parental stage: some evidence from national surveys. *Journal of Marriage and the Family*, 37:105–10.

Keddy, B.A., and Singleton, J.F. (1991). Women's perceptions of life after retirement. *Activities, Adaptation, and Aging*, 16:57–65.

Larson, R., Mannell, R. and Zuzanek, J. (1986). Daily well-being of older adults with friends and families. *Psychology and Aging*, 1:117–126.

Lublin, J.S., and Markels, A. (1995). Retired CEOs find big jobs hard to forgo. *The Wall Street Journal*, 14 April.

Luckey, E.B. (1966). "Number of years married as related to personality perception and marital satisfaction." *Journal of Marriage and the Family*, 28:44–48.

Morrow-Howell, N. and Leon, J. (1988). Life-span determinants of work in retirement years. *International Journal of Aging and Human Development*, 27 (2):125–140.

Palmore, E.B., Fillenbaum, G.G., and George, L.K. (1984). Consequences of retirement. *Journal of Gerontology*, 39:109–116.

Parnes, H.S. (1981). From the middle to the later years: Longitudinal studies of the pre-and post-retirement experiences of men. *Research on Aging*, 4:387–402.

Payne, E., Robbins, S., and Dougherty, L. (1991). Goal directedness and older-adult adjustment. *Journal of Counseling Psychology*. 38:302–308.

Reitzes, D., Mutran, E., and Pope, H. (1991). Location and well-being among retired men. *Journal of Gerontology*, 46:S195–203.

Richardson, V., and Kilty, K.M. (1991). Adjustment to retirement: Continuity vs. discontinuity. *International Journal of Aging and Human Development*, 33(2):151–169.

Sagy, S., Antonovsky, A., and Adler, I. (1990). Explaining life satisfaction in later life: The sense of coherence model and activity theory. *Behavior, Health and Aging*, 1:11–25.

Salokangas, R.K., and Joukamaa, M. (1991). Physical and mental health changes in retirement age. *Psychotherapy and Psychosomatics*, 55:100–107.

Salokangas, R., Mattila, V., and Joukamaa, M. (1988). Intimacy and mental disorders in late middle age: Report of the TURVA Project. *Acta Psychiatrica Scandinavica*, 78:555–560.

Seccombe, K., and Lee, G.R. (1986). Gender differences in retirement satisfaction and its antecedents. *Research on Aging*, 8(3):426–440.

Sonnenfeld, J. (1988). *The hero's farewell: What happens when CEOs retire.* New York: Oxford University Press.

Spanier, G.B., Lewis, R.A., and Cole, C.L. (1975). Marital adjustment over the family life cycle: the issue of curvilinearity. *Journal of Marriage and the Family*, 37:264–275.

Sperry, L. (1993). Psychiatric consultation in the workplace. Washington, DC: American Psychiatric Press.

Sporaskowski, M.J., and Hughston, G.A. (1978). Prescriptions for happy marriage: Adjustments and satisfactions of couples married for 50 or more years. *Family Coordinator*, 27:321–328.

Szinovacz, M. (1989). Retirement, couples, and household work. In S.J. Bahr and E.T. Peterson (eds.), *Aging and the family.* Lexington, MA: Lexington Books.

Taylor, S.E. (1983). Adjustment to threatening events: A theory of cognitive adaption. *American Psychologist*, 3(8):1161–1173.

Thomas, J. (1990). Grandparenthood and mental health: Implications for the practitioner. *Journal of Applied Gerontology*, 9:464–497.

Toughill, E., Mason, D.J., Beck, T.L., and Christopher, M.A. (1993). Health, income, and post-retirement employment of older adults. *Public Health Nursing*, 10(2):100–107.

Van Haitsma, K. (1986). Intrinsic religious orientation: Implications in the study of religiosity and personal adjustment in the aged. *Journal of Social Psychology*, 126:685–687.

Vinick, B.H., and Ekerdt, D.J. (1991). Retirement: What happens to husband-wife relationships? *Journal of Geriatric Psychiatry*, 24:16–23.

———. (1992). Couples view retirement activities: Expectations versus experience. In

M. Szinovacz, D. Ekerdt, and B. Vinick (eds.), *Families and Retirement*, 129–144. Newbury Park, CA: Sage.

Wright, L. (1990). Mental health in older spouses: The dynamic interplay of resources, depression, quality of marital relationship, and social participation. *Issues in Mental Health Nursing*, 11:49–70.

Humor and Enhanced Well-Being in the Later Years

Robert R. Cadmus

"You don't stop laughing because you grow old. You grow old because you stop laughing." To some this is just another catchy phrase designed to placate the elderly. However, to an increasing number of perceptive gerontologists, geropsychiatrists, and other health care professionals, humor and laughter are fast becoming medical realities.

The word "humor" has roots deep in history. Medieval medicine was known for its humors and its vapors, but that humor was drastically different from the humor we think of today. The medieval versions were blood, phlegm, yellow bile, and black bile. The modern version is, in formal terms, words or situations that are sufficiently amusing to elicit a paroxysmal flutter of the diaphragm causing the sound we call laughter.

Laughter comes naturally. It's part of our human heritage. Fortunately, evolution was sufficiently kind to us so that we neither purr nor wag our tails to demonstrate pleasure or to react to humor. Rather, we laugh. Our genes are programmed so that we begin to smile at three to five weeks after birth and develop the ability to laugh aloud by four months. It is a uniquely human trait.

Although our forefathers nourished and perpetuated this gift of laughter, most people throughout our long history considered it to be merely a simple response to something humorous—nothing more, nothing less. However, a few visionaries recognized that humor and laughter did something more than just make us laugh. They sensed that laughter was good for us; that it could favorably affect both our minds and our bodies; that it could enhance our well-being and even play a part in the prevention and treatment of disease. They felt it could permit us to enjoy life more fully and find sunshine where there was only darkness. As Joseph Addison, a seventeenth century writer, put it, "Mirth is like a flash of lightning that breaks through a gloom of clouds and glitters for a moment."

Perhaps the earliest written recognition of this power is in the Bible. Proverbs 17:22 states, "A merry heart doeth good like a medicine." Years later the eighteenth century German philosopher, Immanuel Kant, in his *Critique of Pure Reason,* claimed, "I never knew a man who possessed the gift of hearty laughter who was burdened by constipation." Sir William Osler, the patriarch of modern medicine, considered laughter to be the "music of life," capable of helping an individual stay young (Cushing, 1940, p. 990). Norman Cousins, in his book *Anatomy of an Illness* (1979), considered laughter essential to our equilibrium and called laughter the great placebo, helping "to mobilize the natural defense mechanisms which are indispensable agents of recovery" (p. 39). He felt that laughter "helps make it possible for good things to happen" (p. 145). Specifically, Cousins reported that ten minutes of genuine belly laughter would give him at least two hours of pain-free sleep. The late Reinhold Niebuhr, a leading Protestant theologian, felt that humor was a prelude to faith and laughter the beginning of prayer. Authors such as Sir Francis Bacon, Robert Benchley, and countless others have endorsed laughter in their writings, and scientists such as Albert Schweitzer and Sigmund Freud have proclaimed its value.

Medical scientists the world over have now confirmed that those visionaries are correct; there is something magical in laughter. Researchers have documented that sustained laughter is a good aerobic exercise strengthening both the heart and the lungs. Laughter not only burns calories but is also helpful in many other aspects of human physiology. Psychiatrists and social scientists vouch for its beneficial effects on mental health, human behavior, and overall well-being. Albeit slowly, the current generation of physicians now recognizes that laughter is more than just an insignificant guffaw. It can help people stay healthy and make illness and disability more tolerable. Indeed, it's even therapeutic.

Before one can elaborate on the benefits of humor, the term must be more clearly defined. The official psychiatric definition, which will be given later, is couched in professional jargon. For the layman's use, the term includes jokes, riddles, comical stories, pictures or cartoons of funny incidents, or even amusing facial expressions, whether a child's, a peer's, or an animal's. In addition, humor includes stories, songs, poems, or words of wisdom that reveal an unexpected twist; situations that amuse and lighten our lives; or experiences that bring on a smile or laughter. Pleasant surprises, sounds that for some reason society considers amusing, funny little nicknames, and numerous other unique circumstances, whether reserved for a single person or humanity at large, cannot be left out. Each of our five senses can be tweaked by this wonderful human trait. If we react with laughter, feel happy, or our lives are made brighter, it's humor. If we react with disgust, feel depressed, or our lives are darkened, it's not.

How the Elderly React to Humor

Healthy seniors see something funny in almost every situation. Each amusing story stirs up memories long forgotten. That's one reason why the elderly prefer to be with people their own age. They laugh together, and laughter is contagious, lifting the spirits of those around them. As Addison said, it's "a flash of lightning that . . . glitters for a moment."

Some observers say that such laughter is a defense mechanism to offset the frightening fate of growing old. Others go so far as to identify it with the unruly child in school who tries to get attention by being silly. Neither fully applies. They may apply to those of lesser years, but not to those in later life. To the elderly, laughter is genuine enjoyment of something funny. It's the essence of humor, yet each individual weaves into the humorous episode the diversity of his or her own personality and experience.

There is essentially no difference between elderly men and women in their reaction to humor. Both laugh equally. Both get the same therapeutic benefits. Both widen their circle of friends by laughter. The subject matter may be different, a bit more risqué in the men, but from current trends that difference may be narrowing. When the younger generation becomes elderly, they may share their humor with fewer gender differences and fewer sexual innuendos.

Certainly, the life of every elderly individual offers many potential circumstances worthy of a good belly laugh. Professional comedians have built their careers by making fun of the elderly. Johnny Carson, Milton Berle, Jonathan Winters, Tim Conway, and scores of others have never been too kind or gentle to those in their later years. They comment on memory loss, napping, physical weakness, slow reaction time, loss of sexual prowess, wrinkles, flatulence, and difficulties with vision, hearing, digestion, and every other minor or major infirmity inherent in old age. Each peculiarity gives the comedian ample opportunity to poke fun at the elderly. The world is full of such stories. For example, one comedian matched up loss of memory and the use of a hearing aid by telling about a daughter visiting her mother. On entering the house, the daughter screams, "Mother, what are you doing with that suppository in your ear?" The mother stops, then slowly answers, "Now I know where I put my hearing aid." Another joked about the elderly's loss of sexual drive by telling the story of the old man walking in the park. He came across a frog who said, "I am under a spell. Kiss me and I shall be your love slave for the rest of your life." After a moment of thought, the old man picked up the frog and put it in his pocket. The frog, from deep down inside his jacket, shouted, "Aren't you going to kiss me so that I can become your love slave?" "No," the old man replied, "At my age I'd rather have a talking frog."

If these two examples were ethnic jokes, the teller would end up in court. Not so with jokes about those in their later years. The elderly tolerate them. Most can, at minimum, relate to them, and many enjoy them and perpetuate them by repeating them to their friends and neighbors. No shame, no hesitation—just the pure enjoyment of living and laughing.

To be effective, laughter need not be raucous. Silent laughter is very typical in some elderly. A restrained twitter is as much as some will muster, and for others, the laughter is altogether silent. Perhaps a close observer might notice a slight smile or lightening of a dour expression on such occasions, but no flutter of the diaphragm. This lack of outward expression should not be taken as an absence of humor. Humor can be thoroughly enjoyed even if given the silent treatment, and the silent individual might later repeat the joke or story as enthusiastically as the more demonstrative character. Reading humor or watching it on TV is more likely to elicit this silent treatment than when experienced in person. Perhaps we are conditioned to consider that the only courteous response to someone who is trying to lift our spirits is to flutter our diaphragms. Without a live storyteller, no flutter. For example, two old folks watching the same humorous TV program may not let out a peep during the show, but when it is over, both will confess they thoroughly enjoyed it.

Our emotions, including the sense of humor, originate in and are shaped during childhood. It appears that once endowed with a sense of humor, always endowed—although people seem to acquire their senses of humor in different degrees. Consequently, some individuals will react wildly to a specific humorous exposure, others with icy restraint. There are clowns, and there are the melancholics, and many shades in between. It appears that once a clown or a melancholic, always a clown or melancholic. Individuals in their later years don't change their spots, at least, in the matter of humor. A sense of humor may be honed, but not taught. If a child shows humor in his formative years, chances are he or she will retain it when he or she matures. It may even grow in intensity as the years pass. Most of the world's comedians apparently were class clowns when they were young. When they matured and reached adulthood, humor became either their professions or, at least, part of their characters.

Of course, outward expression of humor can be modified. For instance, a giggler may consciously learn restraint; the individual prone to tasteless and discriminatory humor that offends every ethnic, racial, sexual, or religious subgroup may learn to temper his or her remarks; and the less demonstrative person can become more animated. Still their basic senses of humor remain intact.

Cheerless souls who try to change their spots in midstream usually fail. Their humor lacks sincerity and authenticity. It isn't natural. It lacks the spark of the real clown, and unlike the clown, the individual also fails to enjoy his or her own humor. In spite of this tendency and its proclivity for failure, it's still good advice to suggest to the cheerless that they lighten up. Like any advice, however, it's easier to say than to do. Certainly, no one wants to turn the world into a parade of clowns, but people, to be normal and happy, must succumb to a belly laugh now and then. Laughter is like a pebble thrown into a mill pond. Ripples spread out in all directions, and the bigger the pebble the further the ripples travel and the more people they touch.

INTENSITY AND ACCEPTABILITY

Humor requires a certain level of intensity before it unfolds, much like a trumpet requires a blast of air before it produces a sound. Humor gains its intensity primarily through relevancy, the listener's ability to relate to the message. For example, to someone unfamiliar with American currency, a joke about a three-dollar bill would evoke little laughter. Intensity is often heightened by outside or external sources. For example, when two laugh together, one the giver and the other the receiver, the personal intimacy tends to increase the intensity of the response. Intensity can also be matched to the quality of the offering. A snicker may be suitable for something mildly amusing; a belly laugh for a prize-winning joke. Of course, the enjoyment of humor continually requires the infusion of new humorous material, as stale humor is no humor.

Stimulation from the outside is particularly necessary for the well-being of the elderly, particularly for those who are either imprisoned within the walls of their own colorless bedrooms or confined to nursing homes. Many such patients are deprived of sufficient humorous stimuli. For example, if an isolated patient is met each morning with the humorless request, "Have you moved your bowels today?" instead of being reminded of the morning sunlight and the twitter of birds outside the window, there will be little humor. With no stimulus there will be no response, no intensity, no beneficial effect. Therefore, the challenge for family, friends, volunteers, and staff—if not overworked or of the wrong caliber—is to feed their charges sufficient merriment to keep their senses of humor well churned. In many fine facilities, the staff does provide the incentive necessary to keep their patients' senses of humor alive and well. Stories, funny hats, cute names, or humorous maneuvers during treatment, each in its own way, can provide such stimuli. If there is even a twinge of a favorable response, keep it up. All is not lost. If the elderly are left unchallenged, the intensity of their sense of humor and the good it brings will fade to naught. An elderly patient with little left to laugh about treasures the presence of someone who shares his or her own lively sense of humor and can apply it even to patient-caregiver interactions, no matter how mundane. In this process, however, one must avoid talking down to the patient or acting like a first-time mother trying to get her kid to eat. Don't let the feeding spoon become an imaginary airplane. That's irritation, not humor.

In addition to intensity, there is an element of acceptability. The elderly, as well as certain ethnic and religious minorities, will find certain pornographic or derogatory humor unacceptable, even offensive. One might think that such unpopular and inappropriate humor would fade away due to its lack of acceptance, but it has not. The numbers tell otherwise. While ethnic jokes have diminished, pornography has increased and now reaches a wider segment of society. Therefore, humor cannot be too rigidly defined, because it is a dynamic force changing with each generation and its societal mores. It is like the woman who said, "My great-grandfather rode horses but was afraid of trains; my grandfather rode trains but was afraid of autos; my father rode autos but was afraid of airplanes; now I ride airplanes but am afraid of horses." Humor will follow a similar cycle as individuals and society evolve and mature.

People are mindful, often consumed, by their own appearances, but they can equally be possessed by the appearance of their physical environment. Can humor be stimulated by appearances? It seems so. Every pediatric ward and pediatrician's office is a showplace of familiar cartoon characters. Such artwork provides a familiar, reassuring face, one that gives pleasure and draws out a smile or a laugh to the young, apprehensive patient.

Consequently, I have often wondered what decorative touches might be appropriate for a geriatric area, and I have failed to find the answer. For some, wallpaper showing a restful outdoor scene might strike a happy chord, yet for someone who once experienced being lost in the woods, it might be less appealing. Certainly, one should avoid dark, depressing colors. Purple is considered the color of the elderly, but not for the environment. I can't think of any cartoon characters I would suggest. Therefore, all we can do is to make the environment bright and cheery, avoiding the typical hospital palette of faded creams and sickly greens. But be reassured that lively, laughing, friendly people brighten an environment better than any paint or fabric ever could.

HUMOR AND MISFORTUNE

As folks move into their later years, there seems to be less to laugh about and more to complain about. As W. Somerset Maugham, the distinguished English author, said on the occasion of his eightieth birthday over forty years ago, "There are many virtues to growing old." As he stood before his audience, about to identify these profound virtues, he slowly pointed to each of his outstretched fingers, but one by one, turned them back as being inappropriate. Finally, he confessed, "I can't think of any." Of course, he was wrong in one fundamental respect. There is no greater virtue than to have the privilege of growing old. In any generation, many of one's peers never reach that goal. Furthermore, Maugham forgot the virtue of laughter (although he used it to make his point).

Much of humor is based on misfortune. To even the most optimistic individual, aging is not all fun and games. Let's not forget that only an apostrophe and a space differentiate the words "man's laughter" from "man-slaughter." Life is filled with tragedies, great and small. Fortunately, humor generally stresses the small. The elderly seem to handle with surprising equanimity most of the medical disasters that come with the aging process. If they were to weep every time they had pain or stiffness, misplaced their glasses, fell asleep in front of guests, failed to completely pull down their skirts or zip their flies, forgot names, or mixed up their checkbooks, the world would be flooded with salty tears. Rather, under such circumstances, we hear the ring of laughter. Most of the stories about their many peccadilloes are funny and fairly accurate, so why not laugh?

One can often see the differences in people's senses of humor by their reactions to relatively serious adversity. One woman who had a colostomy—a depression-maker if there ever was one—referred to it as her "calamity," a nice play on words. She didn't use it with a voice of despair, but used a normal conversational tone as if that were the accepted scientific terminology. Her approach confirms that humor aids communication. Humor also breaks down the age, sex, race, and social barriers that we see in many people, certainly in patients. Humor has no bounds. It becomes everyone.

It is often said that hospitalized elderly can lose all sorts of innards without a peep, but if they lose their slippers or false teeth, there's hell to pay. Those with a sense of humor seem to adjust to adversity. The issue matters little. They play down all things great and small. They concentrate on the insignificant and make light of it. Our challenge is not only to feed our patients and clients sufficient merriment to keep their senses of humor well honed, but also to let them know that humor is welcomed, beneficial, and acceptable in a professional environment.

Asking questions seems to be characteristic of the healing professions. However, if the questioner becomes too probing or too invasive in his or her questioning of the elderly, he or she may not get the correct answer. Although there are a few seniors who will tell the unadulterated truth, eager to answer fully and correctly every medical question, most elderly reveal only what they want to reveal. They have a penchant for fabricating, exaggerating, or denying the truth when pinned down. They hold their cards very close to their chests and play their little games in such a convincing manner that the questioner is often fooled. To put it bluntly, the elderly can be consummate liars if they want to be. Tempered by years of experience, the elderly have learned that under certain circumstances it is better to limit one's confessions and to shade the truth. Insurance, government regulations, and the lack of confidentiality are responsible for much of this behavior, but the cause is irrelevant. When they're through with their deceptions, they'll laugh about them and share their experiences with their friends.

Because of their tendency to laugh, some elderly are misunderstood when they attend the funerals of their friends. Many elderly, both men and women, do not weep, do not break down, do not need physical support to keep them on their feet, nor do they clutch handfuls of wet facial tissue. They are respectful, of course, but they laugh as they relive past experiences and pleasant memories. The memories that stay in their minds are not only the funny times, but also the good deeds the departed has shared with them and others. As George Bernard Shaw once said, "Life does not cease to be funny when people die any more than it ceases to be serious when people laugh."

At funerals, seniors may be glad to see one of their own relieved of their years of suffering. Depending upon their spiritual backgrounds, they may envy the deceased and be happy for them. For many of the surviving elderly, it's not a period of loss; it's a time of release. Consequently, people shouldn't condemn the elderly who leave the church or funeral home in small knots laughing and talking as if they were leaving a party. They're not disrespectful. They feel their loss, yes, but they understand and accept the reality of the situation. Some might call this a defense mechanism. A careful observer witnessing such funerals and memorial services over the years would accept that behavior as a mature expression of love and remembrance, not a defense against morbid fears.

I recall one such memorial service for an elderly, highly respected local sports announcer. Just as the last prayer was said and the attendees were about to rise to exit, the booming strains of "On Wisconsin" were heard from the back of the church, and two tuba players decked out in red uniforms marched down each side aisle and crossed in the front of the church. Then the four, in cadence, strutted up the center aisle blasting away their heady tune. The assembled mourners emptied the church like children following after the Pied Piper. With that kind of humor, I can't call them mourners; they were loving friends reliving the memory of a wonderful guy. Realizing that the deceased himself had preplanned that part of the service, one must recognize there is no time or place that dignified humor can't be lovingly used.

Seniors have faced the fact of their own mortality. Many youngsters have not. The elderly know they are born naked and need clothes; born hungry and need food; born exposed and need shelter; and they know they are born mortal and don't expect immortality. The elderly have faced the biological facts of life. Although they try to stretch out their lives, particularly if they are enjoying the added years, they don't expect the impossible. Therefore, they can laugh at life.

For some years, I presented a seminar on aging to a group of second-year medical students. One year I brought three elderly folks with me. During the discussion, one young student asked a lady in her high eighties, "How often do you think about death?" Apparently, the student felt that the elderly live in a humorless world of fear and despair. Her answer went something like, "Daily, of course, but what can you do about it? I'm happy with my life. I live each day to the fullest. I'm not obsessed with death. Are you?"

HUMOR AND THE HANDICAPPED

Many of the things handicapped seniors do are funny, but anyone with compassion recognizes that not all amusing things are truly funny. Senility, whether it be due to Alzheimer's disease, multiple small infarcts in the brain, or a handful of other medical reasons, is not funny. Disability at any age is not funny. Illness is not funny. These are therapeutic challenges, not grist for the comedian's sharp tongue.

Although making fun and telling derogatory jokes about people with disabilities are unwarranted, laughter is almost a necessity for the disabled. It matters little how severely handicapped the individual may be or from what cause (mental or physical): Laughter works its salutary wonders. Humor provides little flashes of relief, little moments of remission from the pain, and a substitute for the stress and alienation that accompany illness and disability. Such bits of humor should be encouraged. Red Skelton hints at this by responding to people who ask to shake his hand with, "Just hold it. It shakes by itself."

Little jokes, humorous expressions or deeds, pleasant surprises, or even cute names can be appropriately used with senile or disabled patients. It's how you do it that matters. It's much like treating a child—laugh with, not laugh at. Constructive humor will always spark a pleasant reaction in the disabled. It may convince lonely and broken patients that they are still involved with life and their own affairs. Chances are remote that if properly done without harsh criticism, such humor will spark anger or violent action. Certainly, in the early stages of most disabilities, many patients offer their own brands of humor, but often in attempts to strengthen their defense mechanisms. President Reagan, as he was entering the operating room after having been shot by an assassin, apparently said to the surgeons, "I hope all of you are Republicans!" It was funny, but I think there might have been a twinge of defense mechanism in making light of something so serious.

For every handicapped individual, there's a caregiver equally in need of respite through laughter. Humor is the tonic, the lifeline for a caregiver. It's a universal language open to the handicapped, their caregivers, and the lucky ones in society. It's a great natural resource. Without humor, the world seems dark, cruel, even unfair. Humor shared with a caregivers' support group is as helpful to the members as it is to the individual offering it. They all need it. They all need to know that they still know how to laugh and enjoy life.

Humor in the Humorless

Unfortunately, there are a few elderly who seem to lack every vestige of humor. They are indeed the sad sacks of the world. They make good role models for comic strips and sitcoms but lousy neighbors—or relatives. Being humorless and a total pain in the neck is uncommendable, but not unconstitutional (except for certain insane individuals!). Their miserable situations often revolve around their ideas of happiness. They feel that old age gives them the privilege of doing what they want even if more rational people feel their destructive behavior threatens their own longevity, happiness, or well-being. To make matters worse, they are often successful at transferring some of their misery to those around them. To let the elderly retreat deeper into their humorless shells is hard to take, but we can't lead another sane person's life, as destructive as it may seem to us. Under no circumstance should aging alone be blamed for this lack of humor.

Can we lose our senses of humor? Many family members and friends believe so as they witness someone whose usual happy nature has turned to sadness. They see an individual who, along with other manifestations, no longer laughs. There are two groups who lose their sense of humor that should concern us as health professionals. The first loses their sense of humor temporarily; the second, more permanently. Both are depressed, but to different degrees and for different reasons.

The first are those who have lost a spouse, been diagnosed as having a chronic or life-threatening illness, suffered pain, or endured some other personal tragedy. They experience sadness and understandably so. During such bouts of misfortune, humor, like all normal and constructive behaviors, is put on hold, but is not lost. With treatment it returns, and, in fact, this return may even portend recovery.

For this first group, medical conditions such as hypothyroidism, anemia, malnutrition, and drug intoxication can cause sadness and despair, so these organic conditions must first be ruled out. If there is no physical cause, laughter can help turn these mildly discouraged souls away from more destructive behavior. They can again link up with the therapeutic forces of humor. They can discover that laughing at trouble helps heal that trouble and that normal behavior includes laughter, joy, and optimism. Humor can put the brakes on their depression and return them to normalcy. Give them time to grieve and to adjust, but don't abandon them.

The other group suffers from true clinical depression, one of the most common diagnoses in the elderly. Many of these individuals have isolated themselves from every outside contact for extended periods of time. They're engulfed in a downward spiral. Frequently the patient's family, as well as his or her friends and associates, tries its own brand of amateur psychiatry in an attempt to help these folks face their world. Every physician has witnessed such behavior and recognizes that these efforts are usually unsuccessful. Individuals this deeply depressed need professional help. They are not the ones to voluntarily join a senior center or a day-care support group. It's too late for humor alone.

The difficulty comes in determining when the depression is merely sadness and is reversible with humor and friendship, or when the flat behavior requires skilled professional therapy. Laughter can be part of the key. The sad respond to it; the depressed do not (though there is a litany of other more important diagnostic signs and symptoms to identify the truly depressed).

There is a potential flip side to either the return of one's sense of humor or the uncharacteristic onset of apparent humor. One must react with caution when a cheerless, depressed, melancholic soul seems to radically change his or her spots and exhibits an outpouring of frivolous humor. This transformation is usually not because that person has, at long last, embraced humor or is showing clinical improvement. Rather, it is more likely a sign that the individual is out of character and is not acting normally. This is a sign of mental imbalance. The individual must seek professional care; another joke won't work.

At other times, an outpouring of humor in an otherwise normal individual might be an attempt to hide something that is truly serious—a terminal illness, a financial crisis, the fear of losing a spouse. Often the elderly try to deny trouble by making light of it. Such behavior may be a sign that problems are being poorly pasted over, not handled. Humor is being used as a tool for a problem to which it was never meant to be applied.

One of the signs of successful aging is the ability to handle loss. Inappropriate laughing is not a rational substitute; having a healthful sense of humor is. Professionals must be constantly on the alert for such neurotic behavior. It is not easy to identify, and it takes careful observation over extended periods to determine whether such humor is genuine or manipulative. Individuals using humor for the wrong reason require psychiatric evaluation and care.

THE PLACE FOR HUMOR

Few alert individuals can miss the increasing mention of humor in the electronic and print media. It's everywhere. The comic strip, *Cathy*, recently presented a situation where Cathy was recovering from the flu. Her message was, "I will release all negative energy and tension through the healthy, healing power of laughter!" There are even reports of "humor churches" (although neither humor nor rattlesnakes seem a firm underpinning for religion).

Periodically hospitals or medical groups offer programs on the therapeutic value of humor to either professional or lay audiences. These seminars are catching on and drawing crowds. An increasing number of physicians, particularly radiologists and oncologists, have begun to sprinkle humorous books around their waiting rooms and to show humorous tapes to reduce stress before and during treatment.

Humor has not only crept into medicine, it has invaded hospitals. The International Institute of Humor, housed in California, recognized this new expansion by presenting its 1991 Humor Award to the St. John's Hospital and Health Center of Santa Monica, California, for its Laugh Channel, a program viewed on its in-house television system. The idea was based on Norman Cousins's laugh-therapy concept. Many hospitals have followed suit, many with individualized programs that are well produced and offer a local flavor. Other hospitals use commercial tapes of popular comedians, although some tend to be a bit too risqué for general use and definitely *verboten* for a hospital sponsored by a religious denomination.

Either a homemade or a commercial program can be a welcome alternative to the soap operas and game shows that seem to occupy the bulk of hospital viewing. Of course, there are educational programs, programs on diabetes, gall bladder disease, and "Your Hospital Bill" on in-house radio or TV systems, but they do little for recovery.

Equally popular are "humor rooms" set aside for patients and their families so that they might visit and read humorous books, see funny movies, and hear or see tapes produced by the nation's best comedians. St. Joseph Hospital in Houston, Texas; the DeKalb Medical Center in Decatur, Georgia; the Sunnyview Hospital and Rehabilitation Center in Schenectady, New York; and the Mesa Lutheran Hospital in Mesa, Arizona, are reported to have such rooms (Buxman, 1991). There are many similar facilities or variations of this idea throughout hospitals both in this country and abroad. Although such rooms have yet to be included in the American Hospital Association's annual *Guide Issue* listing each hospital's facilities, I predict they will in due time.

Humor rooms should be colorful, conveniently located, and designed for optimum effect. Don't just move a VCR and a few joke books into an unused patient room with chipped beige paint and an inoperative call-button dangling from the wall and call it a humor center. Do it right! Use humorous imagination. To control costs, seek volunteers to staff it. They'll love it.

The Morton Plant Hospital, in Clearwater, Florida, has a "comedy cart" from which patients can select humorous materials. The Medical Center of Vermont, in Burlington, has a similar program in its intensive care unit. The Ball Memorial Hospital in Muncie, Indiana, has established a Library of Life, Love, and Laughter, filled with humorous tapes.

Those who have studied such facilities and services vouch for their help in recovery, staff morale, and hospital reputation. With short stays in hospitals and the increasing use of ambulatory surgery, such humor rooms seem particularly suited for those with long stays and those in rehabilitation hospitals and nursing homes. Humor can also be built into the programs of adult day care centers with promise of good results. If a hospital has a patients' library, it should certainly contain books of humor. If not, the public library is a potential source of humorous material in the form of books and tapes. There is no excuse for not being able to add some spice to the hospital routine, and no excuse for not being able to laugh when ill or injured.

The American Journal of Nursing, in its December 1991 issue, carries a full page of "Resources for your Humor Room." It lists over twenty-five books—there are more now—and offers list upon list of magazines, newsletters, audiocassettes, movies, and organizations promoting the advantage of humor (Buxman, 1991).

The Humor Project, Inc. (110 Spring Street, Saratoga Springs, NY 12866), one of those organizations mentioned in the foregoing reference, publishes a quarterly newsletter, sponsors conferences, and assists in the development of humor services and resources. They can offer private practices or institutions much helpful advice. Then there are the American Association of Therapeutic Humor in St. Louis, Missouri; the Laugh Prescription Newsletter in Rancho La Costa, California; and the Journal of Nursing Jocularity in Mesa, Arizona.

Today, entrepreneurs have turned humor into an industry. The most isolated of us are aware of the national computerized data networks into which those of us with a computer and a modem can obtain all sorts of information and receive it directly on our screens in truck-sized lots. *The Internet Yellow Pages,* published by the Osborne McGraw-Hill Company, devotes eight pages to humor resources. Within that listing, there is much material suitable for the hospital market.

When on their own, the elderly seek out their own brands of acceptable entertainment much as they select friends, food, and where they want to live. Generally, they prefer light comedy; popular music, particularly music like Lawrence Welk playing tunes they remember; realistic movies about the elderly, such as *Driving Miss Daisy;* current events, travel and nature programs; and good books, fiction and nonfiction—works that amuse or educate, but do not depress. Still others enjoy the inspirational programs of classical music, religion, and history. This sounds as if the elderly enjoy everything. At first blush, nothing seems to have been excluded, yet you would not think so if you sat on a committee to select the weekly movies at a senior center. It's beyond frustration!

Some demographers predict that by the beginning of the twenty-first century those individuals above sixty-five years of age will account for approximately 14 percent of this country's population. Certainly, those who planned for Social Security in 1935 underestimated the numbers. Present-day demographers may be equally conservative. However, the numbers really don't matter. What does matter is that the number of elderly is growing by leaps and bounds, that all fields of medicine will have to adjust to this increase, and that laughter will be a new and increasingly important therapeutic medium for those in their later years. Now and in the future, a sense of humor, good health, and well-being will go together.

HUMOR IN THE DOCTOR'S OFFICE

It is the widespread impression among physicians that patients with a sharp sense of humor do better in respect to their health than those humorless souls who mope around turning off every bit of the sunshine they find. Consequently, physicians generally prefer patients addicted to laughter. Happy patients are more agreeable to the rigors of diagnosis and treatment; they get along better with the staff; and their final outcomes are predictably better. I knew a patient who started every visit to her doctor with a joke or some humorous story. Her visits were anticipated by everyone in that office. Her appearance was a bright spot in a long day of "organ recitals."

It is not only the patients who should sharpen their senses of humor, but those who take care of them as well. The public assumes a physician to be serious, intellectually alert, even a bit haughty. Few would believe that his or her day is "a tour through the museum of humor, containing situational comedy, comedies of manners and errors, humor that is low, high, dry, wry, sly, underhanded, heavy-handed, farcical, absurd, slapstick, silent, tragic, and black" (Editors, JAMA 1992). In medicine you see it all. Consequently, no one should be surprised that many physicians and other health care workers use humor to put their patients at ease. Voltaire, the eighteenth-century French writer, summed it up by saying, "The art of medicine consists of amusing the patient while nature cures the disease." Of course, science has come a long way since his generation, but the relationship between humor and cure continues.

Don't look for humor in the physician's bookshelf. Few, if any, medical textbooks list humor in their indices or mention it in their texts. The current medical self-help tomes published for the layman by the nation's major medical centers are no better. They offer more medical knowledge than most laymen can assimilate, but nothing about humor. In contrast, the research literature, particularly in the field of psychiatry and psychology, increasingly mentions laughter as a rational addition to the therapeutic armamentarium. For example, a recent search of MEDLINE revealed some twenty-six journal references to humor over the past five years—not many, but a good start.

ON THE CUTTING EDGE

Compared with the field of pediatrics, the specialty of geriatrics is a newcomer. Obviously, the diseases of those in their later years have long been recognized and treated, but only the present generation considers both aging and humor as subjects worthy of investigation. Scientists around the world are involved in anatomical, physiological, and psychological studies of the relationship between humor and health. Humor is becoming recognized as a modality preventive medicine as well as an adjunct to therapy in the clinical practice of medicine. It has been said that "Laughter may not be the best medicine, but its positive effects on your mind and body are no joke" (Garrity, 1993). Dr. Harry Prosen of the Department of Psychiatry and Mental Health at the Medical College of Wisconsin has stated that "A sense of humor is a sign of health." As others, he believes humor is not only good for mental health, but physical health as well.

The *Diagnostic and Statistical Manual of Mental Disorders* (*DSM - IV*) lists humor as one of the adaptive defense mechanisms. It defines humor as when "the individual deals with emotional conflicts, or internal or external stressors, by emphasizing the amusing or ironic aspects of the conflict or stressor" (First, 1994, p. 755).

Dr. Arthur Stone of the Department of Psychiatry and Behavioral Science at the State University of New York at Stony Brook and others have studied the destructive effect of stress on the immune system (Stone and Bovbjerg, 1994). If such studies are true, it is logical to assume that by reducing stress through humor, one can simultaneously protect the immune system.

Dr. William Fry, Jr., of Stanford University, defined humor physiology as "those events occurring in our bodies in association with humorous experiences" (1992, p. 1857). His studies indicate that laughter stimulates both pulse and respiratory rates and by aiding circulation, enhances the delivery of oxygen and nutrients throughout the body. He feels laughter can help break the pain-spasm cycle seen in neuralgias and rheumatism. Although laughter is a motor reflex involving contractions of some fifteen facial muscles as well as the diaphragm and other skeletal muscles, it is not, of course, a substitute for sustained exercise.

Many of the studies of laughter are reported in the psychiatric literature. One such study, from Eastern New Mexico University, annotated sixty-seven references between 1970 and 1990. From such research in laughter the researchers theorized that humor could be a potential modality in psychotherapy (Shaunessy and Wadsworth, 1992).

Science has yet to unravel the full biochemical relationship between one's state of mind—humorous or otherwise—and physical health. Nevertheless, during the past few decades, scientists have confirmed that emotions, certainly laughter, can not only affect the body's chemistry, particularly the immune system, but can also exert a beneficial effect on both physical well-being and pain. By its ability to increase catecholamine production, laughter may sufficiently stimulate the central nervous system to favorably affect certain mental functions, such as alertness and memory. The study of this interesting relationship between the brain and the immune system is now known as psychoneuroimmunology.

It is popular to implicate the endorphins, those polypeptide hormones secreted by the anterior lobe of the pituitary and serving as neurotransmitters, as being somehow involved in this process, but proof eludes the scientists. Nevertheless, the Mayo Clinic Health Letter confirms that "Researchers are trying to determine whether humor and laughter increase certain brain chemicals (endorphins) which are your body's natural pain fighters." The same reference also quotes other research saying that "laughter can temporarily increase the concentration of immunoglobulin A in your saliva. Immunoglobulin A apparently helps your immune system fight off colds, flu, and sinus problems" (Garrity, 1992, p. 6). It may well be that laughter restrains the excessive production of cortisol and adrenaline, both of which can suppress the immune system and cause tension and stress. Although no one has yet bottled any of these substances for home consumption, most physicians, if only from observation, know that a true relationship exists between laughter and well-being.

The increasing documentation of the healthful effects of laughter seems to suggest that physicians might not only use laugh therapy on their patients, but also on themselves so that they too may taste its benefits. Many patients, particularly the elderly, complain that physicians and their associates are humorless souls acting like a bunch of cold fish. Patients like doctors who are competent and who take time to listen, but they also like them to be witty, upbeat, and not always wringing their hands each time they add a new diagnosis to an already long list.

There are no reports in the literature of any adverse effects of laughter, although there are a few anecdotal reports that individuals with already compromised hearts and circulation have sustained a transient elevation of blood pressure, a cerebrovascular accident, or a myocardial infarction while laughing. The key words here are "with already compromised hearts and circulation." Of course, common sense suggests that laughter is not the therapy of choice in individuals immediately following abdominal, pelvic, or rib cage surgery, or in patients with asthma or other forms of acute respiratory distress—but it can't hurt in everyone else!

SUMMARY

Although modern laughter therapy encourages humor, it alone is not the total answer, nor in some cases even a partial answer, to all of the ills of man. It is an addition—a pleasant and palatable addition—to the physician's growing armamentarium, but it has to be placed appropriately in the full panoply of medicine. Let's not develop a cult of laughology (though the study of laughter in medicine has already been christened *gelotology* from the Greek root meaning "laughter." Humor is an important and documented adjunct in the life of both the well and the unwell, but as a therapy it rarely can stand alone. It should not be naively endowed with unwarranted or unrealistic powers that cannot be scientifically supported.

Like so many things in medicine, laughter has both an up and a down side. Research has documented the benefits of laughter. They are clear. The rational individual can respond to genuine humor and be favorably affected by laugh therapy. On the down side, physicians, particularly psychiatrists, frequently see individuals who exhibit an insincere, inappropriate, or untimely form of laughter. This is not a lucid reaction to humor but rather the symptom of an unbalanced mind. Such patients need psychiatric treatment. They are not candidates for laugh therapy. With modest observation it should not be difficult to distinguish between the two.

The benefits of laughter, whether for patients, caregivers, or health care workers themselves, are piling up too fast for any health professional to ignore. In medicine we have long heard the cliché that "He who treats himself has a fool for a doctor." Perhaps in laugh therapy we have an exception: "He who treats himself with laughter has a genius for a doctor."

We should recognize humor for what it is. We should seek it out, let it surround us, and feel its therapeutic warmth. By encouraging people, sick or well, to make laughter a larger part of their lives, we are, indeed, practicing good medicine.

REFERENCES

Buxman, K. (1991). Make room for laughter. *American Journal of Nursing,* 91:46–51.

Cousins, N. (1979). *Anatomy of an illness.* New York: Norton.

Cushing, H. (1940). *The life of Sir William Osler.* New York: Oxford University Press.

Editors (1992). A funny thing happened on the way to recovery. *Journal of the American Medical Association,* 267:1856.

First, M.B. (ed.). (1994). *Diagnostic and statistical manual of mental disorders.* (DSM-IV) 4th ed. Washington, DC: American Psychiatric Association, 755.

Fry, W.F. (1992). The physiologic effects of humor, mirth, and laughter. *Journal of the American Medical Association,* 267:1857.

Garrity, R. (1993). Laughter. *Mayo Clinic Health Letter* (March):6.

Shaughnessy, M.F., and Wadsworth, T.M. (1992). Humor in counseling and psychotherapy: A 20-year retrospective, *Psychological Reports* (June):755–762.

Stone, A.A. and Bovbjerg, D.H. (1994). Stress and humoral immunity: A review of the human studies. *Advances in Neuroimmunology,* 4:49–56.

Expanding Knowledge of Older Gay Men and Lesbians

Retrospect and Prospect

Jeanne L. Thomas

Introduction

Lisa and Victoria have been partners for over forty years; they brought up their children together. When Victoria enters a nursing home following a stroke, Lisa is forced to sell their home.

Richard's partner of thirty years died a few weeks ago. Richard is having difficulty coping with his grief and consults his pastor. The pastor suggests that Richard join the church's bereavement support group, composed entirely of widows.

Following complications from her bypass surgery, Joan is placed in intensive care for several days. Hospital policy allows only immediate family to visit patients in the ICU. Ruth, Joan's partner, is not allowed to visit.

These vignettes illustrate only a few of the problems raised by "heterosexism" in services provided for older adults. As practitioners and policy makers, we have worked hard to develop networks of services and supports to meet the medical, social, and emotional needs of older people. We have become more sensitive to ways in which race, class, ethnicity, and gender color the experience of aging, and the implications of these impacts for practice.

However, it is unkind but not unfair to say that gerontologists have yet to fully consider the heterosexism that often guides decisions in work with elderly adults. Open acknowledgment of older people as sexual beings is difficult for many people, and some are uncomfortable with the notion of homosexuality at any age. Correspondingly, attention to the needs and resources of older gay men and lesbians has been lacking.

This chapter will provide an overview of what we know about older gay men and lesbians, and what we need to know. We begin by identifying points that are prominent in earlier work, and proceed to discuss issues likely to be of special concern for older gay men and lesbians. We also discuss future needs and identify resource organizations.

The Theme of Historical Context

In virtually every scholarly discussion of homosexuality and aging is the reminder to be mindful of the historical circumstances in which contemporary elderly gay men and lesbians grew up and grew old (e.g., Kimmel, 1993; Kimmel and Sang, 1995; Reid, 1995; Sang, 1993). To be sure, homophobia is alive and well in contemporary America: Every openly gay person undoubtedly represents several others who feel compelled to keep their sexual orientation hidden. But as we consider the steps that remain to be taken to achieve a nondiscriminatory society, we must remember the progress that has been made—and the level of hostility and repression that elderly gay men and lesbians have survived.

The litany is familiar. Psychiatry defined homosexuality as a mental illness until the 1970s. In the past, virtually all religions condemned same-sex unions as crimes against nature; some denominations still do. Throughout most of this century, people in general reacted to gay men and lesbians with pity or ridicule at best, or rage and loathing at worst.

In most cities there was little if any visible gay/lesbian community. With the exception of dimly lit bars in run-down areas, there were few gathering places. And prior to the 1950s, there were virtually no organizations of gay men and lesbians. For gay men and lesbians in this decidedly homophobic atmosphere, remaining closeted was a rational survival strategy.

Historical context has at least two implications for practitioners. First, scholars routinely note the difficulty of building representative samples of older homosexuals for research. Virtually all we know about aging in these populations is drawn from studies of relatively advantaged Caucasian men and women living in large cities on the East or West Coasts. Practice with other sorts of populations may bring different issues to light than those identified in prior research, and demand different responses.

Second, contemporary homosexual young and middle-aged adults experience a different social context. As Kimmel and Sang (1995) explain in their discussion of homosexuality in middle and old age:

> Persons who are between age 40 and 60 today reached sexual maturity before the impact of the 1969 protest demonstrations following a police raid on the Stonewall bar. That event began to change the

social construction of homosexuality from a personal pathology to minority group membership. . . . middle-aged lesbians and gay men were in the prime of middle adulthood when the AIDS epidemic emerged. Many have been personally touched by the AIDS epidemic. Survivors of this cohort will enter old age and be followed by a cohort of middle-aged lesbians and gay men with different historical and cultural experiences. (p. 191)

As in most aspects of gerontological work, we must be prepared to adapt our experiences with current cohorts to meet the needs of "post-Stonewall" cohorts of older gay men and lesbians. More older gay men and lesbians in the future are likely to have been "out" for more of their adult lives, and to be more adept than their predecessors at managing financial and legal issues of special concern for homosexual elders (e.g., Adelman, 1991).

The Theme of Adjustment

Stereotypes of homosexuals in old age are negative, as Berger (1982) describes in his landmark study of older gay men:

He becomes increasingly effeminate with age, he is alienated from friends and family alike, and he lives alone, not by choice but by necessity. At thirty he is old. Since he is no longer sexually attractive to other homosexuals, he is forced to prey on children and to pursue anonymous sexual contacts in public places such as restrooms and parks. He is desperately unhappy. (p. 15)

Findings of research on psychological adjustment among older gay men and lesbians stand in stark contrast to this portrait, however. Kimmel (1993) reminds us that thinking of elderly adults as a homogenous group is a serious misconception. Just as "the elderly" have only their age in common, lesbians and gay men similarly share only their sexual orientation. Both groups include a wide range of backgrounds, interests, attitudes, and life styles. There are, then, many ways to grow old as a homosexual—and most lead toward relatively high levels of life satisfaction in old age (e.g., Berger, 1982; Deevey, 1990; Friend, 1990, 1991; Kimmel, 1993; Quam and Whitford, 1992).

Given the historical context that we have reviewed, how can we understand these findings? Friend (1990, 1991) posits that, ironically, it may be the long-term confrontation with heterosexism and homophobia that contributes to well-being in old age. Friend identifies coming to terms with one's homosexuality as a life crisis. This crisis may include family disruption and even alienation from the family, and inevitably demands managing intense emotions. Weathering this storm provides a sense of competence, preparing the individual to confront future crises associated with aging.

Friend (1990, 1991) further suggests that gay men and lesbians reach old age with a lifetime of experience in challenging traditional gender-role definitions. This experience provides the freedom to learn nontraditional skills. Furthermore, Friend proposes that elderly homosexuals have, of necessity, honed their ability to deconstruct society's negative images of gay and lesbian people, and reconstruct affirmative self-images. These capacities can be transferred to the task of replacing society's pejorative images of older people with more positive ones. Thus, Friend (1991) explains older gay men's and lesbians' adjustment in old age:

> Crisis competence, flexibility in gender role, and reconstructing the personal meanings of homosexuality and aging so they are positive have powerful effects on the individual psychology of older lesbian and gay people. At a cognitive level there is the adoption of a set of beliefs that affirm personal worth. At a behavioral level, adaptive skills which promote both daily living and a sense of competence and empowerment are developed. . . . these cognitive and behavioral dimensions impact positively on emotional factors such as self-acceptance and self-esteem. (p. 111–112)

Thus, prior research paints an optimistic picture of aging for most gay men and lesbians as regards mental health. It is clear, though, that older homosexuals share with other elderly adults the practical, social, and emotional needs that old age can entail. And just as ethnicity and class may affect the degree to which available services are accessible and acceptable, so too may sexual orientation itself, the wish to keep one's orientation private, or the fear of homophobia on the part of service providers, family, or friends.

MEETING THE PRACTICAL AND SOCIAL NEEDS OF GAY AND LESBIAN ELDERLY CLIENTS

Are the Issues Different?

On the one hand, sexual orientation casts a unique hue on the manner in which age-related crises are experienced. Life-span scholars have taught us that the experience of later life reflects the impact of events earlier in the life span. For example, an older gay man's transition to retirement is shaped by the long-term character of his involvement in work, the extent to which homophobia and discrimination have impeded his career advancement, his integration into the gay/lesbian community, and his ties to the broader community.

Furthermore, psychologists (e.g., Friend, 1990, 1991; Kimmel, 1978, 1993; Kimmel and Sang, 1995; Sang, 1993) describe unique patterns of development in early and middle adulthood for homosexuals. Kimmel (1978, 1993; Kimmel and Sang, 1995), for example, identifies coming out as a nonnormative life crisis: Since approximately 10 percent of the population is homosexual, most people do not come out; the experience can occur at any point in the life cycle; and—for those who do come out—the experience affects the character of subsequent development.

On the other hand, the issues that homosexuals face in old age are far from unique. Older gay men and lesbians, as noted above, confront changes in health and vigor, the transition to retirement and reduced income, and bereavement. The age-related crises with which gerontologists are familiar, then, are crises for this population as well. But how does sexual orientation shape responses to these experiences?

Legal and Financial Issues

The most pressing legal issues for older gay men and lesbians typically surround relationships with a partner, inheritance, and protection of jointly-owned assets. It is essential that older homosexuals know their rights and options in these areas, that they understand the urgency of making their wishes known in a formal manner, and that they have access to professionals who support their wishes and are skilled in effecting the necessary legal arrangements. For example, without a power of attorney for health care, an elderly lesbian may be prevented from visiting her partner in an intensive care setting or from contributing to decisions about her care. Similarly, state law controls distribution of assets should an older homosexual man or woman die without a will; the deceased individual's partner may receive no share of the estate unless prior arrangements have been made.

Unmarried people and women, generally, confront old age at a financial disadvantage. Current tax and inheritance laws operate to the disadvantage of unmarried individuals (e.g., higher inheritance taxes for unrelated persons). Monthly Social Security and (with few exceptions) pension income can go only to a surviving spouse. Many contemporary older lesbians face still another hurdle, since American women have traditionally been relatively uninformed about financial matters, including investment options and risks.

What can practitioners do to address these issues? First, practitioners can be advocates for the equal financial and legal treatment of homosexuals of all ages. Widespread support for domestic partnership policies extending insurance, pension, and other employment-related and Social Security benefits to unmarried same-sex partners is critical. Second, practitioners can identify attorneys and financial advisors who are knowledgeable about the special circumstances confronting older gay men and lesbians and who are supportive of their needs.

Housing and Community Issues

Most older adults, of course, live in their own homes—which are typically unmortgaged older, single-family residences. Older homosexuals in this circumstance probably confront few housing-related problems outside of the regular maintenance needs with which every homeowner is faced. For some older adults, however, congregate housing is a sound choice due to the individual's physical frailty, cognitive limitations, or desire. Surveys inform us that the heterosexual atmosphere of existing residential facilities is distasteful to some older gay men and lesbians and that older gay men and lesbians would prefer to have "homosexual only" age-segregated housing available (e.g., Quam and Whitford, 1992; Lesbian Aging Issues Forum, 1993). At present, such facilities are virtually unavailable.

The most vulnerable elderly homosexuals, those so frail that they must enter a nursing home, confront still more problems—and so do their partners. Elderly lesbians, in particular, may enter old age following a lifetime of "women's work"—either child rearing and unpaid work in the home, or work at jobs with low wages and few, if any, pension benefits. In such a situation, the only option may be to rely on public assistance for nursing home care. Public policy in many states requires sale of a home owned by a nursing home resident whose care is state-funded (unless the home is occupied by a spouse, minor, or disabled child). As the vignette that opened this chapter describes, the lesbian or gay partner of a nursing home resident may thus be rendered homeless by the partner's need for care.

Even older gay men and lesbians in more advantaged circumstances are not free of problems related to nursing home residence. Certainly, most nursing home administrators have worked hard to create policies that respect residents' dignity, individuality, and privacy. It is likely that Kimmel's (1993) description, however, applies to most nursing homes' readiness to meet the social and emotional needs of gay and lesbian residents:

> Assuming that similar proportions of gay persons are in nursing homes or other chronic care facilities as in the general community,

about 10 percent of nursing home residents may be assumed to be homosexual. Yet, no provision is made for these persons. Nursing homes often do not recognize the sexual/affectional needs of their heterosexual residents, let alone the needs of homosexual persons. Even nursing homes that allow private conjugal visits would not be likely to allow this for a homosexual couple. Moreover it is often possible for a relative of the resident to prevent visits by a homosexual friend or lover. (p. 532)

Again, what steps can practitioners take to address these issues? In some cities, there are burgeoning efforts within the gay/lesbian community to establish residential facilities for older members (e.g., Kimmel, 1993; Lesbian Aging Issues Forum, 1993). These efforts face uphill battles, to say the least, and could benefit from support in revision of zoning ordinances (to increase the numbers of unmarried persons permitted to share a home) and of public housing policies (to allow for occupancy of a single unit by maritally unrelated persons). Other advocacy needs include revision of public medical assistance guidelines to protect a partner's life tenure in a jointly-owned home following institutionalization, and establishment of an accepting climate for sexual expression on the part of nursing home residents.

Health and Caregiving Issues

Older gay men and lesbians, of course, share the predominant health-related concerns of all older adults (e.g., increased incidence of chronic disease and comorbidity; use of multiple medications; medical costs not covered by Medicare, Medicaid, and/or private insurance). However, these issues become more complex in the case of the older homosexual for at least two reasons. First, older gay men and lesbians confront psychic and often financial barriers to health care access that are not present for heterosexual elderly people. Second, there are medical problems—including AIDS and HIV infection—that are particular threats for older gay men and lesbians.

Deevey (1990) writes with moving sensitivity of older lesbian women as an "invisible minority" in health care settings. She notes that the nursing literature has heretofore provided little guidance toward improving care of older lesbian patients. And she warns that significant percentages of nursing educators express negative stereotypes of lesbians.

Given this context, it is not surprising that many older gay men and lesbians hesitate to be "out" with health care providers (e.g., Lesbian Aging Issues Forum, 1993; Quam and Whitford, 1992). Actual homophobia and presumed homophobia set up psychic barriers between elderly homosexuals and health care professionals. What may be an even more significant barrier to health care access is the elderly homosexual's inability to cover a partner under a family health insurance plan, or to cover younger partner's care under Medicare.

Despite the "invisible" status that older gay men and lesbians share vis a vis the health care profession, medical conditions for which these individuals are at high risk have been identified (e.g., Berger, 1982; Deevey, 1990). These conditions include breast cancer, pharyngeal and anal gonorrhea, anal fissures, alcohol/other drug dependence, and AIDS/HIV infection. The latter, of course, has been the focus of monumental research efforts since the early 1980s. However, very little work focuses specifically on the implications of the AIDS epidemic for older people in particular (see Riley, Ory, and Zablotsky [1989] for an exception). Ironically, one group of public health scholars pointed out that those developing long-term care policies for PWA (persons with AIDS) could do well to consider the lessons learned through long-term care practice with the elderly (Crystal, 1989).

Currently, most cases of HIV infection are identified in younger cohorts; there are relatively few instances of individuals living with AIDS in their sixties, seventies, or beyond (e.g., Riley, Ory, and Zablotsky, 1989). It is reasonable to expect that the numbers of older PWA may increase in coming decades, however. Though progress in identifying effective treatments for AIDS is slow, more PWA are surviving longer each year. As this trend continues, caregiving in the face of AIDS will become a more widespread experience among older adults.

Caregiving—and care-receiving—as a response to chronic illness is, of course, a major issue for contemporary older adults and their families. Like the other age-related concerns that we have considered, caregiving presents particularly vexing problems for gay and lesbian older adults. At a recent forum, older lesbians noted that:

Aging lesbians who are in relationships are still considered single women. If we have parents who need care, society expects the single daughters to shoulder this burden. A lesbian who is with a partner may need to take a parent into her home. If she is not "out" to her parents, and many of us who are older have not "come out," she may be forced to hide and deny her relationship in her own home. The problem can become even harder if she herself is in need of care and her children decide to take her into one of their homes. If she is not out to them, this can mean that she could be forced to leave her partner . . . if both of them are in need of care, the children of one may not want to take them both, as they would if it were a hetero-sexual married couple. (Lesbian Aging Issues Forum, 1993, p. 17)

As is the case with legal, financial, and housing-related issues, prac-titioners' most important contribution may be that of advocacy for unbi-ased treatment of older homosexuals. Health care professionals can help further through continuing professional education programs that present homosexuality in an honest, positive manner. Finally, practitioners involved in long-term care and caregiver support services should be prepared to iden-tify and meet the special needs of older gay and lesbian clients (see Deevey [1990] for specific suggestions).

Bereavement Issues

Scholars disagree concerning the extent to which bereavement poses greater challenges for homosexual elders as compared to their heterosexual coun-terparts. On the one hand, Berger (1982) suggests that older gay men may enjoy certain advantages in adapting to the death of a partner:

> Although death of friends and family is a burden shared by older het-erosexuals and homosexuals, the older homosexual is less likely to invest himself in a single spouse. . . . the homosexual, aware of his isolation at an early age, is perhaps more likely than the heterosexual to have developed strong friendship bonds, and these friendships are then used as a resource in crisis situations. Furthermore, because of the greater similarity in life expectancies for two men, the phenom-enon of one spouse (the female) outliving the other is less typical. (p. 194)

However, others disagree. Kimmel (1993) points out that death of a long-term partner may well involve many of the problematic issues that we have already considered (e.g., legal and financial issues related to inherit-ance; threats to home ownership; access to a critically ill partner in a hospi-tal or nursing home). And most scholars stress the emotional anguish (and sometimes physical effects) that older gay men and lesbians experience upon the death of a long-term partner. As Kehoe (1989) describes:

> The survivor of a couple that had lived together for 44H years ad-mits that her most serious problem is still loneliness, long after the woman she loved died. . . . The devastation of losing the most impor-tant person in one's life can also have its physical effects. On the af-

termath of such an experience, another respondent said "I've since retired and through all the stress of this negativism have a chronic lung problem." (p. 49)

The absence of bereavement counseling and other forms of support specifically tailored to the needs of older homosexuals is another oft-cited problem (e.g., Berger, 1982; Deevey, 1990; Galassi, 1991; Kehoe, 1989; Kimmel, 1993). Certainly, practitioners need to make establishment, support, and promotion of such services within the aging and the gay/lesbian support networks a high priority. Advocacy for equal legal treatment of homosexual widows and widowers, as noted above, is also important.

PROSPECT: OLDER GAY MEN AND LESBIANS IN THE NEXT MILLENNIUM

Within gay/lesbian communities across the country, there is growing recognition that attention to the needs of older members—and enrichment from the resources that they offer—needs nurturing. SAGE (Senior Action in a Gay Environment) is probably the best known response to this recognition (e.g., Gwenwald, 1984). SAGE is dedicated to meeting the social, educational, and service needs of older gay and lesbian adults, and to providing educational programs for professionals and the general public. Support groups and social organizations for elderly homosexuals are available in some cities, as are programs for training practitioners likely to work with elderly gay and lesbian clients (e.g., Berger, 1982).

What can contemporary young homosexuals expect in old age? Our younger counterparts encounter discrimination, homophobia, and well-meant insensitivity, to be sure. But they have not had to grapple with the level of invisibility, isolation, and condemnation that today's elderly gay men and lesbians remember. We can hope that elderly homosexuals in the future will benefit from growing old in a more accepting climate that includes visible and viable gay/lesbian communities in many cities.

The Appendix to this chapter lists national resource organizations with a focus on the needs of older homosexuals and practitioners who work with them.

APPENDIX

National Organizations with a Focus on Gay/Lesbian Aging Issues
GLOE (Gay and Lesbian Outreach to Elderly)
1853 Market St.
San Francisco, CA 94103

Golden Threads Friendship Club
P.O. Box 3177
Burlington, VT 05401

NALGG
National Association for Lesbian
and Gay Gerontology
1853 Market St.
San Francisco, CA 94109

SAGE (Senior Action in a Gay Environment)
208 W. 13th St.
New York, NY 10011

Stonewall Union Task Force on Lesbian and Gay Aging
P.O. Box 10814
Columbus, OH 43201-7814

OLOC (Old Lesbians Organizing for Change)
P.O. Box 980422
Houston, TX 77098

Dignity Task Force on Aging
235 S. 23rd St.
Philadelphia, PA 19013

Older Women's League
730 11th St. NW
Suite 300
Washington, DC 20001

Women's Initiative Network
AARP
601 E St. NW
Washington, DC 20049

Gray Panthers
1424 16th St. NW
Washington, DC 20036

National Gay/Lesbian Task Force
2320 17th St. NW
Washington, DC 20009

Lambda Legal Defense & Education Fund
666 Broadway
New York, NY 10012

National Action Forum for Midlife and Older Women
Box 816
Stony Brook, NY 11790

REFERENCES

Adelman, M. (1991). Stigma, gay lifestyles, and adjustment to aging: A study of later-life gay men and lesbians. *Journal of Homosexuality*, 20:7–31.

Berger, R.M. (1982). *Gay and gray: The older homosexual man.* Urbana: University of Illinois Press.

Crystal, S. (1989). Persons with AIDS and older people: Common long-term care concerns. In M.W. Riley, M.G. Ory, and D. Zablotsky (eds.), *AIDS in an aging society: What we need to know,* 147–166. New York: Springer.

Deevey, S. (1990). Older lesbian women: An invisible minority. *Journal of Gerontological Nursing*, 16:35–39.

Friend, R.A. (1990). Older lesbian and gay people: Responding to homophobia. *Marriage and Family Review*, 14:241–263.

—— (1991). Older lesbian and gay people: A theory of successful aging. *Journal of Homosexuality*, 20:99–118.

Galassi, F.S. (1991). A life-review workshop for gay and lesbian elders. *Journal of Gerontological Social Work*, 16:75–86.

Gwenwald, M. (1984). The SAGE model for serving older lesbians and gay men. *Journal of Social Work and Human Sexuality*, 2:53–61.

Kehoe, M. (1989). *Lesbians over 60 speak for themselves.* New York: Harrington Park Press.

Kimmel, D.C. (1978). Adult development and aging: A gay perspective. *Journal of Social Issues*, 34:113–130.

——— (1993). Adult development and aging: A gay perspective. In L.D. Garnets and D.C. Kimmel (eds.), *Psychological perspectives on lesbian and gay male experiences*, 517–540. New York: Columbia University Press.

Kimmel, D.C. and Sang, B.E. (1995). Lesbians and gay men in midlife. In A.R. D'Augelli and C.J. Patterson (eds.), *Lesbian, gay, and bisexual identities over the lifespan: Psychological perspectives*, 190–214. New York: Oxford University Press.

Lesbian Aging Issues Forum. (1993). *Report from the Forum held at Madison, Wisconsin, March 6, 1993.* Madison, WI: AgeAdvantAge.

Quam, J.K. and Whitford, G.S. (1992). Adaptation and age-related expectations of older gay and lesbian adults. *The Gerontologist*, 32:367–374.

Reid, J.D. (1995). Development in late life: Older lesbian and gay lives. In A.R. D'Augelli and C. J. Patterson (eds.), *Lesbian, gay, and bisexual identities over the lifespan: Psychological perspectives*, 215–240. New York: Oxford University Press.

Riley, M.W., Ory, M.G., and Zablotsky, D. (1989). *AIDS in an aging society: What we need to know.* New York: Springer.

Sang, B.E. (1993). Existential issues of midlife lesbians. In A.R. D'Augelli and C.J. Patterson (eds.), *Lesbian, gay, and bisexual identities over the lifespan: Psychological perspectives*, 500–516. New York: Oxford University Press.

Relationships with Children, Grandchildren, and Great-Grandchildren

Today and Tomorrow

Jeanne L. Thomas

Introduction

Sandy and Jim see their daughter, son-in-law, and grandchildren every few days; hardly a day goes by that they don't talk on the telephone. Sandy says that her children and grandchildren are her best friends. And Jim is never happier than when he is helping his son-in-law and granddaughter with a carpentry project.

Shirley, at age ninety-two, needs help from her children to do housework and cooking. Because she no longer drives, her children and grandchildren take her shopping, to the doctor's office, to church, and visiting. One of her children, grandchildren, or great-grandchildren stops by every day to see what she needs and be sure that she is all right.

Eighty-year-old Bill loves and fears his son Charlie. He counts on Charlie to help out with house and yard chores, and he needs to borrow money every now and then. Charlie always comes through on these occasions. But Charlie sometimes flies off the handle. When that happens, he ridicules and humiliates Bill and sometimes strikes him. The last time, Bill had to have twelve stitches in his forehead.

These vignettes illustrate the importance of older adults' relationships with the younger generations in their families. Nearly all older people have living children, grandchildren, and/or great-grandchildren. These relationships almost always provide satisfaction and support. Sometimes, too, however, children, grandchildren, or great-grandchildren create stress in older people's lives.

This chapter provides an overview of these relationships. Throughout, we consider implications for psychologists, psychiatrists, other practitioners, and older people and their families. The chapter concludes with a discussion of unanswered questions that are important to professionals who work with older adults.

Are elderly people abandoned and neglected by their children? Many people think so. Supposedly, geographic mobility has put great distance between older people and their offspring, and prevents them from seeing one another often. These images are surprisingly tenacious, given the volume of data that soundly contradicts them.

Geographic Proximity

Among the best-documented findings in family gerontology is that older people and their adult children prefer to live near one another but not with one another, and that most families are successful in implementing that preference (e.g., Bengtson, Rosenthal, and Burton, 1990). About three out of four elderly parents live within a half-hour of at least one of their children (e.g., Shanas, 1979), although many also have other children living at greater distances (Moss, Moss, and Moles, 1985). Although this close intergenerational proximity applies to older people of all ethnic backgrounds, older Hispanic-Americans generally live closer to kin than do non-Hispanic older people (Markides and Mindel, 1987).

Getting Together

Older adults generally see their sons and daughters frequently. Most older people see at least one of their adult children on a weekly basis, and many see an adult child nearly every day (Bengtson, Rosenthal, and Burton, 1990; Treas and Bengtson, 1987; Crimmins and Ingegneri, 1990; Shanas, 1979). What determines just *how* often older people get together with their children? As the vignettes that opened this chapter suggest, older parents and adult children get together because they think they should, because they need to help one another, and because they enjoy being together (Roberts and Bengtson, 1990).

Feelings between Older Parents and Their Children

How older people and their sons and daughters feel about one another is potentially the most important part of their relationship, but probably also the least tangible aspect. Typically, both elderly parents and adult children report strong feelings of affection for one another (e.g., Bengtson, Rosenthal, and Burton, 1990; Treas and Bengtson, 1987). How much affection older parents and adult children feel toward one another does not necessarily depend on how often they see each other. Elderly parents describe their relationships with geographically distant, infrequently seen children as close and satisfying, much like their relationships with children living nearby that they see more often (Mercier, Paulson, and Morris, 1989; Moss, Moss, and Moles, 1985).

Helping Each Other

Nearly all older adults continue to help their children and grandchildren and receive help from them (e.g., Hill, 1968). One gerontologist describes these exchanges as a long-term "support bank" that operates on an unconscious level (Antonucci, 1985, 1990). In their forties, fifties, and sixties, Sandy and Jim, described at the outset of this chapter, make "deposits" into the support bank by helping their own parents and grandparents as well as their children and grandchildren. They can then anticipate "withdrawing" help from children, grandchildren, and great-grandchildren when they are themselves older and in greater need of help. Of course, the types of help Sandy and Jim give and receive, and the balance between giving and receiving help, will change over the life cycle as their own and their relatives' needs and resources change.

Middle-aged people are especially important actors in these networks of intergenerational support (e.g., Bengtson, Rosenthal, and Burton, 1990; Brody, 1981; Hill, 1968; Nakao, Okabe, and Bengtson, 1988). In most families, individuals in their forties, fifties, and sixties give more help to the younger and older people in the families than they receive from them. And in most families, the youngest and oldest generations in the family more often exchange help with middle-aged relatives than they do with each other.

Is reciprocity in family support important? Common sense may suggest that an older person's ability to "repay" younger relatives' help would be important to his or her morale, but surveys have not supported this notion (Lee and Ellithorpe, 1982; McColloch, 1990). However, elderly parents reporting an even balance between the amounts of help that they gave to children and help that they received from children were more satisfied with children's help than were parents reporting less balanced exchanges (Thomas, 1988).

Family Caregiving

Many people assume that most frail elderly people who need regular assistance with activities such as housework, shopping, bathing, and toileting receive help from formal sources—a home health aide or health care professionals in a nursing home. Actually, though, the family provides such long-term care far more often (Brody, 1981; Chappell, 1990; Penning, 1990; World Health Organization, 1980).

A caregiver may be the aged spouse or sibling of the person receiving care—or a middle-aged child or grandchild, a more distant relative, or even a friend or neighbor. Although most caregivers are women, men take on caregiving responsibilities as well. The need to provide care may arise from an elderly person's physical incapacity, dementia or other mental impairment, or a combination of frailties. The course of physical aging is so variable that very old parents may need to provide care for their aged children. And, of course, family caregiving occurs in all racial and ethnic groups, and all social classes.

Being a caregiver can be difficult. Compared to people not providing care, caregivers report higher levels of depression, demoralization, grief, despair, hopelessness, physical illness, and weakened resistance to disease (e.g., Pruchno et al., 1990; Schulz, Visintainer, and Williamson, 1990). Using a stress and coping model, a caregiver's feelings of burden reflect the impacts of 1) an objective event (the elderly person's incapacitating illness), 2) stressors that are consequences of that event (the older person's symptoms, tasks that the caregiver performs, changes in the caregiver's life), 3) the caregiver's perception of these consequences, and 4) the resources available to him or her (e.g., Gatz, Bengston, and Blum, 1990).

What challenges confront caregivers who are employed, in addition to carrying out their caregiving responsibilities? Paid employment apparently has little impact on women's caregiving, but fulfilling both roles may exact a heavy cost from the caregiver. Comparisons of caregivers who do and who do not work outside the home reveal few differences in how much care they give elderly parents. Employed caregivers manage by maintaining rigid personal schedules and by giving up time for their own rest and enjoyment (e.g., Brody, 1985; Chappell, 1990; Stoller, 1983).

Caregivers do not, then, neglect frail elderly relatives in order to pursue careers. However, being a caregiver affects caregivers' work. Brody (1985) compared working and nonworking women caring for their elderly mothers, and found that nearly a third of the nonworking women had left their jobs to meet their mothers' needs; similar numbers of working women were considering giving up their jobs, and many had already reduced their work hours. More recently, Scharlach and Boyd (1989) reported that employees with caregiving responsibilities were more likely than other employees to miss work or to take time off because of caregiving. These employees also admitted that they were sometimes so exhausted from caregiving that it was difficult for them to do their jobs.

The problem of role conflict is not simply one of competing demands of work and caregiving. Elaine Brody (1981) proposes a broader notion of role conflict in her discussion of "women in the middle." These middle-aged women provide support to their husbands; they may have children (even preschool-aged children) still living at home; and they also are often pursuing careers while caring for their elderly parents and/or parents-in-law. Clearly, these women are caught in the middle of a complex set of demanding roles within the family and outside it.

Other Reactions to Caregiving

Although caregiving is stressful for most, many caregivers also identify ways in which providing care is gratifying. Some find that they become closer to the elderly person receiving care, or that the family as a whole becomes closer (Kinney and Stephens, 1989; Motenko, 1989; Stoller and Pugliesi, 1989a, 1989b). Others take comfort in the assurance that their elderly relative is receiving good care (Kinney and Stephens, 1989). For some, providing care brings pride in managing a difficult challenge, or an opportunity to learn new skills and experience personal growth (Brody, 1985; Davies, Priddy, and Tinklenberg, 1986; Schulz, Visintainer, and Williamson, 1990; Stoller and Pugliesi, 1989a, 1989b).

Implications for Practitioners: Minimizing Caregiver Burden

Just as gerontologists have documented the extent of caregiver burden, they have also identified means through which professionals can minimize burden. Family counseling is often helpful (e.g., Gatz, Bengston, and Blum, 1990; Toseland and Smith, 1990). In this case, however, the counselor's goal is not the traditional effort to enhance personality and behavior, but rather to help the family deal with a situational problem.

Other approaches are more innovative. For example, Goodman and Pynoos (1990) described a telephone information and support program for caregivers of Alzheimer's disease patients. In this program, caregivers could either participate in a peer network that engaged in regular telephone conversations about caregiving, or they could listen to informational minilectures delivered by telephone. Both telephone-based interventions increased caregivers' knowledge about the disease and their satisfaction with the help that they received from family and friends.

Another common intervention is a caregiver support group. In these groups, caregivers can receive information about specific disorders, share social support, and exchange ideas about how to manage problematic behaviors. Respite care is one of the services that caregivers request most often (Chappell, 1990; Gatz, Bengston, and Blum, 1990). In respite care programs, the primary caregiver can take a break from his or her responsibilities when a volunteer (or sometimes a professional) temporarily takes over caregiving duties. Respite may be provided for a few hours, or as much as a few days, and it may be provided in the home or in a group setting, depending on the program.

Elder Abuse

Even though most older people have warm relationships with adult children, conflicted relationships also obviously exist between the aged and their children. Probably the most extreme hostility is acted out in cases of elder abuse. Elder abuse encompasses several kinds of victimization of older people, including physical violence, psychological abuse, financial exploitation, or theft of material resources.

As with other forms of family violence, it is difficult to know how often elder abuse occurs. Reported cases probably only represent a fraction of all instances. One recent study of a random sample of over 2,000 community-dwelling elderly people indicated a prevalence rate of thirty-two instances of abuse for every 1,000 persons (Phillemer and Finkelhor, 1988). The typical victim is often a particularly vulnerable older person. The victim is often in advanced old age or physically quite frail, and may suffer from chronic disease or from mental impairment (e.g., Phillemer and Finkelhor, 1988; Rathbone-McCuan, 1986).

Several explanations have been proposed for elder abuse (e.g., Rathbone-McCuan, 1986). The abuser may have been mistreated by the elderly victim in the past, or violence may be the main way in which family members have learned to deal with stress. Occasionally, a caregiver abuses an elderly relative under his or her care. In these instances, the abuse may stem from the stress of caregiving, from not receiving enough help from family and friends, or both. Others propose that a personality disorder or substance abuse problem may cause the abuser's behavior.

Implications for Practitioners: Interventions in Cases of Elder Abuse

Those who work with older adults must be alert for signs of physical abuse (e.g., repeated unexplained injuries), and careful to follow up on any statements that suggest the possibility of emotional abuse or financial exploitation. Several states have enacted mandatory reporting laws for suspected cases of elder abuse; even when the law does not demand reporting suspected abuse, common decency and concern for older adults' welfare does. Practitioners should be familiar with the appropriate authority to whom suspicions should be reported, as well as any legal protection the state offers to reporters.

Practitioners who want to provide the greatest long-term benefit to an abused older person will probably do best by considering the abuse as the symptom rather than the disease. Intervention almost certainly needs to be made in the kinds of expectations that the older person and the abuser have for one another, the means through which they communicate their expectations, and the strategies that they have for solving problems in their relationship. If the abuse stems from a substance abuse problem or some form of psychopathology, then treatment obviously needs to focus on that situation.

GRANDPARENTHOOD AND GREAT-GRANDPARENTHOOD

The media conveys a sentimental image of grandparents. Grandmothers are portrayed as plump, gray-haired, bespectacled bundles of nurturing thoughts and deeds, tirelessly baking cookies and Thanksgiving turkeys, reading stories, and treating grandchildren's cuts and scrapes with Band-Aids, kisses, and hugs. Grandfathers, too, have the girth, gray hair, and glasses of old age. Some grandfathers teach grandchildren fishing and carpentry, some are mischievous companions who indulge grandchildren with treats and outings, and all tell fascinating stories of the "good old days."

Although these images may have once had a realistic basis, they do not describe many contemporary grandparents. Today, grandparents better fit a far more youthful image, as the transition to grandparenthood now typically occurs in the forties. A forty-five-year-old grandmother today probably devotes more time to her career than to baking cookies; her husband may be more concerned with his own parents' and grandparents' increasing frailty than with his granddaughter's interest in woodworking.

Grandparenthood and Mental Health

Is it true, as bumper stickers proclaim, that "Happiness is being a grandparent"? Does having grandchildren benefit the grandparent's mental health? Recent research suggests that it does. What grandparents find *symbolically* important about having grandchildren is important, but in different ways for women and for men (Kivnick, 1982a, 1982b; 1985). Grandmothers stress the symbolic importance of grandchildren to compensate for such age-related stresses as chronic illness, limited finances, and widowhood. However, grandfathers who find grandparenting most pleasant and important are those who most enjoy life in general. Furthermore, concrete relationships with specific grandchildren are related to grandparents' mental health. The grandparent's feelings of satisfaction and nurturance in these relationships are positively associated with mental health, although the extent to which the grandparent wields authority in the relationship (by disciplining the grandchild, for example) is not (Thomas, 1990b).

Overgeneralizing about relationships with grandchildren is risky—even within a single grandparent's experience! Grandparents describe relationships with different grandchildren quite differently (e.g., Cherlin and Furstenberg, 1986; Thomas, 1982). Many grandparents make "selective investments" by developing particularly close, satisfying relationships with one or a few of their grandchildren. Even if the grandparent lives far away from some grandchildren, or doesn't get along with some, she or he may have strong relationships with other grandchildren.

Great-Grandparents

Prior to the twentieth century, great-grandparents were a rarity. However, increased life expectancy has changed that situation. Today, nearly everyone aged sixty-five and older who has living children also has grandchildren; nearly half of all grandparents are also great-grandparents (Shanas, 1980). For most, being a great-grandparent is important more for symbolic reasons than because of the personal relationships with great-grandchildren. Great-grandchildren can be symbols of family success and vitality, personal and family renewal, and longevity (Doka and Mertz, 1988; Wentowski, 1985).

Implications for Practitioners: Grandchildren and Great-Grandchildren

As a sound treatment plan invariably rests on a thorough assessment, mental health practitioners working with older adults will want to develop a clear picture of the client's family context—including relationships with grandchildren and great-grandchildren. Reactions to these and other family relationships often reflect much more general values regarding family closeness and support, and the extent to which generations agree on these values (Rodeheaver and Thomas, 1986; Thomas, 1982). The clinical interview, then, needs to encompass not only the client's family circumstances but also his or her views of ideal family circumstances. Children, grandchildren, and great-grandchildren should also be interviewed whenever possible.

Authority in grandparent-grandchild relationships may be a fruitful arena for therapeutic exploration. Disciplining grandchildren and advising parents about their care is an aspect of grandparenthood from which grandparents typically derive little satisfaction (e.g., Thomas, 1990b). Furthermore, parents who believe that their own parents are "interfering" in how the grandchildren are brought up (perhaps by disciplining the grandchildren, or by giving advice) often voice dissatisfaction with this aspect of their relationships with their own grandparents (Thomas, 1990a).

Gazing into a crystal ball is always risky. But it is no risk to predict that older adults and their families will continue to turn to health and mental health professionals as they encounter age-related challenges, and that professionals will need a well-honed repertoire of skills to meet these needs. Practitioners looking ahead to work with older adults in the twenty-first century can frame their expectations using known demographic and social trends.

Gerontologists regularly direct our attention to the rapid growth in the oldest segments of the population. As these "oldest old" cohorts continue to expand, the challenges inherent in providing services to these individuals and their families may become more complex in at least two respects. First, caregiving for frail elders may become a prolonged process—at least for older people who live more years in frailty rather than living a longer *and* healthier life. Practitioners and policy makers must engage in ongoing processes of exploring and evaluating strategies for combining community-based and institutional long-term care, for merging care provided by professionals and by family and friends, and for financing long-term care.

Second, increased life expectancy could yield more complex family caregiving networks to the extent that members of more generations share caregiving duties. In particular, elderly people caring for still older relatives and friends is likely to become a more frequent phenomenon. These caregivers may need support of various kinds—physical assistance, practical information, service referrals, emotional support, financial help, and the like—in order to provide care. Thus, finding cost-effective means of enabling older caregivers should become a priority for research and funding.

All of these possibilities suggest that families will continue to need professional support as they care for frail older relatives, and that professionals may be confronted with more imposing caregiving-related situations. We also know that the oldest segment of the population, like the American population generally, is becoming more diverse in race and ethnicity. Furthermore, family forms have grown more varied (at least among younger cohorts) with gay and lesbian households, single-parent families, one-child families, and blended families growing far more common than was once the case. These trends, too, confront practitioners of the future with new challenges. To serve such a rich and varied population effectively, professionals will need to be knowledgeable concerning ways in which such dimensions as race, class, sexual orientation, and family size affect individual and family functioning in old age.

Other trends form a broader context from which to consider aging in the twenty-first century. Technology is revolutionizing education at all levels, corporate and manufacturing operations, and health care. It is almost inevitable that technology will transform the lives of older adults and their families as well. Caregivers in the twenty-first century may rely on communications technology to receive information and contact health and social service professionals. Those who lived most of their lives in the computer age may "surf the Net" during retirement, electronically taking courses, keeping in touch with friends and relatives, and pursuing personal interests. There may be electronic "virtual support groups" for caregivers and electronic bulletin boards allowing professionals who work with the aged to exchange information. Sophisticated robotics may be used to provide assistance to those with mobility impairments.

Throughout the twentieth century, the importance of adopting a global perspective—considering issues in terms of their international and intercultural implications—has become increasingly clear. This trend is reflected in the growing significance of cross-cultural and cross-national comparisons of family forms and service approaches in gerontology. As the world continues to shrink, metaphorically, we can predict that older adults and those concerned with their welfare will benefit from the enhanced understanding of aging that a global perspective provides.

Being an older individual and meeting the needs of older people will likely, then, be more challenging in the twenty-first century than they are today. However, the future also offers expanded resources for meeting the challenges of aging in the twenty-first century.

REFERENCES

Antonucci, T.C. (1985). Personal characteristics, social support, and social behavior. In R. H. Binstock and E. Shanas (eds.), *Handbook of aging and the social sciences*, 94–128. 2nd ed. New York: Van Nostrand Reinhold.

———. (1990). Social supports and social relationships. In R.H. Binstock and L.K. George (eds.), *Handbook of aging and the social sciences*, 205–226. 3rd ed. San Diego: Academic Press.

Bengtson, V., Rosenthal, C., and Burton, L. (1990). Families and aging: Diversity and heterogeneity. In R.H. Binstock and L.K. George (eds.), *Handbook of aging and the social sciences*, 263–287. 3rd ed. San Diego: Academic Press.

Brody, E.M. (1981). Women in the middle and family help to older people. *The Gerontologist*, 21:471–480.

———. (1985). Parent care as a normative family stress. *The Gerontologist*, 25:19–29.

Chappell, N.L. (1990). Aging and social care. In R.H. Binstock and L. K. George (eds.), *Handbook of aging and the social sciences*, 438–454. 3rd ed. San Diego: Academic Press.

Cherlin, A.J. and Furstenberg, F.F. (1986). *The new American grandparent*. New York: Basic Books.

Crimmins, E.M. and Ingegneri, D.G. (1990). Interaction and living arrangements of older parents and their children: Past trends, present determinants, future implications. *Research on Aging*, 12:3–35.

Davies, H., Priddy, J.M., and Tinklenberg, J.R. (1986). Support groups for male caregivers of Alzheimer's patients. In T.L. Brink (ed.), *Handbook of clinical gerontology*, 385–395. New York: Haworth Press.

Doka, K.J. and Mertz, M.E. (1988). The meaning and significance of great-grandparenthood. *The Gerontologist*, 28:192–197.

Gatz, M., Bengtson, V.L., and Blum, M.J. (1990). Caregiving families. In J.E. Birren and K.W. Schaie (eds.), *Handbook of the psychology of aging*, 404–426. 3rd ed. San Diego: Academic Press.

Goodman, C.C. and Pynoos, J. (1990). A model telephone information and support program for caregivers of Alzheimer's patients. *The Gerontologist*, 45:399–404.

Hill, R. (1968). Decision making and the family life cycle. In B.L. Neugarten (ed.), *Middle age and aging*, 286–295. Chicago: University of Chicago Press.

Kinney, J.M. and Stephens, M.A.P. (1989). Hassles and uplifts of giving care to a family member with dementia. *Psychology and Aging*, 4:402–440.

Kivnick, H.Q. (1982a). Grandparenthood: An overview of meaning and mental health. *The Gerontologist*, 22:59–66.

———. (1982b). *The meaning of grandparenthood*. Ann Arbor: University of Michigan Research Press.

———. (1985). Grandparenthood and mental health: Meaning, behavior, and satisfaction. In V. L. Bengtson and J.F. Robertson (eds.), *Grandparenthood*, 151–158. Beverly Hills: Sage.

Lee, G.R. and Ellithorpe, E. (1982). Intergenerational exchange and subjective well-being among the elderly. *Journal of Marriage and the Family*, 44:217–224.

Markides, K.S. and Mindel, C.H. (1987). *Aging and ethnicity*. Newbury Park, CA: Sage.

McColloch, B.J. (1990). The relationship of intergenerational reciprocity of aid to the morale of older parents: Equity and exchange theory comparisons. *Journal of Gerontology: Social Sciences*, 45:S150–155.

Mercier, J.M., Paulson, L., and Morris, E.W. (1989). Proximity as a mediating influence on the perceived aging parent-adult child relationship. *The Gerontologist*, 29:785–791.

Moss, M.S., Moss, S.Z., and Moles, E.L. (1985). The quality of relationships between elderly parents and their out-of-town children. *The Gerontologist*, 25:134–140.

Motenko, A.K. (1989). The frustrations, gratifications, and well-being of dementia caregivers. *The Gerontologist*, 29:166–172.

Nakao, K., Okabe, T., and Bengtson, V.L. (1988). Reciprocity across generations in social support. Paper presented at the annual meeting of the International Network for Social Network Analysis, Sunbelt Social Network Conference, San Diego.

Penning, M.J. (1990). Receipt of assistance by elderly people: Hierarchical selection and task specificity. *The Gerontologist*, 30:220–227.

Phillemer, K., and Finkelhor, D. (1988). The prevalence of elder abuse: A random sample survey. *The Gerontologist*, 28:51–57.

Pruchno, R.A., Kleban, M.H., Michaels, J.E., and Dempsey, N.P. (1990). Mental and physical health of caregiving spouses: Development of a causal model. *Journal of Gerontology: Psychological Sciences*, 45:P192–199.

Rathbone-McCuan, E. (1986). Elder abuse resulting from caregiving overload in older families. In N. Datan, A.L. Greene, and H.W. Reese (eds.), *Life-span developmental psychology: Intergenerational relations*, 245–264. Hillsdale, NJ: Lawrence Erlbaum.

Roberts, R.L. and Bengtson, V.L. (1990). Is intergenerational solidarity a unidimensional construct? A second test of a formal model. *Journal of Gerontology: Social Sciences*, 45:S12–20.

Rodeheaver, D.A. and Thomas, J.L. (1986). Family and community networks in Appalachia. In N. Datan, A.L. Greene, and H.W. Reese (eds.), *Life-span developmental psychology: Intergenerational relations*, 77–98. Hillsdale, NJ: Lawrence Erlbaum.

Scharlach, A.E. and Boyd, S.L. (1989). Caregiving and employment: Results of an employee survey. *The Gerontologist*, 29:382–387.

Schulz, R., Visintainer, P., and Williamson, G.M. (1990). Psychiatric and physical morbidity effects of caregiving. *Journal of Gerontology: Psychological Sciences*, 45:P181–191.

Shanas, E. (1979). Social myth as hypothesis: The case of the family relations of old people. *The Gerontologist*, 19:3–9.

Shanas, E. (1980). Older people and their families: The new pioneers. *Journal of Marriage and the Family*, 42:9–15.

Stoller, E.P. (1983). Parent caregiving by adult children. *Journal of Marriage and the Family*, 45:851–858.

Stoller, E.P. and Pugliesi, K.L. (1989a). Other roles of caregivers: Competing responsibilities or supportive resources. *Journal of Gerontology: Social Sciences*, 44:S231–238.

———. (1989b). The transition to the caregiving role: A panel study of helpers of elderly people. *Research on Aging*, 11:312–330.

Thomas, J.L. (1982). The development of grandparents' relationships with their grandchildren: A qualitative study. Ph.D. diss., West Virginia University, 1982. Abstract in *Dissertation Abstracts International*, 43:4211–4205B.

———. (1988). Predictors of satisfaction with children's help for younger and older elderly parents. *Journal of Gerontology: Social Sciences*, 43:S9–14.

———. (1990a). The grandparent role: A double bind. *International Journal of Aging and Human Development*, 31:169–178.

———. (1990b). Grandparenthood and mental health: Implications for the practitioner. *Journal of Applied Gerontology*, 9:464–479.

Toseland, R.W. and Smith, G.C. (1990). Effectiveness of individual counseling by professional and peer helpers for family caregivers of the elderly. *Psychology and Aging*, 5:256–263.

Treas, J., and Bengtson, V.L. (1987). The family in later years. In M.B. Sussman and S.K. Steinmetz (eds.), *Handbook of marriage and the family*, 625–648. New York: Plenum.

Wentowski, G.J. (1985). Older women's perceptions of great-grandmotherhood: A research note. *The Gerontologist*, 25:593–596.

World Health Organization, Regional Office for Europe. (1980). *Appropriate Levels For Continuing Care of the Elderly*. Report of a WHO Working Group, Berlin: ICP/ADR o26 4566B.

THE FUTURE OF GEROPSYCHIATRY AND GEROPSYCHOTHERAPY

Geropsychiatry Research in the Twenty-first Century

George H. Pollock

Not only is the world on the threshold of, or already beginning, a new era, but the medical health care field similarly is poised for change—some of it driven by economics, some by biotechnology, some by increased longevity and health and newer concepts and approaches to disease. I use "disease" here as a general category—namely, disease agents, deterioration, absence of preventive prior care, or the result of the complex interreactions of various factors that combine to result in dysfunction, disturbance, and eventually disease.

Some theories, theoreticians, practices, understandings, and utopic explanations and therapies of the not so distant past have become less relevant. The ideas of Einstein, Freud, and Marx are being questioned. What is valuable is retained to form the basis of new studies, but serious rethinking, reexamining, and researching are necessary in an era when fiscal restraints, priority evaluation, and professional boundaries themselves are in states of transition. If we are to avoid disorder and disillusionment we must articulate what is going on and what we hope can result.

To sharpen our focus, I turn to a statement by David Magnusson, an internationally known gerontologist. He notes that:

> For a long time, research on developmental issues in the biological and social sciences was mostly concerned with the early parts of life, such as infancy and adolescence. Studies paying full attention to people after they had passed through late adolescence were rare even though we all know that humans continue to develop. The dynamics of adult life can be as forceful and full of transitory states as is life before 20. Individual development is a lifelong process: from the moment of conception to the moment of death. Recently, more and more researchers have turned their attention to the problems of de-

velopment and aging in later periods of life. This increased interest is caused partly by growing social demands from the aged generations in many Western countries and partly by the fact that longitudinal research endeavors have now started to yield impressive results concerning life-span development. (1990, p.xi)

One can add to the variables mentioned by Magnusson; additional ones include, for example, increase in the length of life; the need for biological, psychological, and social baseline data so that we can differentiate successful aging from unsuccessful aging; the importance of economic and political changes as a result of older populations the world over, such as the need for a greater labor force in Japan as its population gets older and is retired. We witness in many of our national and international situations transformations in intimacies and trust. As Giddens (1990) elaborates on this theme, the trust issue involves, for example, personal relations, personal identity, global issues, scientific papers, even educational institutions of the highest reputation, and political and economic leaders and systems. We are in several states of personal, familial, national, international, and ecological transitions.

What previously seemed secure and trusted now presents us with threat, danger of risk, and uncertainty. And yet by extending our horizons, reexamining our assumptions and institutions, thinking anew about our values and goals, we can envision new possibilities that are not chaotic or nihilistic. We can reflect upon the past and think of the present and future. New knowledge, new collaborations, new applications, and new appreciations can help us attain our objectives and deal with challenges as opportunities and not defeats.

Two important documents for those working with older adults are the National Institute on Aging's *Special Report on Aging 1990* (1990a) and *Progress Report on Alzheimer's Disease* (1990b).

In a recent letter to members of the Society of Biological Psychiatry, John Greden, president of the society and chairman of the Department of Psychiatry at the University of Michigan, notes that:

Four salient features of pathophysiology receive inadequate attention in biological psychiatry. First, most psychiatric disorders have relatively characteristic ages of onset. Second, most have a lifetime course. Third, the clinical phenomenology associated with a given diagnosis tends to change as the person ages. Fourth, gender and reproductive milestones strongly influence clinical onset, features and course. These

observations suggest that neurobiological changes in the brain associated with aging and development are profoundly important in understanding pathophysiology and clinical presentation of psychiatric
disorders. What are these neurobiological changes? When and where
in the brain do they occur? Can they be predicted? Recognized clinically? Identified by laboratory tests? Altered by treatment? . . .
(L)ongitudinal course may be the most important aspect of clinical
psychiatry. (1991, p. 1)

This clinical research endeavor involves outcome follow-up studies with initial criteria and predictions of outcome noted beforehand and checked as
development unfolds.

Greden goes on to write:

Longitudinal patterns are important. They are relevant to diagnosis
and prognosis. They have made the development of laboratory tests
more difficult, since "normal" results often change with aging. Perhaps most importantly, different longitudinal patterns probably have
major treatment implications . . . (C)linicians . . . should give more
attention to the question of which patients require ongoing medication, often including lifetime medication. (1991, p. 3)

Greden implies, but does not say, that developmental psychiatry (infant, child, adolescent, geriatric) subspecialization parallels a longitudinal
concept of individual development, except subspecialties develop their own
languages and become more isolated from colleagues of different
subspecialties, and this fragmentation can be detrimental to joint efforts in
research and clinical work. Thus the longitudinal approach to aging must
also consider the other side of the coin, the "experts" in particular age or
developmental groups. He suggests that "considerable data suggest that clinical features for a given diagnosis are not the same at all ages" (1991, p. 12).
Thus an eighty-year-old who is depressed presents a different pattern than
an eight-year-old. In our research on duodenal ulcer, we observed that prior
to age nine, the presenting symptoms were much different from those seen
in adults with such a disease. We work on classificatory schemas but the base
developmental data (normal and/or deviant) are not yet systematically collected and available. I have modified Engel's bio-psycho-social model to include a fourth component—developmental. Using such a bio-psycho-social-
developmental model along with a further breakdown into predispositional,
precipitating, and perpetuating factors, acting singly or in combinatorial

fashion, can allow us to collect meaningful information that is useful in comparative as well as outcome studies.

Aging-related concerns involve many different disciplines, professions, and biomedical and psychosocial specialties. Not so long ago we had severe stigmatization of older adults. Aging was equated with aged. Aged was equated with disease and infirmity that was beyond hope. Successful and healthy older adults seemed beyond belief. There were discriminatory health care practices and now, because of economic pressures, these are surfacing again—for example, age limitation on coronary bypass surgery, renal dialysis, cataract surgery. So while we make progress in some sectors, in others we find reversals. There may be less active evaluation and treatment of older adults who can benefit from care.

We need to deal with family despair, depression, and dilemmas when confronted by the sick parent, sibling, spouse, and now even the ill child who may be in his or her sixties when the competent parent is in his or her late eighties. We involve ourselves in team efforts to study the sites of care—home care, nursing homes—and caretakers who are empathic and realistic. We are involved with the economics of aging, be it a preventive program, a health care program, a heart-hypertension-stroke or malignancy program. Our social scientists—psychologists, educators, sociologists, economists, political scientists, anthropologists, historians—are ever increasing their involvement in the study of applications of knowledge of healthy aging and its discontents and diseases. Our colleagues in the humanities are studying literature, poetry, art, and aesthetic creativity as it relates to aging. Those in the fields of medicine, pharmacology, physiology, biochemistry, immunology, molecular biology, endocrinology, brain imaging, genetics, epidemiology, biological "rhythmology," and somnographics are joining the psychiatrists, neurologists, and neuroscientists in pursuing joint efforts to understand the healthy older adults who are productively contributing to our society and culture, and who can teach those younger about the paths they themselves have traversed and what the future may hold for our society—not only in this land of ours, this continent in which we are based, but the world over, which is becoming smaller as we have rapid communication, quick transportation, and greater mobility.

With the increase in divorce and other significant alterations in family cohesiveness, our theories of emotional development will be challenged and perhaps modified. Our belief systems and our religious involvements are already undergoing major shifts—these may be the beginnings of new investments we will have in positive, hopeful, altruistic pursuits. This reaction is a swinging of the pendulum away from only self-involvement or involvement with only one's own group. Who would have believed that in our life-time we would see the demise of a major powerful political and military force (Germany first, the U.S.S.R. second)? Who would have believed that we would land men on the moon and are now extensively exploring outer space? Many of our older adults lived through the major economic depression in the late twenties, the Second World War, the demystifying of sex, the appearance of the scourge of AIDS—how did and do these stresses, stressors, and strains affect our attitudes, our philosophies of life?

Man in the generic sense can now study, think about, and research what goes on in the cell during learning; what goes on in the various phases of the life course; what other worlds may be like. We are living in a most exciting period in history—technical, theoretical, clinical, and research advances have opened new vistas and domains for us. Now for an action plan that can initiate the changes we need and want.

The fear and stigma of nursing home placements and who cares for these patients must be studied. Another area of possible stigmatization involves the availability of rehabilitation care for individuals having, for example, emotional, medical, or neurological disorders. Not only do we have to be concerned with after-care, but research and especially clinical studies are also needed. Here the comparison of what is normal for different age groups and different social and ethnic groups is basic if we can identify those who deviate from the norms and what can be done about the situation.

In the realm of the dementias, the National Institute on Aging (NIA) reports on studies of the prevalence of Alzheimer's disease in different groups and countries, biological markers for Alzheimer's disease, and basic studies of calcium-regulating systems. "Defective calcium regulation provide(s) an interesting . . . speculative, explanation . . . of the Alzheimer puzzle" (1990b, p. 9). Research on memory enhancement; drug reactions and interactions in older adults; how to help families handle the stress involved in dealing with impaired, chronically older adult relatives; the importance of virus-induced changes in the brain in chronic fatigue syndrome; falls; arthritis; heart disease; personality; the various kinds of depressions and the disabilities they produce; psychiatric therapy with patients having malignancies—these and many other projects give us hope to enhance the partnership of clinical and research methodology.

Since the fairly new blood test for detecting early prostatic malignancy has gained greater acceptance and utilization, the need for treatment of positive testers, including psychiatric treatment, is a new horizon. We see similar situations in early detection of breast, uterine, ovarian, and colonic malignancies. Previously well-known diseases such as non-insulin dependent diabetes management through diet and exercise, obesity, the hypertensions, strokes and their rehabilitation, glaucoma, and hearing problems are not neglected in our clinical investigative activities. In all of these we find the role of the psychiatrist, psychologist, social worker, and other mental health professionals to be of pivotal importance.

The mental health clinicians have their particular areas of specialization, such as the depressions, the dementias, and the stress disorders. But psychiatric illnesses from earlier periods of life may either persist or return and require treatment and outcome follow-up research.

Thus we begin to delineate various areas where psychiatric-psychologic research, clinical application, prevention, and collaboration with other disciplines—all in the service of knowing more about aging—are coming to the forefront. Since the U.S. Bureau of the Census expects the percentage of the population over age sixty-five to increase from 12.6 percent in 1990 to 21.8 percent in the year 2030, we are, we must, and we can address the many issues this demographic shift will affect. We are also interested in the older rural populations and different ethnic groups.

I have emphasized various biological dimensions to the study of aging and the aged. I now wish to shift the focus to the psychological, which is intimately connected with the biosocial spheres of emphasis but which also has some of its own unique features.

To summarize some of these conclusions in a somewhat telegraphic form, in an etiological perspective one has to consider the following in working with the older adult:

1.   Antecedent psychopathology, either manifest or latent; compensated or pathologically defended; and detected or undetected (the latter as a result of favorable life situations).

2.   Situational crises, acute or chronic, that strain the ego's ability to maintain equilibrium. Age, physical health, and intactness of support systems are but a few of the variables one must keep in mind as contributing to signs and symptoms of psychic distress or illness.

3.   Organic illness (neurological and other bodily systems) that can increase reactive symptoms, such as depression, and psychosocial needs. Helplessness, isolation, fear of loss of basic controls, and hopelessness are a few of the emotional anxieties observable. There can be regressions to earlier fixations, and if the reality disruptions are severe and persistent, these regressions can become chronic and return the individual to infantile levels of functioning.

4.   As Abraham (1919) observed, age in and of itself need not pre-

clude psychoanalytic treatment. Indications for, and anticipations of, successful psychoanalytic treatment depend upon the individual's psychological construction as well as the nature of the subsequent psychic distress. In successful work with middle-aged and older adults, some in their eighties, I have found:

A.   The capacity for, and utilization of, insight.

B.   The capacity for utilization of therapeutically induced transferences.

C.   The capacity to dream and fantasize and the ability to relate these dreams and fantasies to the therapeutic process, as well as to one's past.

D.   The mobilization of motivation to change, to examine goals and values anew, and to make new social relationships or restructure those of the past in more positive ways.

E.   The capacity for self-observation in the present as well as a retrospective view, more or less objective, of how one handled significant life relationships in the past, and how these can be changed in the present. Retrospective introspection assists in current retrospective activities, as well as in prospective planning.

F.   The mobilization of libidinal and constructive aggressive "energies" in ways that make life more creative and satisfying, and allow the individual to face the inevitable traumas ahead with less anxiety, depression, and pain.

G.   The institution of a mourning-liberation process that allows the past to appropriately become past and allows for "investment" in the present and future.

H.   In the treatment situation, the elderly easily distinguish between the facade of interest and genuine caring and involvement on the part of the therapist. Older patients wish to be useful and respected, and to preserve their dignity. What seemingly concerns them most is fear and pain and suffering, helplessness and isolation and loneliness, physical and mental hopelessness, impairment, loss of competency and adequacy, and the need to rely upon those who may abandon them. Unlike younger patients, the elderly do not fear death. At times, they may welcome it as a relief from pain and anguish. Death may be a completion—a freedom.

This picture is not one that can apply to all older individuals, but can do so in selective instances (as is true of all patients), and therapists should not a prior be therapeutically nihilistic about what can be accomplished with psychotherapy and psychoanalysis. Elderly people may be understood in different ways, but they *can* be understood, and with that understanding they often can be helped.

At a recent meeting in Chicago that addressed issues of mental illness, several facts from NIMH emerged that are pertinent to our topic.

1. Depression is one of the major symptoms (not diseases) seen in this country. I emphasize its symptomatic character rather than it as a disease, and see it in conjunction with associated symptoms. There may be more than one disease that has symptoms of depression—endogenous, reactive, depressive, depressive character structure, viral disease of the brain—these all have areas in common, perhaps common pathways. Their treatments may vary—ranging from electroconvulsive therapy to psychoanalysis, from viricidal agents to pharmacological medication. Older adults may have one or more of these depressive disorders present at the same time and may need multiple simultaneous therapies.

2. As many as four million Americans now have serious mental illness. This includes approximately one-third of the nation's homeless.

3. In 1988, the cost of treating mental illness, including income lost due to the illness, exceeded $129 billion (the direct-care cost was $55 billion).

4. Only about 20 percent of adults with mental illness receive any treatment, even though one in five Americans will have some form of mental disturbance at some point in their lives.

These rough figures and projections clearly underline the imperative to pay close attention to the older adult population—in all ways including service, research, education, communication, and liaison with other specialties and disciplines.

As more adults live longer, even in the absence of pathology, choices and additional dilemmas and needs are demanded of the caretakers, the individuals themselves, and of society. Even the most healthy of the oldest adults cannot maneuver as autonomously as they could in their fifties, sixties, and even seventies. Issues of gender, widow- and widowerhood, retirement activities, loneliness, retirement adaptations, and deficits in sensory apparatuses increase. Health monitoring, preventive care, and reassurance when minor deficits of memory or diminished energy become evident call for families and sometimes even professionals who are empathic, knowledgeable, and desirous of helping without diminishing the esteem of the older adult. Financial guidance and assistance with forms for insurance, Medicare, and Medicaid is needed; so is care in selecting trustworthy and competent specialists. Who will do this? On what basis will such selections be made? What research and clinical investigations are needed to render these yielded data useful? These are our challenges.

REFERENCES

Abraham, K. (1919–1927). The applicability of psychoanalytic treatment to patients at an advanced age. In *Selected papers of Karl Abraham*, 312–317. London: Hogarth Press.

Giddens, A. (1990). *The consequences of modernity.* Palo Alto, CA: Stanford University Press.

Greden, J.F. (1991). *President's letter.* Ann Arbor, MI: Society of Biological Psychiatry.

Magnusson, D.L. (1990). Foreword. In P.B. Baltes and M.M. Baltes (eds.), *Successful aging: Perspectives from the behavioral sciences,* ix. Cambridge, England: Cambridge University Press.

National Institute on Aging. (1990a). *Special report on aging 1990.* Washington, DC: U.S. Government Printing Office.

National Institute on Aging. (1990b). *Progress report on Alzheimer's disease 1990.* Washington, DC: U.S. Government Printing Office.

EMERGING TRENDS IN GEROPSYCHIATRY

Jerome Yesavage

In the preceeding chapter, Pollock presents a number of useful insights about many of the issues challenging gerontologists today, and then he ends with the question, "What research and clinical investigations are needed to render these data useful?" He raises a couple of ideas that I think are worth developing.

First of all, he provides the useful insight that, "Unlike younger patients, the elderly do not fear death. At times they may welcome it as a relief from pain and anguish." Thus we realize that the elderly are perhaps more concerned with the quality of their lives than the fact that their lives are close to ending. There are several issues which gerontologists can address in future research that will improve that quality of life and make life worth living for these elders.

One issue of major import to which Pollock alludes is depression. He states that an "eighty-year-old who is depressed presents a different pattern [of depressive symptoms] than an eight-year-old." Our own development of a Geriatric Depression Scale (Brink et al., 1982) suggested this. We found that the use of somatic complaints to identify depression in the elderly was a red herring. Most elderly already had somatic complaints whether or not they were depressed. This led us to empirically develop a scale not based on these issues but on other items more closely linked to issues of subjective well-being.

In any case, the identification of depression in the elderly is crucial. Although the prevalence may be no higher in younger patients, it is often less well recognized. This is tragic since there are effective psychological, pharmacological, and physiological methods for treating it. This area is rife with potential research projects to better identify depression in certain elderly populations and to develop better ways of delivering treatment.

A second major area of research in gerontology that can immediately add to the quality of life of the elderly has to do with memory. Many elderly are more afraid of losing their memories than losing their lives. Although no more than 10 percent of the elderly population develops Alzheimer's disease, and most of those are individuals in their eighties, 90 percent of elderly seem to think they are in the early stages of decline. This is particularly distressing for the elderly because their memories may have declined a bit with normal aging, what psychiatrists call "age-associated memory impairment." The physician says it's nothing to worry about because it is not Alzheimer's, but this does little for the original complaint.

There are a number of reasons for these age-related changes, but it is important to emphasize that not all of these changes are physiological. Many are psychological and reversible. For example, many elderly fail to use image association techniques commonly used by younger people to register and recall information. Common mnemonic techniques can be used, for example, to recall names and faces. Thus the changes associated with aging are not permanent and may be remediated by psychological interventions. Development of such interventions is particularly timely since, as Pollock notes, there will be a need for an increased labor force in many societies, just as those societies become geriatric. Some who would normally retire will be asked to continue to work and methods of keeping cognitive performance at optimal levels will be important for such older people.

All in all, Pollock's paper sets the right tone for this section of the book. He shows what we have learned is substantial, but his closing question is crucial: What areas are most important to target our future research efforts? I hope that I have suggested a few areas in which to concentrate our efforts.

REFERENCE

Brink, T.L., Yesavage, J.A., Lum, O., Heersema, P., Adey, M., and Rose, T.L. (1982). Screening test for geriatric depression. *Clinical Gerontologist* 1:37–43.

Geriatric Psychiatry in the Private Sector

Donald P. Hay
Linda K. Hay

It is apparent that older adults are a rapidly expanding segment of the population who need psychiatric services and are not being served adequately as a result of inadequate access to mental health care. The diagnosis and treatment of the geriatric psychiatric patient was formerly felt to be an extension of care of the adult psychiatric patient; however, practitioners had a limited knowledge base of diagnosis and treatment possibilities and even fewer were interested in or able to provide adequate care for these individuals. With the emergence of increasing absolute numbers of this group, the general population has become increasingly aware of the specific problems of older adults, and the medical community has exhibited an increased interest. In addition, both basic and clinical research have developed rapidly.

The rapidly developing field of geriatric psychiatry is, in essence, an interface of medicine and psychiatry (Cohen, 1989). The resulting services have been affected by the steady increase in elderly populations and the evolution of health care facilities, both medical and psychiatric, inpatient and outpatient. It would appear, however, that the number of individuals requiring geriatric psychiatry care and treatment is increasing at a more rapid rate than programs and clinicians (Smally, 1983; Kane et al., 1980; Murray, 1979; Arie and Jolley, 1983; Jackson, 1978).

The problem, then, of providing adequate care for this dramatically increasing population may be viewed as part of a larger problem. Inadequate funding from Medicare for health care professionals and for institutions creates a disincentive for growth of programs. Thus the complexity of care, the increasing work load, and the inadequate funding have all resulted in fewer and fewer physicians, including psychiatrists, wishing to work with the elderly population (Freudenheim, 1990).

The challenge at hand is to create psychiatric programs within the existing system of reimbursement that are able to provide the comprehensive care that an older individual with multiple medical concerns requires. This is especially difficult for the private practitioner who is dependent on the minimal reimbursement of Medicare while being expected to provide comprehensive care that is more demanding and time-consuming than for younger patients.

This report presents various issues of models of practice for the private sector. From the perspective of geriatric psychiatry as an interface of medicine and psychiatry, it becomes important to discuss the following: the implementation of geriatric psychiatry services in the general hospital and in the freestanding psychiatric hospital (proprietary or private), the role of the geriatric psychiatrist as consultant or attending, various aspects of inpatient programs, and the equally important role of outpatient services. The extension of services to nursing homes is also an important aspect of the geriatric psychiatry model.

The implementation of services is predicated upon the financial structure that defines them. Medicare, commercial insurance, Medicaid, HMOs and private-pay options are discussed as the underpinnings for the design of the model for the private practitioner in geriatric psychiatry.

The discussion of the development of models of care for older adult programs in psychiatry is preceded by a review of the literature, which reflects the opinions of individuals involved in geriatric psychiatry around the country. The creation of new models is best implemented by understanding what has been observed by others.

REVIEW OF THE LITERATURE

The literature on care for the mentally ill elderly describes the need for comprehensive systems. The essential components of the system and, in particular, the need for an interdisciplinary approach are also emphasized by many authors.

A general overview of mental health services for the elderly is included in *Essentials of Geriatric Psychiatry* (Lazarus, 1988). In the tenth chapter, a summary of abstracts is presented from a symposium held in October of 1986 during which a multidisciplinary group discussed the development of mental health services for the elderly. They supported the notion that comprehensive systems are needed because of the complex and extended needs of the elderly.

A joint report of the Royal College of Physicians and the Royal College of Psychiatrists (1989) includes a description of the need for more expanded services for the older psychiatric patient and a description of the key elements in a comprehensive psychiatric service. The report recommends that the style of service include the treatment of remediable functional illness, the prevention of crises, and the alleviation of intractable problems in the community.

A report by Greene, Wagner, and Johnson (1986) describes the successful development of a psychogeriatric unit in a community nonprofit hospital and included several important factors in delivery of acute services to older Americans with combined medical and psychiatric dysfunction. This report stresses the importance of a comprehensive assessment protocol as well as psychiatric and medical training for the staff. The authors also state that it is essential for the program to provide a sense of security for the patients by attention to perceptual confusion of milieu, design issues, and control of access or egress from the unit.

McClelland (1984) describes the geriatric mental health care professional as a member of a service provider team. Three major components of a bio-psycho-social model are identified. The functional role includes data collection, referral, advocacy, and home health care. The affective role refers to the therapeutic alliance and the community-integrative role refers to the method by which the patient is maintained in follow-up in the community.

Alter (1988) describes the development of elderly service delivery systems. The major components of an interorganizational system are defined as size, centrality (having the patients flow through one organization), differentiation (service provided as distinct roles, such as intake, assessment, treatment), and integration of the types of methods used to coordinate and control its parts. The type of elderly service systems seen today are described as centralized, differentiated, and smaller, but capable of delivering a greater amount of service than previously.

Berger and King (1990) describe elements of geriatric service programs. Planning involves market research to determine the wants and the needs of the community as well as a business plan regarding the financial structure of the system providing the service. It is essential to determine which service to emphasize. Diversification and provision of services that are affordable and that are reimbursable is critical.

An innovative community-based health care program for the elderly is described by Timms (1990). Critical elements of the program include community support, guidelines for care, community needs assessment, determining scope of service, marketing strategies, and provision for faculty and student development.

The interdisciplinary approach is a constant theme in the literature. One report describes this as the focus of an urban geriatric home care system (Zink and Bissonnette, 1990). Another program specific for the needs of Alzheimer's patients is reported by Schneider (1990). The reported program is interdisciplinary and includes neurologists, a geriatrician, neuropsychologists, social workers, a gerontological nurse practitioner, a master's-level community health nurse, and bachelor's-level home health and acute care nurses. A clinical psychologist, psychiatrist, and nutritionist are all available as consultants.

Another theme in the literature is the medicalization of services to the elderly, which has been promoted by the policies of Medicare reimbursement (Binney, Estes, and Ingmen, 1990). It is stated that the restructuring to provide acute medical services takes away from the broader range of social and supportive systems. Further research is suggested to determine the effects of this shift, but it appears that demographics and policy trends may be at cross-purposes.

Financial issues in providing care for the elderly psychiatric patient are written about by Freudenheim (1990), Barsa et al. (1985), and Gottlieb (1988). In a chapter entitled "Financial Issues Affecting Geriatric Psychiatric Care" in *Essentials of Geriatric Psychiatry* (Lazarus, 1988) Gottlieb delineated the economic structure underlying geriatric care delivery systems. The older adult proportion (11.9 percent) of the population consumes more than 30 percent of the United States' health care services. Older adults are discussed as suffering from mental health problems but not seeking traditional mental health treatment. He notes that an ever increasing high-risk population is presently underserved in the area of mental health.

Gottlieb goes on to report that most older adults use Medicare as the main form of payment for health services, and reimbursement for psychiatric services is less and more limited than medical and surgical coverage. Inpatient hospitalization is encouraged and outpatient treatment is severely limited. Medicaid and private insurers function as secondary providers after Medicare, and are limited in their reimbursement of psychiatric services.

Medicaid is regulated by individual states, but in general pays for deductibles and copayments. Medicaid may provide reimbursement when the 190 lifetime days of Medicare have been used, but this varies greatly among different states. As with Medicare, Medicaid reimbursement for psychiatric services is significantly below prevailing fees.

Private health insurance in most cases for the elderly falls into the category of "medigap" coverage. These policies usually pay Medicare and therefore are minimal in what they add to psychiatric coverage.

Federally qualified HMOs contract directly with Medicare but are more likely to encourage outpatient primary care, which is more cost-efficient for the HMO as compared with more expensive specialty services such as geriatric psychiatry. In many cases, the HMO contracts with less expensive mental health providers such as social workers and psychologists. Since many of the patients may have mental illness requiring medication or other somatic treatment (such as electroconvulsive therapy [ECT]), this limits the access of older adults to the type of specialty care they may require.

Gottlieb reported on financial issues in *Comprehensive Review of Geriatric Psychiatry* (Sadavoy, Lazarus, and Jarvik, 1991). He stressed that poor reimbursement and "perverse incentives" have led to barriers to the care of the older adult population.

There are many other reports in the literature that have addressed the issue of development of models of practice for geriatric psychiatry. Blalock and Dial (n.d.) reported a preliminary analysis of differences in practitioner characteristics and found that elderly use psychiatric services in hospital settings more and use private psychiatric services less. Many overviews of the issue of development of geriatric services have been published, including Cohen (1989), Smally (1989), Rowe (1987), Hay (1988), and Rodenburg (1985). Hay (1984) described physicians' resistance to treating the elderly. Training issues have been addressed by Gatz and Pearson (1985), Hickey and Fatula (1975), Taintor et al. (1984), Spar, Ford, and Liston (1980), Ford et al. (1980), Lieff (1983), and Schulman et al. (1986). Consultation by geriatric psychiatrists was described by Liptzin (1983), Ruskin (1985), Rosse, Ciolino, and Gurel (1986), and Mainprize and Rodin (1987). Nursing home practice was reported by Jacobson and Juthani (1978), Gurian and Chanowitz (1987), and Bienenfeld and Wheeler (1989). The attitude of professionals toward working with the elderly has been addressed by Jones and Galliard (1983), Ingstad and Gotestam (1987), and Hay (1984). Day-hospital provision was reviewed by Peace (1982).

In summary, the literature on programs for the delivery of psychiatric services to the elderly contains two themes. The first is that this population is currently in need of extensive comprehensive service programs to encompass the complicated needs of the elderly individual. The second is that the financial reimbursement for service to the elderly, and especially the elderly with psychiatric problems, is inadequate.

MODELS OF PRACTICE: THE PRIVATE SECTOR

The challenges involved in providing psychiatric care for the older adult are defined by the need for comprehensive services that are able to address multiple body system problems as well as decreasing social support networks.

These challenges are superimposed upon a limited and deficient financial reimbursement system for the care providers.

Salaried individuals in the public sector can and will continue to provide services through state, county, and Veterans' Administration (VA) facilities. The private practitioner, however, is restricted in serving this population because there are a variety of disincentives. The literature has pointed out the disparity of the reimbursement for nonpsychiatric as compared with psychiatric medical services as defined by Medicare. In addition, there is a social disincentive in working with the elderly when one considers the stigma of working with patients who may be viewed as less attractive, less socially appealing, lacking status in our society, and less intelligent (e.g., dementia patients).

Programs

The best model of practice for the private practitioner, therefore, must include a comprehensive system as described in the literature such that the psychiatrist is not facing the challenge alone, but as part of a team. The essential elements of a comprehensive geriatric psychiatry approach include an evaluation and outreach team, a centrally based organizational unit that coordinates communication and organizational activities, extended sites in the community with community outreach activities, and liaison with hospitals, nursing homes, and other agencies involved in the care of the older adult. The total organization of such programs includes personnel dedicated to coordinating the various aspects of service. This necessitates the support of hospitals or agencies who commit themselves to providing these services. Thus the psychiatrist in the private sector can provide proper treatment for the older adult if he or she links up with such a comprehensive system. Such a system must indeed be viewed as "user-friendly" by the private psychiatrist, who is usually overwhelmed by the extensive demands on time and resources for the geriatric patient, and faced with the constant disincentive of inadequate financial reimbursement.

Specific geriatric psychiatry programs can enhance the desirability of working with the geriatric patient. Such programs may include specialized inpatient units, outpatient treatment facilities, programs for teaching, training and research, liaison programs for linkage with other medical services within the hospital, and outreach and community based programs to establish connections with long-term care facilities in the community.

Inpatient Care

In areas where the population is sufficient, the establishment of specially designated geriatric psychiatry inpatient units may be extremely helpful for diagnosis and treatment of this special population. A cadre of highly trained specialists including psychiatrists, nurses, social workers, and related discipline therapists (occupational, music, rehabilitation) is critical to meet the needs of this unique group.

Outpatient Services

A geriatric psychiatry outpatient clinic is essential for the provision of linkage with the community for easy entry into and egress from the program, as well as for linkage with the inpatient treatment program and community-based long-term care facilities. Staffed primarily by nurses with special expertise in geriatric psychiatry, the outpatient clinic is an integral component and the hub of a geriatric psychiatry program.

Teaching and Education

Learning specialized needs of this population and developing an expertise in the diagnosis and treatment of geriatric psychiatry illnesses is enhanced by an active teaching program for medical students, psychiatry residents, and, especially, geriatric psychiatry fellows. With the assistance of the American Association for Geriatric Psychiatry (AAGP) and the Council on Aging of the American Psychiatric Association, attention has been focused on the need to improve the quality and availability of geriatric psychiatry residency training and fellowship training programs in geropsychiatry. Geriatric medicine fellows and family practice residents may also be part of and complement and enhance the general teaching program of a geriatric psychiatry program. Inservice training for the staff within a geriatric psychiatry program is also essential. Ongoing teaching for staff, residents, and fellows contributes to the excitement and enhances enthusiasm for working daily in a difficult area.

Geriatric Psychiatry Clinical Research

Another area for improving care for the elderly, as well as for on-the-job satisfaction and esteem, is the development of clinical research possibilities. The development of diagnostic and treatment techniques within particular programs can lead to heightened enthusiasm and awareness on the part of staff and students alike. Research possibilities abound, particularly in the area of psychopharmacology, as there are very few research protocols addressing the effects of psychotropic medications in the elderly. Other research possibilities are ECT for major depression, movement disorders, the agitated patient with major affective disorder, among others (Hay, 1989; Hay et al., 1990). There are also endless possibilities of research into nursing and other staff behaviors and patient interaction methods (Hickey and Fatula, 1975; Ingstad and Gotestam, 1987).

CONCLUSION

Psychiatric care for the elderly is at risk due to the increasing needs of this population, the lack of services available, and the lack of financial support. The literature describes the need for comprehensive programming to encompass the variety of issues involved in assisting and treating older adult patients. The ideal model for the private practitioner requires a team approach, which can be organized around a hospital or other coordinating and sponsoring agency.

If reimbursement for private practitioners is reinforced and systems of care are encouraged, quality psychiatric care for the elderly may grow and improve. If, however, financial support for the private practitioner and for the hospitals he or she serves continues to diminish far below parity with care for other sectors of the population, psychiatric care for the elderly may steadily diminish and result in inadequate services being available for this most significant population subgroup of our country.

REFERENCES

Alter, C.F. (1988). The changing structure of elderly service delivery systems. *The Gerontologist,* 28(1):91–99.

American Psychiatric Association. (1986). The role of psychiatrists in diagnosing and treating mental illness in the elderly. *The APA Task Force on Psychiatric Services for the Elderly.*

Arie, T., and Jolley, D. (1983). The rising tide. *British Medical Journal,* 286(29):326–27.

Barsa, J.J., Kass, F., Beels, C.C., Gurland, B., and Charles, E. (1985). Efficient psychogeriatrics services. *American Journal of Psychiatry,* 142(2):238–241.

Berger, S., and King, E. (1990). Designing services for the elderly. *AORN Journal,* 51:2.

Bienenfeld, D., and Wheeler, B.G. (1989). Psychiatric services to nursing homes: A liaison model. *Hospital and Community Psychiatry,* 40(8):793–794.

Billig, N., and Leibenluft, E. (1987). Special considerations in integrating elderly patients into a general hospital psychiatric unit. *Hospital and Community Psychiatry,* 38(3):277–281.

Binney, E.A., Estes, C.L., and Ingman, S.R. (1990). Medicalization, public policy and the elderly: Social services in jeopardy? *Social Science & Medicine* 30(7):761–771.

Blalock, R., and Dial, T.H. (n.d.). Psychiatry and the elderly: A preliminary analysis of differences in practitioner characteristics. CNIMH report.

Cohen, G. (1989). The interface of mental and physical health phenomena in later life: New directions in geriatric psychiatry. *Gerontology and Geriatrics Education,* 9(3):27–38.

Ford, C.V., Spar, J.E., Davis, B., and Liston, E.H. (1980). Hospital treatment of elderly neuropsychiatric patients: Initial clinical and administrative experience with a new teaching ward. *Journal of the American Geriatrics Society,* 28(10):539–543.

Freudenheim, M. (1990). Medicare's woes found worsening. *The New York Times,* 6 Sept.

Gatz, M., and Pearson, C.G. (1985). Training clinical psychology students in aging. *Gerontology and Geriatrics Education,* 6(2):15–25.

Gottlieb, G.L. (1988). Financial issues affecting geriatric psychiatric care. In L. Jarvik, J. Foster, J. Lieff, and S. Mershon (eds.), *Essentials of geriatric psychiatry.* New York: Springer Publishing Company.

———. (1991). Financial issues. In J. Sadavoy, L. Lazarus, and L. Jarvik (eds.), *Comprehensive review of geriatric psychiatry.* Washington, DC: American Psychiatric Press.

Greene, J.A., Wagner, J., and Johnson, W. (1986). *Development of a psychogeriatric unit at HCA Park West Medical Centers.*

Gurian, B., and Chanowitz, B. (1987). An empirical evaluation of a model geropsychiatric nursing home. *The Gerontological Society of America,* 27(6):766–772.

Hay, D.P. (1984). Physician resistance to treating the elderly: Facing our own future. *Wisconsin Medical Journal,* 83(10):33–37.

———. (1988). Trends in care for the elderly in geriatric psychiatry. *Wisconsin Medical Journal,* (December):87(12):22–28.

———. (1989). Electroconvulsive therapy in the medically ill elderly. *Convulsive Therapy,* 5(1).

Hay, D.P., Hay, L.K., Blackwell, B., and Spiro, H. (1990). ECT and tardive dyskinesia. *Journal of Geriatric Psychiatry and Neurology,* 3(2):106–109.

Hickey, T., and Fatula, B. (1975). Nursing staff training for an effective geropsychiatric environment. *JPN and Mental Health Services,* (Jan/Feb.).

Ingstad, P.J., and Gotestam, K.G. (1987). Staff attitude changes after environmental changes on a ward for psychogeriatric patients. *The International Journal of Social Psychiatry,* 33(3):237–244.

Jackson, S.L. (1978). Fall in admission rate of old people to psychiatric wards. *British Medical Journal,* 1(6112):580.

Jacobson, S.B., and Juthani, N. (1978). The nursing home and training in geropsychiatry. *Journal of the American Geriatrics Society,* 26(9):408–410.

Jones, R.G., and Galliard, P.G. (1983). Exploratory study to evaluate staff attitudes towards geriatric psychiatry. *Journal of Advanced Nursing,* 8(1):47–57.

Kane, R., et al. (1980). The future need for geriatric manpower in the United States. *New England Journal of Medicine,* 302(24):1327–1332.

Kennedy, G., and McKegney, F.P. (1990). Psychogeriatric practices among consultation/liaison services. *APA Task Force on Models of Geropsychiatric Practice.*

Kral, V.A., Palmer, R.B., and Yakovishin, V. (1986). A psychogeriatric outpatient service in a general hospital: Is it medically worthwhile? *Psychiatric Journal of the University of Ottawa,* 11(3):140–142.

Lazarus, Lawrence W. (eds.). (1988). *Essentials of geriatric psychiatry.* New York: Springer Publishing.

Lieff, J.D. (1983). Interdepartmental training program for the geropsychiatrist. *Gerontology and Geriatrics Education,* 3(3):237–241.

Liptzin, B. (1983). The geriatric psychiatrist's role as consultant. *Journal of Geriatric Psychiatry,* 16(1):103–112.

Mainprize, E., and Rodin, G. (1987). Geriatric referrals to a psychiatric consultation-liaison service. *Canadian Journal of Psychiatry,* 32(1):5–9.

McClelland, G. (1984). The geriatric worker in a community-based out-patient geropsychiatry clinic: A conceptual model. *Social Work in Health Care,* 10(2).

Murray, P. (1979). Aging Britain: Failing to count the days. *Health and Social Service Journal,* 89(4628):157–159.

Peace, S.M. (1982). Review of day-hospital provision in psychogeriatrics. *Health Trends,* 14(4):92–95.

Rodenburg, M. (1985). Psychiatric and nonpsychiatric facilities in the care of psychogeriatric patients. *Canadian Medical Association Journal,* 132(3):244–246, 248.

Rosse, R.B., Ciolino, C.P., and Gurel, L. (1986). Utilization of psychiatric consultation with an elderly medically ill inpatient population in a VA hospital. *Military Medicine,* 151(11):583–586.

Rowe, J. (1987). Interface of geriatric medicine and geriatric psychiatry. *Journal of Geriatric Psychiatry,* 20(1):3–9.

Royal College of Physicians of London and Royal College of Psychiatrists. (1989). *Care of Elderly People with Mental Illness.*

Ruskin, P.E. (1985). Geropsychiatric consultation in a university hospital: A report of 67 referrals. *American Journal of Psychiatry,* 142(3):333–336.

Schneider, C. (1990). The Rush Alzheimer's Disease Center. *Nurse Administrator Quarterly,* 14(2):54–57.

Schulman, K.I., Silver, I.L., Hershberg, R.I., and Fisher, R.H. (1986). Geriatric psychiatry in the general hospital: The integration of services and training. *General Hospital Psychiatry,* 8.

Smally, G. (1983). Health manpower shortage in geriatric psychiatry. *Archives of General Psychiatry,* 40.

Smith, S.A., and Marshall, W.L. (1989). Alternative programs in a psychogeriatric hospital. *Dimensions,* 66(2):17–19, 33.

Spar, J.E., Ford, C.V., and Liston, E.H. (1980). Hospital treatment of elderly neuropsychiatric patients: Statistical profile of the first 122 patients in a new teaching ward. *Journal of the American Geriatrics Society,* 28(12):539–543.

Timms, J. (1990). Innovative community-based health care for the elderly: A university-community partnership. *Nurse Administrator Quarterly,* (Winter):14(2):75–78.

Taintor, Z. et al. (1984). Evaluation of training in geriatric consultation: Development of assessment measures. *Gerontology and Geriatrics Education,* 5(1):73–81.

Wasylenki, D.A., Harrison, M.K., Britnell, J., and Hood, J. (1984). A community-based psychogeriatric service. *Journal of the American Geriatrics Society,* 32(3):213–218.

Zink, M., and Bissonnette, A. (1990). A unique multidisciplinary approach for urban geriatric home care. *Nurse Administrator Quarterly,* 14(2):69–73.

Wellness Consultation with the Elderly

Today and Tomorrow

Richard H. Cox

The growing awareness of health possibilities for the elderly in our society has rapidly increased available options for healthier living throughout the entire spectrum of life. Service providers and senior citizens alike are becoming increasingly aware of the many options resulting from this new awareness, producing both opportunity and responsibility for continuous education. Health care providers and organized institutions have learned that services can best be offered and research developed by giving careful attention to the needs and requests of the elderly; important education comes about by listening to the elderly population. Senior citizens have grown increasingly aware of opportunities for healthier and happier living and are making greater contributions toward bringing that about as well as making increasing demands upon health care providers and the government for such services and opportunities. Many of these senior citizens are living longer, healthier lives, and are very bright, well educated, alert, and capable of bringing about a new world for themselves. This is in contrast to only a few decades ago, when the elder person was considered to be feeble, absent-minded, and valuable only as a retired grandparent. "Until quite recently, the concept of senescence included the idea that aging inevitably led to increased physical and mental disability that resulted in death . . . there has been an abrupt about-face regarding this issue" (Zarit and Molar, 1987, p. 18).

Service providers to the elderly also have an increasing demand placed upon them to consider the medical, psychological, social, and ethical impacts of their decisions. Human services are always rendered within a spoken or unspoken, but nonetheless real, context of values and hierarchy of needs. However, as techniques and possibilities for longevity increase, so will our need to cope with the many dilemmas produced by the geometric and logarithmic nature of opportunities and conflicts arising out of the quest to do "what is right." Many times that which appears to be appropriate from the medical point of view is in conflict with the psychological, and both of those are frequently in conflict with social conscience. There seems to be a huge gulf between the academic ethicist and the daily practitioner who must make and assist families in making tough, pragmatic decisions.

Furthermore, with culture changing and expanding within the Western world, that which seemed to be a more homogeneous society a few years ago now has virtually every known race, religion, value system, and ideation present within it. Therefore, it is no longer possible to discuss "American" medicine or "the Western way of life." It is now necessary to bring into the context wide and frequently disparate points of view among providers, recipients, third-party payers, and institutions that provide and govern such services.

Governmental involvement shows no sign of decrease, but on the contrary appears to be growing in regulatory areas and increasingly assuming public responsibility; that is, the government is more and more looked upon as the caretaker for the public and the public more and more looks upon the government not only for regulation but the wherewithal to carry out services. As the financial burden of the elderly increasingly falls upon governmental shoulders, obviously more and more "outside" influence and control will dictate models of care. This is, of course, in conflict with the traditional "American way" of doing things. Western society has wanted to enjoy the free enterprise approach to life from cradle to the grave.

One cannot ask the government to pay for services without having a voice in those services. However, the conflict that this will present far exceeds any possibility of discussion at this point. The impact produces potential conflict not only with health care services, but housing, welfare, and research; as each domino falls, a very long line of dominos falls, producing a rippling effect that cannot be stopped. The hope is that those interested in health care services will be able to keep service paramount in spite of bureaucratic entanglements that are bound to increasingly thwart attempts at quality care.

The American family has, to a very large extent, disenfranchised itself from care for the elderly. The past several generations in our western culture have given little attention to the care of, services for, or, for that matter, respect for senior citizens. The "graying of America" has crept up upon Western society. All of a sudden, it would seem, senior citizenhood has become a majority factor. With insufficient planning, insufficient knowledge, and an insufficient data base, we must enter an era when responsibilities are great and knowledge is limited.

Families who are now becoming aware of the complexities of the aging population range in desire to care for senior citizens, as might be expected. While some hardly know of the problem, others are enmeshed with caring for their own parents while at the same time caring for their children, thus creating what has been termed the "sandwich" generation. Others are elderly themselves while caring for even more elderly parents. Due to the healthier longevity of the human race, new variations and complexities of family relationships have developed and our culture has not developed adequate methods for coping. A reorganization of our "usual and customary" social system allows for what appears to be dysfunctional behavior of the elderly to become fully functional. Such reorganizing includes the utilization of "networks, subsocialization groups and volunteers" (Litwak, 1985, p. 228). Further, public education regarding the vast array of possibilities and problems for senior care is insufficient. A much more vigorous public education program is needed if we are to hope for the average American family to become involved with its own senior members.

The recognition of a normal developmental process of aging is a very new consideration. "Our knowledge of normal aging is still in its infancy." (Carstensen and Edelstein, 1987, p. 30) Just as children are recognized to move through developmental stages, we are learning to recognize the maturing patterns through later life, rather than to conceive of that portion of existence as one stage.

Although we do not become angry with a small child who has a problem with urinary incontinence, for instance, but see that as a normal developmental process, we continue to see elder persons with similar developmental problems as in "deterioration" rather than in a developmental stage. Likewise, an infant whose closely bonded mother dies is acknowledged as suffering from normal grief, even though considerable regression may occur. The elder person, on the other hand, who loses a lifelong partner in death may be viewed as pathologically depressed. There is still in our society abhorrence and disdain for recognizing with equality the full spectrum of human existence, therefore allowing for behaviors that differ from the "norm" on both ends.

We do not allow the same latitude in all ages for similar behaviors, because it is new for us to deal with a fully developmental context of human existence. We often see journal articles and book titles with references such as "adulthood and aging" or "adult development and aging," as if failing to recognize that aging is part of adult development and vice versa. The difficulty is that we believe that only the middle of the spectrum to be the "norm." Therefore, we perceive children as developing toward that norm and the elderly as developing away from it, rather than recognizing that the norm extends throughout the spectrum. Therefore, a behavior such as memory loss in the elderly is not abnormal, but within the norm for that developmental stage.

Fortunately, recognizing aging as a process rather than a defined "stage" offers more opportunities for care giving and opens many doors for educating the public on how to deal with senior citizens. "Most older people are not depressed, neglected, and alone. The majority of older persons continue to function well and lead productive, meaningful lives. Nevertheless, in our enthusiasm to view old age in a more positive light and to root our 'ageism,' we must not ignore the vulnerability of the elderly that is due to the many changes and losses in their liver" (Whanger and Myers, 1984, p. 3). By the same token, this stuff in perspective opens many doors for senior citizens by not lumping them all together in the same group. We have been able to strip away the chronological aspects of aging and look more at the human process without reference to birthdays.

Just as we consider the normal developmental stages of aging, we must recognize that with extended life, certain patterns, pathologies, and handicaps occur that would not be necessary for our consideration with a younger demise. By surviving formerly fatal diseases senior citizens create entirely new contexts. New medical problems, intriguing social constellations, fascinating psychological pathologies, and more importantly, exciting new awarenesses present themselves with extended life patterns. Yet, of course, we must develop methods of coping with all of these complexities.

It is important that we not label conditions "pathological" too quickly. Our current codifications, and diagnostic criteria do not fit much of what occurs in senior citizenhood. As a matter of fact, from the psychological/psychiatric point of view, the *Diagnostic Statistical Manual of Mental Disorders* (Fourth Edition) is woefully lacking in recognizing the combination of factors present in seniors. As a result, with much too little evidence, such persons are classified as "organic," or suffering from "dementia," without recognizing that certain aspects of aging behavior may be no more "dementia" than are the actions of a child who has not yet learned material development. Many older adults actually suffer from "presbyophrenia (literally, old mind), and not aberrant, pathological conditions" (Verwoerdt, 1976, p. 53).

In the immature child's mind, ideas of reference, fantasy, and delusions are expected; they are considered healthy and within normal development. We must recognize both ends of the human spectrum and come to expect and accept as normal the behavior of the over-mature brain just as we do the immature.

Granted, these are opportunities for vigorous discussion, and will produce robust disagreements. It is precisely in that hope that such comments are made—so that they will spur us to a new level of consciousness and thinking regarding senior citizenhood.

REFERENCES

Carstensen, L L., and Edelstein, B.A. (eds.). (1987). *Handbook of clinical gerontology.* New York: Pergamon.

Litwak, E. (1985). *Helping the elderly.* New York: Guilford.

Verwoerdt, A. (1976). *Clinical geropsychiatry.* Baltimore, MD: Williams and Wilkins.

Whanger, A.D., and Myers, A.C. (eds.). (1984). *Mental health assessment and therapeutic intervention with older adults.* Rockville, MD: Aspen.

Zarit, J.M., and Molar, S.M. (eds.). (1987). Aging: The physiology and psychology of normal aging. In L.L. Carstensen and B.A. Edelstein (eds.), *Handbook of clinical gerontology*, 18. New York: Pergamon Press.

The Development of Wisdom in Later Years

Harry Prosen

The discussion of wisdom in the aging person is controversial and can be followed from several points of view. A historical perspective shows that in many cultures and societies, wisdom was taken for granted as a natural development in the elderly. The aged person was looked to as the seer or prophet in some societies, and especially respected. There have also been periods of time in our own society when the aged person has been looked at as helpless and even infantile; disregarded, and pushed aside. Particularly in the United States and Canada, as well as in some European cultures, the elders have become vigorous, politically active, and have left no doubt about their wisdom when it comes to representing themselves and their own concerns.

Major psychological research, particularly in cognitive areas, has been particularly significant in attempting to elaborate on the development of creativity, and there is much argument as to whether creativity evolves into wisdom, continues as creativity, or just disappears. Questions are left unanswered as to whether wisdom increases with longevity or stagnates. Too often the tendency is to see all older people as gradually deteriorating intellectually with a cognitive outcome of stasis; any ability to develop new ideas, fresh approaches, and wisdom is seen as simply the product of a long life. This is the concept of the wise elder.

RETIREMENT

For many reasons, retirement is an idea that is currently and vigorously being debated. Retirement is questioned by many as a social experiment that both is contrived and in itself contributes to intellectual deterioration and depression. Retirement has been seen as a dream to look forward to by many, but it also represents the imposition for some of an enforced state of giving up career, thinking, and risk. For these people, retirement is an artificial state bearing no relationship to the actual life cycle of those who may yet expect to live for ten or more years and who may want to work for a good part of those years. For many, it is insufficient to sit back and be wise (and dependent), and it is important to be seen as contributing. We see this more often in religious leaders and politicians, in whom it seems to be acceptable to be older and in whom age is thought to bring wisdom.

THE NATURE OF WISDOM

There are many different definitions of wisdom. Clayton (1982) defines wisdom as the ability to grasp human nature, which is paradoxical, contradictory, and subject to continual change. Clayton discusses research into wisdom and describes wisdom as a term used liberally "in contemporary and historical literature to describe a number of behaviors that have not yet received recognition from psychologists" (p. 315). She is careful to state that the literature does not always show the old to be wise or the young to lack wisdom.

Wisdom seems to have a function throughout life in terms of guiding development. One cannot discuss wisdom without discussing Erikson's theory of human development, especially his original eight stages of development (Erikson, 1950, 1959). Erikson has, in his works, discussed thoughts about his own wisdom; and one gets the opinion that wisdom, from Erikson's point of view, contains much compromise on rather than solution to life's major problems.

Research originating in the Max Planck Institute for Human Development in Berlin (Smith, Dixon, and Baltes, 1985) has investigated wisdom, looking at the relationship between intellectual growth and decline over the life span. The question about wisdom naturally evolving from intellectual aging is not really settled in this or other work, and wisdom is defined differently from mechanical and pragmatic points of view.

Simonton (1990) discusses "creativity and wisdom in aging" and states that the capacity of the human is wisdom. He reflects that, rather than living "from moment to moment with minimal reflection and even less foresight, human beings can acquire a broad perspective on life, discerning a larger view of life's meaning than permitted by a hand-to-mouth subsistence" (p. 320). He relates wisdom to creativity, looking at psychometric indicators and plotting intellectual creativity against age. He determines that precocity and production of intellectual material remains strong throughout life in higher intellectual groups. "Those who are precocious also tend to display longevity, and both precocity and longevity are positively associated with high output rates per age unit" (p. 324).

The amount of writing on wisdom is far less then on creativity and far more speculative. Energy and the aggression to produce and be creative are more likely to occur at a younger age. There are, nevertheless, great artists who have had long periods of unproductivity after initial artistic masterpieces who then, when older, go on to produce final artistic masterpieces.

Generally, development in the later part of life has not been discussed in nearly the same way as cognitive skills and personality in younger life. More recent research, however, does challenge the view that the intellect deteriorates with age. Clayton and Birren (1980) present "evidence for the plasticity of intelligence as well as demonstrating the large influence that contextual variables may have when compared with the role of biological factors in the adult intellectual performance."

As has been alluded to earlier in this chapter, with more of our population becoming older, retirement has lost much of its utility as a phase of demarcation in life and it has become important to find meaningful activities and roles for those who are older. Identifying wisdom with these older individuals offers a further dimension of usefulness and contribution. It may not exactly be knowledge, although certainly knowledge is part of it; the mastery of previous life and the maturation of view can certainly be seen as part of wisdom. As Meacham (1983) points out, the constructs of intelligence and knowledge "take on diverse meanings as they are considered within changing social and historical contexts" (p. 111). He has a number of suggestions as to further research in order to define wisdom better. What is obvious is that new knowledge and wisdom are easier to acquire when there is already a solid previous foundation; wisdom does not therefore suddenly occur as a product of aging.

How does aging affect these issues? The nature of social transactions does change with age. The nature of understanding and using new knowledge changes with age. Although elsewhere in the chapter it is stated that research shows that personality does not change, we cannot be sure that this is absolutely reliable information and models of wisdom do tend to show a relationship between knowledge, personality, and action.

CENTERS FOR THE STUDY OF AGING

Centers for the study of normal aging or aging and development, such as the Foley Center in Milwaukee based at the Medical College of Wisconsin, are becoming more common. They have tended to concentrate in the main on cognitive factors, although more recently some very significant work has been done on personality and what happens to personality throughout the life span.

Elsewhere in this volume is a description of the work of the Baltimore Longitudinal Study of Aging (BLSA), which is now past its thirty-fifth birthday and still grows and changes. It has contributed a great deal to the biomedical literature on aging and, as its staff states, findings have helped change aging research, clinical practice, and the way aging is viewed. The study was almost fortuitous, in that it originally formed a group of patients for research on measurements of an enzyme that was predictive of prostate cancer. As more people came back and more new ones came in, the research began to involve a measurement of physical fitness and physical decline. Later on, there was an approach to what was called the aging mind. The work done was related primarily to cognitive features, although coincidentally it was discovered that mental skills probably decline much less than commonly believed and that the decline was probably much later than believed. From the perspective of this chapter, however, their most important finding was the stability of personality over the life span. Also, the study has examined the aging spirit. In the GRC's Laboratory of Personality and Cognition one stereotype after another has exploded. As BLSA participants age, they are not more conservative or cranky or prone to complaining about their health than they were when young. The five-factor model of personality was used, which measures neuroticism, extroversion, openness, agreeableness, and conscientiousness. As described in the above mentioned chapter in this volume, the dimensions of neuroticism and extroversion were found to be powerful predictors of psychological well-being; it was also found that "the ability to cope with stress does not decline with age"—at least according to the data. Wisdom as a specific aspect of the study was not discussed, although it can be read into the implications of those with stable personalities.

In contrast to the Baltimore studies, more recent findings that have not yet been published tend to indicate that in fact some degree of isolation and obsessionality may be protective as far as the life span is concerned, and in fact may be contributory factors to wisdom. The belief here is that some guardedness leads to taking precautions and care in living. Developing observational features about life in general is one part of a looser definition of the development of wisdom.

AGING SCHOLARS

Birren (1990) has explored the creative potentials and activities of senior scholars. Birren did a study in which he discussed the productivity of thirty- and forty-year-old scholars. He then asks questions such as, "Should the emeritus professor be provided with an office and secretarial support, and access to a laboratory, to continue research?" (p. 28). He states that "the scholarly career is odd in that it tends to bring about its own demise. That is, the quest for knowledge implies the goal of eventually rendering one's own knowledge obsolete" (p. 28). There have been notions that there are cycles in the academic world of senior scholars and that periods of research and scholarship expand and contract, which results in a considerable amount of diversity—a lot of it depending upon individual variations in health. He then comments, however, that health has been overemphasized in this group and, quoting research done in Sweden, he states that physical changes associated with advancing age "do not become a predominant limiting feature of life for most persons until 85 years of age, and may occur even later for some academics" (p. 28). This is extremely important thinking; he goes so far as to suggest that "academics have a preferred way of life with regard to life expectancy" (p. 29). He believes that academics are information seekers with less "exposure to noxious conditions of the environment. Thus, senior scholars, with long life expectations and living a favorable lifestyle, are not typical of the average trends in the population" (p. 29). The point is that senior scholarship and productivity may not only be possible, but may be common up to the age of eighty. It can be quite tragic for scholars to leave universities too young—say, age fifty-five. The encouragement of scholarship must occur throughout the life span, with the enabling of senior scholarship to the benefit of both the individual and society.

Although an attempt has been made to define wisdom above, when one looks at different definitions and concepts of wisdom, perhaps the best one can do is to call wisdom a variety of human behaviors. Sternberg (1990) examined wisdom from many different perspectives, from the cognitive trait of ability to problem-solve to more complex characteristics influenced by affective and motivational elements. Sternberg (along with Birren) comments that the older scholar may also show wisdom through an increasingly desirable balance in behavior, in which rash and impulsive acts diminish and interest in analyzing the broader significance of events and behavior, rather than merely participating in them, grows. Another aspect of productivity is the fact that the wise older person can become an effective mentor of the young (p. 37).

MENTORSHIP

Mentorship as an aspect of wisdom is well recognized. Older scholars, if supported, are generally more loyal to academic principles, bring with them a depth of experience, and understand academic values (which are particularly important nowadays when traditional academic values are being reconsidered and questioned). Older scholars are often only too willing to talk and reason about these values.

Smith, Dixon, and Baltes (1985) state that "clearly, wisdom-related knowledge does not include only aspects of information search but also aspects of advice giving and judgment" (p. 16). Information searching seems to be an important aspect of a research measurement for wisdom; it was found that reserve capacity for average intellectual functioning goes on at least into the sixties. With aging "there is often change in structure of life goals, from school-related performance to pragmatic skills." With aging, "increased vulnerability and decreased maximum levels of performance" occur. On the other hand, these investigators believe that this can be balanced by "selective optimization of functioning" (p. 16).

Meacham's (1983) paper "Wisdom in the Context of Knowledge: Knowing That One Doesn't Know" mentioned previously, makes the point that "the relationship between the constructs of intelligence and knowledge, on the one hand" (p. 111), and its social and historical context, on the other, can only be understood by producing interpretations that give meaning to the behavior. Interpretations are affected by their historical settings. Thus, intelligence and knowledge have different meanings in different situations. If one accepts this, then the problem of doing reliable research becomes evident. Research will be based upon the values and interpretations used at a particular age or in a particular society. No matter how scientific the presentation, the context of history and developmental knowledge changes the findings and definitions of knowledge and wisdom.

Optimism and Pessimism about Aging

Clayton (1975), in her paper "Erikson's Theory of Human Development As It Applies to the Aged: Wisdom as Contradictive Cognition," seems to have a pessimistic view. The paper is a nice discussion of Erikson's ideas about human development including wisdom. Other authors who have commented on some of the same issues as Erikson are mentioned and the author seems to conclude that there really are no wise men. She states,

> It should be evident that interest in wisdom is tantamount to a search for the reasons why many individuals do not seem to reach the last stage of development in Erikson's model. Perhaps the reason we do not seem to find many wise old men is that most people fail to develop solutions which are appropriate to the crises they encounter as they chronologically age. That is, few individuals successfully resolve

the last developmental crisis because they remain fixated at earlier stages. (p. 126)

She feels that the blockage is probably most common in the adolescent years and that the adolescent years now are more conflict-laden then they were some years ago. Thus, we have a view that would cause us to see less wisdom in our elderly than in previous ages. This view is in contrast and contradictory to others' and this author's view. People often make choices that have to do with ways of moving on and compromising. Seldom are conflicts completely resolved before movement along the life span continues. Clayton states that complete crisis resolution is unrealistic. Perhaps if crisis resolution occurred, wisdom could not develop; perhaps some crisis needs to be left unresolved for wisdom to grow.

REFERENCES

Achenbaum, W.A., and Orwoll, L. (1991). Becoming wise: A psycho-gerontological interpretation of the Book of Job. *International Journal of Aging and Human Development*, 32 (1):21–39.

Bailey, W.T. (1991). Knowledge, attitude, and psychosocial development of young and old adults. *Educational Gerontology*, 17:269–274.

Birren, J.E. (1990). Creativity, productivity, and potentials of the senior scholar. *Gerontology and Geriatrics Education*, 11(1–2):27–44.

Birren, J.E., and Fisher, L. (1990). The elements of wisdom: Overview and integration. In R. Sternberg (ed.), *Wisdom: Its nature, origins and development*, 317–332. New York: Cambridge University Press.

Clayton, V. (1975). Erikson's theory of human development as it applies to the aged: Wisdom as contradictive cognition. *Human Development*, 18:119–128.

———. (1982). Wisdom and intelligence: The nature and function of knowledge in the later years. *International Journal of Aging and Human Development*, 15(4):315–321.

Clayton, V.P., and Birren, J.E. (1980). The development of wisdom across the life span: A reexamination of an ancient topic. *Life-Span Development and Behavior*, 3:103–135.

Connidis, I. (1989). The subjective experience of aging: Correlates of divergent views. *Canadian Journal on Aging*, 8(1):7–18.

Erikson, E.H. (1950). *Childhood and society*. New York: Norton.

———. (1959). Identity and the life cycle. *Psychological Issues*, 1(1), Monograph 1. New York: International Universities Press.

Guyot, R.S. (1993). A new theory about the ages of man. *International Journal of Aging and Human Development*, 36(2): 91–96.

Kastenbaum, R. (1989). Old men created by young artists: Time-transcendence in Tennyson and Picasso. *International Journal of Aging and Human Development*, 28(2):81–104.

———. (1991). The creative impulse: Why it won't just quit. *Creativity*, 15(2):7–12.

Keller, M.L., Leventhal, E.A., and Larson, B. (1989). Aging: The lived experience. *International Journal of Aging and Human Development*, 29(1):67–82.

Lasher, K.P., and Faulkender, P.J. (1993). Measurement of aging anxiety: Development of the anxiety about aging scale. *International Journal of Aging and Human Development*, 37(4):247–259.

Meacham, J.A. (1983). Wisdom and the context of knowledge: Knowing that one doesn't know. *Contributions to Human Development*, 8:111–134.

Munnichs, J.M.A. (1990). The senior scholar: A three-sided mirror for society. *Gerontology and Geriatrics Education*, 11(1–2):53–66.

Netz, Y., and Ben-Sira, D. (1993). Attitudes of young people, adults, and older adults from three-generation families toward the concepts "ideal person," "youth," "adult," and "old person." *Educational Gerontology*, 19:607–621.

Pollan, S.M. (1995). The rise and fall of retirement. *Worth* (December/January):64–74.

Rosel, N. (1988). Clarification and application of Erik Erikson's eight stages of man. *International Journal of Aging and Human Development*, 27(1):11–23.

Ryan, E.B. (1992). Beliefs about memory changes across the adult life span. *Journal of Gerontology: Psychological Sciences*, 47(1):41–46.

Simonton, D.K. (1990). Creativity and wisdom in aging. In J.E. Birren and K.W. Schaie (eds.), *Handbook of the psychology of aging*, 349–360. 3rd ed. San Diego: Academic Press.

Smith, J., and Baltes, P.B. (1990). Wisdom-related knowledge: Age/cohort differences in response to life-planning problems. *Developmental Psychology*, 26(3):494–505.

Smith, J., Dixon, R.A., and Baltes, P.B. (1985). *Expertise in life planning: A new research approach to investigating aspects of wisdom*. Berlin: Max Planck Institute of Human Development and Education.

Sternberg, R. (1990). *Wisdom: Its nature, origins and development*. New York: Cambridge University Press.

Thomas, J.L. (1992). *Adulthood and aging*. Needham Heights, MA: Allyn and Bacon.

Thomas, L.E. (1991). Dialogues with three religious renunciates and reflections on wisdom and maturity. *International Journal of Aging and Human Development*, 32(3):211–227.

Tornstam, L. (1992). The quo vadis of gerontology: On the scientific paradigm of gerontology. *The Gerontologist*, 32(3):318–326.

Empathy, Aging, and Intergenerational Issues

Harry Prosen

Introduction

Empathy for the self is an important developmental component of maturation and successful aging. It is not only a precursor to insight but, in fact, may represent a component of insight in itself. The concept of interpretation as generally viewed in dynamic psychiatry has strong verbal connotations of cognitive understanding, even if the therapist must reach in the interpretation for affective penetration and meaning for the interpretation. Empathy for the self thus signifies an understanding that cuts across all levels of intellectual and sensory understanding. If such understanding occurs, there also occurs an acceptance of the self. Such understanding is neither sympathetic or pathetic. Successful psychotherapy viewed from a developmental perspective requires such empathy, at all levels of psychological development up to the current point in the life of the patient.

An added task of therapy is the development of empathy to one's future self, which may have a connection to a sense of optimism. This idea is both the introduction and conclusion of this chapter. It is essential to start with this conclusion in order to understand the importance of an integrated view of the developmental stages of life and intergenerational issues, particularly intergenerational crises in families. Many therapists who approach their understanding of patients from a developmental perspective have made a transition of sorts in the manner in which they conduct psychotherapy. A developmental view is often superimposed on a background of education in psychoanalytically oriented psychotherapy. Intrinsic to these ideas is the development of a notion of developmental deficit, which will be discussed later. Finally, empathy for the self in the patient is a necessity for successful, dynamically oriented psychotherapy, as well as in most other forms of therapy.

CLINICAL ISSUES

In the paper "The Remembered Mother and the Fantasized Mother" (Prosen, Martin, and Prosen, 1976) the authors reviewed a group of male patients they had seen who came into treatment both complaining of and being threatened by what at first appeared to be the rather sudden onset of promiscuous behavior in mid-life after having previously led monogamous and rather conservative lives. The interpretation made of this behavior was based on a concept called "the remembered mother and the fantasized mother." This idea is an oedipal one, consisting of the concept that the memory that nearly all adults have of their mothers is of an aging woman, fading in attractiveness and sexual appeal. The fantasized mother is the mother of early and distant memory, perhaps as seen in photographs when she was young, or as dimly and distantly remembered. The explanation given with these patients was that as their wives aged, they began to seem more like the men's actual mothers. This feeling of being married to one's mother, with its ramifications, activated a search in these male patients to discover again their more attractive and stimulating younger mothers. The explanation also dealt with the ego aspects of mid-life. In fact, this rather general explanation of the etiology of promiscuity in mid-life was seen as having as much, or more, to do with the ego aspects of life review (Butler, 1963) such as dissatisfaction with having failed to achieve earlier and well-established ego ideals, notions of aging, diminished time left to live, and so on.

DEVELOPMENTAL IDEAS

David Gutmann (1987) had previously and continues to conduct significant research with men and women in this field. Erik Erikson (1950) gave us impetus to regard life developmentally. He introduced psychosocial concerns as being of fundamental importance, and also introduced the notion of life stages, each with their specific life tasks. His conception of epigenetic development with life stages progressively developing, each based upon the previous, is similar in many ways to Freud's basic conception of childhood development. Erikson's work, although creative and a major contribution, was at the same time limited by his inability to break freely into a completely "new" developmental theory. His work, nevertheless, encouraged others to combine developmental psychosocial considerations with intrapsychic metapsychology.

Gutmann (1987) did cross-cultural studies in which he illustrated his belief that there were typical and replicable stages of development in adult life in a number of cultures. His first work was done with men and was later followed by studies with women. He elaborated upon at least three stages of development during adulthood, and most recently he, and others, have talked about the need to conceptualize older life as still having its own appropriate developmental aspects with equally appropriate tasks.

Physical maturation—the end of active physical growth—does not end development. We are accustomed to thinking of development as being linked with physical change or change in physical competence. In the middle years especially, there is little that changes form. Rather, the same psychological structures are changed in the ways that they are organized.

The emphasis of life cycle theory has been more on individuals' experiences of not only their own life cycles, but also the interactions of their life cycles with the life cycles of others, particularly in family settings. In a family, members are at different developmental stages and there are, therefore, interrelationships between the various life cycles of family members. One might visualize this as a kind of "Rube Goldberg" factory, with all kinds of wheels cogging with each other, influencing the entire machinery.

MATURATIONAL TASKS

The maturational tasks of different family members are continuously at variance, and the conflicts are often clearly evident, although perhaps not recognized in developmental terms. There is always an interrelatedness between the life cycles of parents and children in the same family. Because of the demands for reevaluation and change brought about by the maturational transitions that are required of both adolescents and middle-aged parents, the upset and turmoil of a life crisis may occur. A life crisis can be defined as a critical problem that disrupts the life style of the individual or family, and threatens physical, emotional, or economic well-being. Some ego aspects of mid-life have been mentioned above. These include a review of one's attainments in life, the struggle surrounding the realization that the early ambitions and plans embodied in the ego ideal will never and can never be met, and the recognition that aging occurs without enough opportunity to reach the ego ideal and to achieve a sense of true ego mastery. There is a resulting and inevitable sense of frustration and disappointment. This sense can result in an adult making sudden changes in direction in order to make up for lost time, and to realize as much achievement as might still be possible in the time left. This not infrequently results in impulsive behavior. Impulsivity is, of course, also characteristic of the adolescent stage of development and basic to both an understanding of mid-life and adolescence, particularly in the sense of the use of time.

A number of authors have talked about mid-life as being characterized by a realization that time to live and accomplish has become shorter. Neugarten (1970) discussed this as a particularly conspicuous feature of mid-life—that is, the change in lifetime perspective to "time left to live," rather than "time since birth." It is recognized that many adolescents again deal with the resurgence of the oedipal conflict around puberty. A third resurgence of the conflict can occur in middle age, particularly when the oedipal situation was inadequately resolved in adolescence. Possible stimuli for this resurgence are the retreat from the aging mate already mentioned or adolescent children who once again awaken the incestuous strivings characteristic of the earlier oedipal conflict. In men, then, we may see the memory of the younger mother, a subjective sense of the shortness of time, and the pressure to act and to risk before it is too late. There is not only a third awakening of the oedipal conflict, but jealousy by fathers of daughters, and mothers of sons.

In this third rekindling, there may be renewed pressure to prove one's role, competence, and prowess. When this occurs in the family setting, the ordinary issues of control and family leadership become contaminated and distorted by issues of jealousy and competition. There results much opportunity for misidentification of the adolescent by the adult, and the adult by the adolescent. There arises also the opportunity for a fluctuating variety of age-related roles adopted by parent and adolescent in the family. These roles may switch, ranging from adult-parent and adolescent-child to adolescent-parent and adult-child.

GROWING UP TAKES A LIFETIME

While middle-aged parents may feel dependent and helpless, adolescent children tend to experience opposite feelings. They are in rebellion, actively questing for their own identities and the right to control and determine their own futures in line with their own goals and dreams. They resent parental authority and control, and indicate that the parents are helpless to influence them. As a result, the helplessness and passivity experienced by the parents is intensified. Added to the passivity of not being able to control one's own life is the passivity of not being able to control one's own children, and added to the anxiety about the uncertainty of one's future is the anxiety about the uncertainty of the adolescent child's future. It should be evident, then, that some of the life-stage tasks and conflicts of adolescent's complement, both positively and negatively, those of the parents. Both youth and parent are involved in working through issues of identity. The youth's task is to form an identity that is secure enough to carry through adulthood. The parent is concerned with the examination of his or her own identity and achievements in the light of his or her own ego ideals.

The adolescent also experiences concerns about sexual intimacy and sexual adequacy. Both adolescent and parent may experience the fear of impotence or sexual failure. The youth's fear is based on uncertainty at the beginning of a new and vulnerable aspect of life, while the parent's (particularly the father's) fear is based on the realization of declining sexuality and the apprehension that sexuality as it represents and symbolizes youth will be sacrificed with passing age. Identity formation in the adolescent usually occurs when parents are approaching or in mid-life. Thus, adolescent identity formation and its critical issues occur against the backdrop of the parent's mid-life reconsideration. Parent and adolescent are both engaged in modifying their views of themselves and each other. Adolescents often fight with their idealization of their parents, and parents often attempt to force their adolescent child to behave in such a way that their idealization of the younger child can continue. The modification required has to do with the idealization, each of the other, that may have existed relatively unchecked by reality until this period of family life.

The adolescent is expected by parents to conform to an ideal. At the same time, this is the period when the adolescent is often most ashamed and disappointed in his or her parents, and experiences them as least understanding. Both parents and adolescent find themselves angry, frequently to the point of death wishes and suicidal thoughts. One can see expression in families of their desire to separate, and increasingly now separation of families does occur. An important loss is that of the idealization of self and others.

A major focus of this chapter is the inability of persons to be empathic to each other and to see their similarities of struggle with identity formation and identity reconsideration. Parents in mid-life, already suffering from the damaging effects of deteriorating self-esteem due to the loss of active ego mastery, are especially vulnerable to injury by their personal disappointment in themselves, added to by the disappointment in them expressed by their children. Ambivalence is a part of the feelings of adolescents towards their parents. Parents' ambivalence towards their adolescent children is equally unpredictable and tumultuous. One would wish to see both a healthy admiration, as well as an empathy, between adolescent and parent. Unfortunately, the opposite is too often present. A therapist, whether working individually with a family member or collectively with the entire family, must possess the capacity to shift empathically and rapidly through various life stages, keeping track of them all simultaneously (Martin and Prosen, 1976).

Lack of empathy to one self has a number of possible origins. At least one of these is the absence of empathy to the life tasks of others in a family, particularly at transitional stages of life. If there is not a developmental deficit, there are nearly always developmental "rough bumps" or at least lacunae in development. Similar ideas have been described in families at all life stages, with considerable recent focus on the empathic deficit that occurs between children, adults, and their aging parents. We all know that it is often easier for there to be empathy between children or adolescents and their grandparents than between adults and their parents.

Elsewhere in this book, this author describes a situation in which a couple married over fifty years, well into their sixties, came for help, having been forced by their children to seek such help when they announced their intention to divorce. These two highly successful parents had three adult married children who, in their attempt to show appreciation for their parents and to ease their parents' lives, had supplied them with many luxuries, but at the same time had put them aside in a manner that made the parents feel unwelcome and more symbolic than real. Each partner in this couple projected his or her anger and frustration on the other. The work with them in traditional couples therapy was initially helpful, but was followed by quick relapse. It took some time to realize that both partners had lost their empathy for each other, but still were suffering similar life crises. They, in fact, had almost identical developmental tasks and it was the introduction of empathy through working with the family together that resulted in amelioration of the parents' problems.

Developmental deficit can be seen as a maturational lag, a deficiency of development of the ego or self. Depending upon the viewpoint and approach, the technical therapeutic efforts vary considerably. Much attention has been paid to deficits in early intrapsychic development, and a great deal of therapeutic attention has been paid to therapeutic methods of dealing with absent development. Goldberg (1990) has written, "Knowing makes for a developmental step and becomes the element consolidating psychic structure; it is an achievement of structure" (p. 64). There may be some argument as to whether knowing itself produces development.

Examples of Deficit

A male patient of thirty-five entered therapy. The therapeutic work with him occurred in several periods over fifteen years. The patient was creative, close to brilliant, and a very conflicted person. With a partial university education, a rather solid but lonely early upbringing on a farm, and some years in the armed services, he eventually began an artistic career. He was highly sought after because of his creative ideas and his fine work. He came to therapy because of periods of depression and difficulty with intimacy.

His early developmental history raised a question as to his fairly solid ego, based upon what initially sounded like deprivation and loneliness. For much of his early childhood, he was left unattended on a farm. As a baby, he spent many hours outside in a carriage. Much of his early childhood found him isolated, having mainly farm animals and scenery as his companions. He recalled his siblings as all much more aggressive than he. They grew up devoted to the farm, but he felt he was different from them. In the early work with him, there was difficulty in getting him to talk, conceptualize, and present himself in ways that were understandable. There were long silences, as well as difficulty in attaching to his therapist. Yet he had astonishingly mature, intellectual development, and was brilliant when he would express his ideas clearly. He possessed, in fact, a level of ego development that seemed quite out of context to either the mothering that he remembered receiving and was told about, or the attention he received from important other persons in his early life.

Somewhere late in the first phase of treatment, the therapist asked him (during a period of long silence) what he was seeing, rather than what he was thinking. It was at this point that it become evident that the patient had intense visual imagery. Though isolated from his family on the farm, he was still left surrounded by much movement and much nonverbal sensory stimulation. His early development was based on intense visual, auditory, and probably olfactory stimulation. It became evident that one could relate to him on this basis by asking him what he felt, sensed, saw, and heard—but not what he thought. Thus, what first appeared to be missing development was later on realized to be more than adequate ego development. Empathy between therapist and patient could only occur after developing a sensory mode of relating to the patient. One might say his understanding of the world was sensory rather than verbal.

A second patient in her thirties spent two years at a well-known hospital following a psychotic episode that was initially diagnosed as schizophrenia. There is reason to doubt the accuracy of that original diagnosis. She was severely depressed and did have a degree of ego fragmentation. As she decompensated, she was hospitalized several times, first in her own city and ultimately at the above hospital, where she remained for two years receiving intensive psychotherapy three times a week. A referral was made for her to receive continuing treatment upon her return home. What was thought to be the necessary kind of therapeutic work at that time involved seeing her initially twice a week and then once a week for a matter of four years. Great attention was paid to further building and reinforcing her defensive character structure. This work seemed successful and she seemed remarkable in terms of her strong, but rigid, defenses. At the same time, however, she was incapacitated in dealing emotionally with her children and husband because of her limited affect and range of feeling. Her empathic deficit protected her from further acute psychiatric illness but had its effects on her family.

During her treatment, the husband requested referral for his own psychotherapy. After the wife's treatment was concluded, the husband asked the wife's therapist for treatment, as his therapist had left the city. They began a period of therapy which continued for several years. This patient was forty years of age when he first saw the second therapist, and was a successful businessman. The patient had a powerful mother, and his father was the one who had originally developed the business. The patient's father died suddenly when the patient was an adolescent, and although he was the youngest child, it seemed that the patient was designated by the mother to be the successor. He became quite successful in his own right; by the time he was sixteen, he was virtually managing the company through the mother. In his twenties, he was in complete charge and rapidly expanding the company. It seemed that he became a man almost overnight. He experienced little of a normal adolescence in any of the usual respects. His reason for entering psychotherapy was his wish to understand himself better and particularly because he recognized that his life, although full of activities and successes, was really without pleasure. His major interpersonal problems occurred when his children became adolescents or his employees entered what could be described as a work adolescence.

Fairly early in this patient's treatment, the therapist made an interpretation that was repeated in its original form some three months later. The patient responded to the second instance by stating that the therapist had already told him "that once." The therapist replied, "You mean that if I tell you something once, you should understand it, accept it, and not ever have to have it repeated again?" He replied in the affirmative. Indeed, he expected his family and his employees to know that he would give them every support, but he failed to see how much they feared disappointing him. In addition, he did not understand how frightened of him they were because he challenged them continuously, was patient with them long past the tolerance of most others, and, when finally fed up with their inability to understand what he really expected of them (which was undoubtedly a repetition of his own effort to attain impossibly high standards and ideals), he would then interrupt or terminate the relationship. Ultimately, all failed him in some manner. Having not had an adolescence of his own, he had an empathic deficit for the adolescence of others.

It seems, therefore, that it is very difficult to convey an intellectual or cognitive interpretation to a patient who has a substantial period of missing development if the interpretation targets that missing period. This patient had mimicked, quickly learned to act mature, and demonstrated what appeared to be mature development. He had, however, not undergone his development in such a way that he could handle empathetically, affectively, or meaningfully those issues related to adolescence in his own children and in others.

Another way of seeing this man was his inability to be empathic to himself. He was superego-driven, unable to enjoy life, unable to experience life evenly, and at his best in intellectual negotiations. He always seemed rational and intellectual to those with whom he negotiated. At times of empathic failure, he would become angry, and would either direct this outward or internally, particularly when he had difficulty in completing a negotiation or when he believed that someone failed to work adequately on his behalf.

Another example with more serious psychopathology occurred in a mother whose daughter had been hospitalized for a schizophrenic episode (which would now likely be diagnosed as a schizophreniform disorder). The mother described a situation in which her daughter came home from school in grade one, at noon, and refused to eat lunch. The mother and daughter never actively communicated about the lunch, although the lunch was prepared each day. The mother said that after a number of days of this behavior occurring, when the daughter entered the house, that she would immediately give the daughter a spanking. The mother did this for a period of a week and then, without words being expressed between them, the daughter started eating. The mother remarked upon how well she had taught the daughter without having to say a word. One might agree that her daughter knew what her mother wanted of her. One cannot know the nature of the empathy between this parent and child, but the mother, in fact, sadistically abused her child and believed the results showed her understanding of her daughter and her daughter of her. One might call this negative empathy; it represents an empathic deficit in the mother for the child.

In these illustrations it seems that there is a relationship between the extent of the empathic deficit and the intensity of the need of the patient for understanding and transferring expressions. Countertransference issues are many and result mainly in a feeling of being unable to reach a patient empathetically, and, indeed, such patients seem almost to have a "learning deficit" in terms of their inability to accept interpretations that have to do with what is essentially a missing period of development. If the therapist has any similar deficit it may lead to major difficulties, and sometimes an impasse, in understanding the implications of a certain part of the life span of a patient.

TREATMENT QUESTIONS

Much of what has been discussed up to this point probably leads to more questions than answers. The real question is whether a severe developmental deficit, or indeed, any developmental deficit can be repaired in psychotherapy. Freud disclaimed this and pronounced patients with more serious deficits as essentially unanalyzable. It is now, however, believed by most therapists that many conditions arising at least partly as a result of developmental deficit are at least partially reparable.

Socialization is a method of development often not sufficiently appreciated. Socialization implies an understanding of the life experiences of others. Without such understanding, empathy and the achievement of intimacy becomes difficult. Productive and complete relationships also become difficult.

PSYCHOTHERAPY SUPERVISION

Psychotherapy supervision conducted from a developmental stance explains many problems that therapists experience and fail to recognize. An example is that of a young therapist being empathic to patients who have had life experiences and have lived through life stages that the therapist has not yet experienced (Martin and Prosen, 1976). There is more complexity to supervision when the supervisor is far removed from the life stage of the supervisee and has a requirement to be empathic both to the supervisee and to the patient whose treatment is being supervised. The understanding of life stages and empathy to the struggles that occur at each life stage is necessary to becoming a mature therapist. In contrast to this, one surely should not have to live through all the stages of life in order to have complete empathic ability. In fact, the longer one lives, the more possible it is that one may lose some empathy to life stages lived through long before.

Patients will occasionally challenge the therapist's empathy to them and use this as a resistance. It is sometimes difficult for male therapists to work in therapy with women who insist that they can only be properly understood and treated by a woman therapist. A not uncommon expression of resistance by patients is an insistence of a lack of understanding by the therapist because of cultural differences, sexual gender differences, financial and educational differences, or simply the inability to understand because patient and therapist are just "so different." A very important part of the therapist's work in dealing with both transference and countertransference must always involve consideration of the current empathic situation between patient and therapist.

CONCLUSION

The challenge presented here is whether a commonly accepted concept of interpretation may be useless in situations (even when it seems to be absorbed and accepted by the patient) when a patient is missing a serious developmental period of life. It is also suggested that a sign of the effectiveness of an interpretation is forward movement in development and signs of increased empathy for the self.

REFERENCES

Butler, R.N. (1963). The life review: An interpretation of reminiscence in the aged. *Psychiatry*, 26(1):65–76.

Erikson, E.H. (1950). *Childhood and society*. New York: Norton.

Goldberg, A. (1990). *The prisonhouse of psychoanalysis*. Hillsdale, NJ: Analytic Press.

Gutmann, D.L. (1987). *Reclaimed powers: Toward a new psychology of men and women in later life*. New York: Basic Books.

Martin, R.M., and Prosen, H. (1976). Psychotherapy supervision and life tasks: The young therapist and the middle-aged patient. *Bulletin of the Menninger Clinic*, 40(2):125–133.

Neugarten, B. (1970). Dynamics of the transition of middle age to old age. *Journal of Geriatric Psychiatry* 4:71–87.

Prosen, H., Martin, R., and Prosen, M. (1972). The remembered mother and the fantasized mother. *Archives of General Psychiatry*, 27:791–794.

REVISIONING PSYCHOTHERAPY WITH OLDER ADULTS

Len Sperry

Old age has been characterized as that period in life with the greatest number of profound crises occurring in multiples and with high frequency (Butler, Lewis, and Sunderland, 1991). It is not surprising, then, that a majority of older adults have various health problems, including 20 to 30 percent who meet the criteria for a psychiatric disorder. Critical psychological events for the elderly involve a wide range of emotional reactions to death and grief, loneliness, disease, dwindling finances, and disability. The nature of their problems ranges from annoying eccentricity to depression or dementia. Unfortunately, the elderly have very low utilization rates for health services, particularly mental health services. Only 1 percent are being treated in psychiatric hospitals and 2 percent in long-term care facilities, with about 3 percent utilizing outpatient mental health services. Only 1.3 percent of federal funds for mental health services are targeted for outpatient psychiatric services for the elderly, and the majority of this care is for organic brain disorders like Alzheimer's disease. Essentially, then, 85 percent of the mental health needs of older adults are not being met (Kermis, 1986). The reason for this underutilization of service is not simply a financial issue (Larson, Whanger, and Busse, 1983).

First of all, older adults have less access to mental health care. Secondly, many older adults have limited knowledge of or biases against psychiatric and psychotherapeutic treatment. And finally, until recently the elderly were commonly designated as "poor" candidates for psychotherapy (Butler, Lewis, and Sunderland, 1991). This pessimism about working with the elderly is usually traced to Freud and the psychoanalytic assumption that those over forty years old were characterologically too rigid to change. However, this pessimistic attitude has never been universally supported by therapists. In fact many have described success in working with older clients (Knight, 1986). For instance, Pollock (1986) reports that many of the elderly he worked with not only had the capacity for insight and self-observation, but also for therapeutically induced transferences and the mobilization of motivation to change.

This essay has two parts: the first part briefly recounts the history of psychotherapy with older adults, while the second part reviews two ways of envisioning psychotherapy with older adults. The assumptions and therapeutic implications of each are briefly discussed.

A BRIEF HISTORY OF PSYCHOTHERAPEUTIC TREATMENT OF OLDER ADULTS

This section selectively recounts the history of psychotherapy with the older adult. As noted previously, Freud was rather pessimistic about the prognosis for older persons in psychoanalytic treatment. Other analysts, like Abraham (1919/1953) and Pollock (1986), opt for a more optimistic view of therapy with older adults. Rechtschaffen (1959) cites others with similar optimism. Clearly, Jung's optimism is evident in articulating the positive developmental role of the second half of life, and his affinity for extending psychotherapy to older adults (1933).

There are two issues regarding psychotherapy with the elderly. First, should it be done at all, and second, how should it be done. Typically, the treatment provided has tended to be supportive, insight-oriented, or problem-focused.

Lillian J. Martin, the great pioneer in geriatric psychotherapy, developed the Martin method in the 1930s. Treatments were brief, lasting only about five sessions, problem-focused, and centered around comprehensive assessment of individual's life pattern. The clinician's role was to emphasize the individual's strengths and encourage and inspire them. Positive affirmation was used as a form of thought-stopping; self-control and homework assignments involving daily activities and future goals were expected (Karpf, 1982). Needless to say, her method was largely ignored by medical and psychological professionals in favor of traditional psychoanalytically oriented approaches. In the past decade, however, group, family, and behavioral approaches have been developed as stepchildren of individual approaches.

In his book *Geriatric Psychotherapy*, Brink (1979) reviews several systems of psychotherapy and other psychosocial treatment methods with the elderly. He concludes that the most clinically useful approaches are problem-centered rather than primarily supportive-, insight- or feeling-centered. He also concludes that aging is a developmental process and that the mechanism for therapeutic efficacy lies in teaching the elderly patients to think and act nonpathologically. Brink has found that the primary reason for the success of geriatric psychotherapy is that a long life constitutes valuable experience in coping, and that brief problem-centered therapy provides the individual the additional training needed to cope with the problems of aging. Brief, problem-focused psychotherapy can be provided in individual, group, family and their youth contexts. Lazarus (1984) describes a brief psychodynamic approach to psychotherapy useful with certain elderly patients. He has also adapted it to the spouses of patients with Alzheimer's disease.

Milieu approaches for the elderly have recently been implemented in long-term care facilities. Often a sizable number of residents of such facilities have Alzheimer's or other organic brain disorders. In the past, only custodial care was extended to these individuals. Brink (1979) describes in detail how a milieu approach has been successfully implemented in several facilities. Research shows that custodial care tends to reinforce the patient-as-victim role, which often results in exaggerated disability and may lead to development of psychiatric disorders in patients who initially entered a long-term care facility for purely medical reasons. On the other hand, Brink proposes that a milieu program should encourage patients to learn to care for themselves and others, instead of how to be cared for by others. Such milieu programs emphasize patient activities: exercise programs, group therapy projects, arts and crafts, and reminiscent groups. Behavioral modification methods have been introduced for many problems, including incontinence, which is a problem for one-third of all patients in long-term care facilities.

Family therapy involving the elderly often is a common intervention in day care programs for the elderly. It is particularly useful in connection with group programs, especially in dealing with the guilt, anger, and frustration that family members have about their elderly relatives. Butler, Lewis, and Sunderland (1991) describe intergenerational family therapy that includes older persons with their adult children, grandchildren, and great-grandchildren, or close friends or relatives considered "family" if they have no living children. Finally, family therapy used on an outpatient basis with the elderly and extended family members has been found to be very effective (Brink, 1979).

WAYS OF ENVISIONING PSYCHOTHERAPEUTIC TREATMENT WITH OLDER ADULTS

This section describes two ways of envisioning psychotherapy with older adults. Both the "traditional" and "emerging" views are discussed in terms of their underlying models and assumptions and their therapeutic approaches and implications.

The Traditional View

Several psychotherapy systems are based on models of personality that focus on childhood development (which extends to early adulthood), with little or no articulation to middle and later adult years. Needless to say, such personality models, and their derived psychotherapy systems, assume that present-day problems and concerns are rooted in or reflect childhood traumas, fixation, developmental delays, maladaptive habits or thoughts, or problems in the family of origin. Although some of the classical cognitive and behavioral therapies emphasize more recent determinants of current problems, others, such as Beck's cognitive therapy of personality disorders (Beck and Freeman, 1990), clearly focus on maladaptive schemas of early childhood. In short, such psychotherapy systems assume a *retrospective* view by relating and explaining adult life experiences to and in terms of childhood experiences.

This retrospective view is quite consistent with many psychotherapists' experience in working with adolescents and younger adults. Specifically, these clients typically struggle with issues that begin in childhood and in their family of origin. Furthermore, because of their young age they have not had sufficient additional life experiences to have problems that could have begun later.

The retrospective model of personality lends itself to the "loss-deficit" view of psychotherapy with older adults (Knight, 1992). Here the normative course of life is viewed as a series of losses, typically resulting in depression. Based on the traditional psychodynamic belief that old age is essentially a regression to increased dependency, psychotherapy could only be conceived of as supportive; the elderly could not be candidates for "real" psychotherapy, since it was assumed that they were too rigid and set in their ways and that their cognitive decline made them no longer capable of insight and change (Knight, 1986).

However, the retrospective view is not as consistent with the experience of psychotherapists who work with older adults. While there may well be "unfinished business" with early life developmental tasks and traumas, older adults can and do experience problems at any point in adult life. Issues may range from unresolved conflicts with accepting death, to failed expectations of children of a mid-life marriage, to delayed grieving following the death of a spouse.

The Emerging View

On the other hand, from a *prospective* or life-span development view of aging (Thomas, 1992), development may become arrested or conflicted at any point in the adult life span. And, since the older adult will have been a member of several family systems throughout life (family of origin, nuclear family, extended family of adult children and in-laws, the dispersed family, and, quite possibly, a blended family), it is more accurate to think of an individual's various family constellations, rather than *the* family constellation, as Adlerians typically do. Bowen's (1978) concept of multigenerational transmission suggests that there is marked consistency from family of origin to nuclear family and so on, unless the pattern of differentiation of self from one's family context is changed. Psychotherapy is but one way of self-differentiation.

The prospective or maturity model of aging is based on the life-span perspective, which, Thomas (1992) notes, emphasizes optimization. Optimization refers to efforts to ensure that developments and aging are as problem-free as possible. More specifically, Baltes and Baltes (1990) describe the "selective optimization with compensation" model for successful aging, wherein older adults select areas of competency that can be optimized by exercise and practice, so that lost or lessened abilities are replaced by compensating strengths.

As mentioned previously, Brink (1979) found that the problem-centered approaches are superior to those that are primarily supportive, insight-oriented, or feeling-oriented because of their hopeful thrust. Knight (1992) also proposes that psychotherapy with older adults be based on a prospective developmental or maturity-based model. He describes the "maturity-specific challenge" perspective and believes psychotherapists better serve their older adult clients by viewing them as mature and strong individuals who are facing specific challenges that occur more frequently in late life. These challenges include disabilities, chronic illness, preparation for dying, and mourning for loved ones.

Pollock's discussion of the mourning-liberation process with psychoanalytic treatment (1986, 1987, 1989) is quite consistent with the emerging vision of psychotherapy with older adults. Pollock believes that successful aging presupposes the ability to mourn what no longer exists in order to be liberated to invest energy in the present and the future. Like others who espouse an optimistic view, Pollock notes that aging is a developmental process (Pollock, 1989).

This prospective and maturity-specific challenge model reminds psychotherapists to think more proactively about their work with the later-life issues of their clients. Viewing aging as a developmental process, wherein maturing is a lifelong task, challenges psychotherapists to assess the strengths and life experiences older clients bring to the task of working out solutions to their problems. Certainly, this view is an antidote to the loss-deficit views of psychotherapy.

CONCLUDING NOTE

The brief historical sketch of psychotherapy and subsequent discussion of different views of psychotherapy suggested that the degree of optimism or pessimism and the type of treatment accorded the older adult is a function of the therapist's vision of the elderly. Thus, therapists who espouse a retrospective and loss-deficit model of aging are likely to be cautious in their optimism but offer primarily supportive treatment. On the other hand, therapists who espouse a more developmental prospective and maturity-based model of aging are quite optimistic and tend to offer problem-centered or insight-oriented treatments, believing that development continues throughout the life span. A major paradigm shift appears to be occurring in our view of the elderly and their treatment (Pollock, 1986; Baltes and Baltes, 1990). If the evolution of therapy continues to mirror the changes that are occurring in our understanding of developmental aging, the next decade may well witness newer and more effective treatment approaches with older clients.

REFERENCES

Abraham, K. (1919/1949). The applicability of psychoanalytic treatments to patients at an advanced age. In K. Abraham (ed.), *Selected papers on psychoanalysis*, 312–313. London: Hogarth Press.

Baltes, P., and Baltes, M. (1990). Psychological perspectives on successful aging: The model of selective optimization with compensation. In P. Baltes and M. Baltes (eds.), *Successful aging: Perspectives from the behavioral sciences*, 1–34. Cambridge, England: Cambridge University Press.

Beck, A., and Freeman, A. (1990). *Cognitive therapy of personality disorders*. New York: Guilford.

Bowen, M. (1978). *Family therapy in clinical practice*. New York: Jason Aronson.

Brink, T. (1979). *Geriatric psychotherapy*. New York: Human Sciences Press.

Butler, R., Lewis, M., and Sunderland, T. (1991). *Aging and mental health: Positive psychosocial and biomedical approaches*. New York: Merrill/Macmillan.

Jung, C. (1933). *Modern man in search of a soul*. New York: Harcourt Brace Jovanovich.

Karpf, R. (1982). Individual psychotherapy with the elderly. In A. Horton (ed.), *Mental health interventions for the aging*, 21–24. New York: Praeger.

Kermis, M. (1986). *Mental health in later life: The adaptive process*. Boston: Jones and Bartlett.

Knight, B. (1986). *Psychotherapy with older adults*. Beverly Hills: Sage.

———. (1992). *Older adults in psychotherapy: Case histories*. Newbury Park, CA: Sage.

Larson, D., Whanger, A., and Busse, E. (1983). Geriatrics. In B. Wolman (ed.), *The therapist's handbook*, 287–324. 2nd ed. New York: Van Nostrand Reinhold.

Lazarus, L. (ed.). (1984). *Psychotherapy with the elderly*. Washington, DC: American Psychiatric Press.

Pollock, G.H. (1986). The psychoanalytic treatment of older adults with special reference to the mourning-liberation process. In J.M. Masserman (ed.), *Current psychiatric therapies*, 87–98. Orlando, FL: Grune and Stratton.

———. (1987). The mourning-liberation process in health and disease. *Psychiatric Clinics of North America*, 10/3: 345–354. Philadelphia: W.B. Saunders.

———. (1989). *The mourning-liberation process*. 2 vols. Madison, CT: International Universities Press.

Rechtschaffen, A. (1959). Psychotherapy with geriatric patients. *Journal of Gerontology*, 14:73–84.

Thomas, J. (1992). *Adulthood and aging*. Boston: Allyn and Bacon.

THE PRACTICE OF PSYCHOTHERAPY WITH THE AGING ADULT

Harry Prosen

OVERVIEW

This chapter will discuss both the use of psychotherapy with older persons—"older," in this case, encompasses the ages of fifty to one-hundred years of age—and the potential for beneficial effects from psychotherapy for such patients. Also discussed are different forms of psychotherapy, some of the changes in thinking about the influence on older people of psychotherapy, and when special treatment approaches should be considered. It will take into account earlier notions of personality development, when it was believed that fundamental personality development was completed in the early years of life, with approximately age six or seven the limit of essential development. There is also some discussion of temperament and of some views that temperament remains essentially unchanged throughout life. Opinions will be mentioned about the hardening of personality and personality defenses with age, not only making the aging person more difficult to get along with, let alone treat, but also tending to reinforce symptoms. It has nevertheless become apparent in recent years that every form of psychotherapy is applicable to people who are aging, including psychoanalysis (Weiner, 1992; Brok, 1992).

The most significant contribution to psychotherapy with older people, and in fact all ages beyond childhood, evolves from the developmental perspective of Erikson (1950, 1959). Erikson not only was the first to suggest a developmental view of life in which psychological development was continuous and did not stop at an early age, but he also contributed the notion of psychosocial concomitants to personality development, which were seen as equally important. This view was then followed and elaborated by many other authors who initially tended to look at specific parts of life, mid-life being one of the first. More recently, as the population ages rapidly, there has been general growth in psychogeriatric medicine and psychogeriatric care. There has developed as well, therefore, an equal need to look at aging as normal, as having its own particular developmental tasks, and as a period of growth and creativity. Here, often psychotherapy is absolutely critical to enabling growth and creativity as well as, of course, being necessary to deal with those losses and self-concerns that occur normally with aging.

DEVELOPMENT IN MID- AND LATER LIFE

Gutmann (1987) has explored developmental perspectives in mid-life. Pollock (personal discussion), with a group of colleagues, has worked extensively on the success of insight-oriented therapy and psychoanalysis with people who would have been thought of, a few years ago, as being extremely old. He has shown that personality can be reshaped, attitudes changed, and productivity and creativity supported. There are at least two groups of authors writing in this area. The younger group often does not seem to have an empathic view; it takes more of a psychopathological or gerontopathological view of the older person. Part of this may be the fact that until they have dealt therapeutically with enough patients who are older than they are, they may tend to transfer and use projective identification related to important older adults in their own lives, such as their parents and teachers, more than do older therapists. On the other hand, older therapists may tend to project many of their own conflicts and issues onto patients who are close to their own age or older. They may also tend to be much more subjective than they realize in their interpretations and advice.

Just as in conducting psychotherapy with younger people, it is important for the therapist to have a broad theoretical background, a knowledge of various therapeutic techniques, and, particularly, a good familiarity with developmental and aging theories. Psychopathology occurs in older people just as it does in younger people and although illness patterns may show a lesser frequency (there may be less late-onset schizophrenia and more late-onset depression), there is no illness that cannot occur for the first time in the older person. Depression is the commonest illness of the elderly and is seen more frequently in women than in men, but on the other hand, depression in men must be taken very seriously because of the high suicidal risk that is often present. The dynamic conflicts are not that much different, but they almost certainly have been present for a good part of the individual's lifetime and therefore have found considerable reinforcement. Thus, the conflicts become so obsessionally imbedded in the patient that they seem to represent a way of approaching life and thinking, which makes such patients frustrating and difficult to deal with. The overlay of depression, loss, and sometimes fear of death always needs to be taken into account and understood.

CHARACTER ARMOR

The concept of character armor (Reich, 1974), is extremely important. Such armor is seen initially as developing necessary defenses for the ego. With aging, what was originally a normal, necessary personality defense may in some cases become heavier, more layered, and obtrusive. It thus gets in the way of relationships and can make people appear to grow more stubborn, more difficult to deal with, more persevering in their ideas. Character can appear to be more heavily armored in the older person than in the younger but this is not necessarily the case—perceptions can be deceptive. The approach in traditional dynamic therapy with the younger person is to work to lessen the armoring that shields the therapist from being able to form a close bond with the patient. Decisions about working in a psychodynamic manner with older people must include the potential for actually getting through the armor or making a decision not only to allow it to exist but somehow or other to see if it is possible to use the defense in the service of the ego.

Having said the above, it is still generally true that therapies that attempt to search for original causes early in life are much less likely to be successful, although as mentioned above, psychoanalysis in carefully selected cases may be as therapeutic as with younger people. Techniques must be chosen that seem applicable to the patient. These techniques also must be used with appropriate respect, and can be very difficult for therapists who do not have a perspective on what it is like to be older or, as mentioned previously, have not yet lived to the age of the older patient (Martin and Prosen, 1976).

As is mentioned elsewhere in this book (see also Martin and Prosen, 1976) a developmental perspective in psychotherapy can also be helpful in understanding the contents of a session. Patients may talk about matters that have occurred at different times in their lives and the unsophisticated therapist may not realize that the same issue, when looked at from different age perspectives, may be presented differently but still represent unsolved tasks carried forward from previous periods of development. A developmental perspective views life as continuously evolving, with different stages of development continuing into adulthood and older life, each stage having its own appropriate tasks. This notion includes the idea that if a task is not solved at the appropriate stage of life, it remains as baggage that accumulates and must be carried along through life. Robert Butler (1963) has stated that those people who age least satisfactorily are those people that carry unsolved life tasks with them from one stage to another. Accretions of unsolved tasks multiply, and, ultimately, when older life is reached, the baggage is so heavy that it makes it very difficult to deal with the problems of aging. Such baggage makes it particularly difficult to be optimistic and creative.

It is mentioned above that there are both transference and countertransference issues to be considered in dealing with older people. There is a suggestion in the literature that seems to indicate that, on balance, it may be better for an older patient to have a younger therapist than a therapist of the same age or older (Teri and Logsdon, 1992). As these authors point out in their discussion of the future of psychotherapy with older adults, there are few control studies, particularly in marital and family therapy, with this group. They discuss the need for rigorous research trials using psychotherapeutic interventions in a controlled way, measuring the outcomes. Most psychotherapy research has been conducted with younger patient groups. Teri and Logsdon further state that they don't believe that there is a single theoretical intervention that is appropriate to all and mention the diversity of issues in psychotherapy, including "chronological age; physical, emotional, and functional health; and social, cultural, and environmental differences" (p. 84). They stress the importance of the diversity of older adults, and that it requires a diversity of approaches. They believe treatment should be founded "in theories of psychopathology as well as in theories of adult development and aging to take into account the range of 'abnormal' and 'normal' psychological processes that occur with age" (p. 84).

The Effectiveness of Psychotherapy

We are only now developing measures that tell us whether psychotherapy is effective or not. We are not always sure of the kind of change that we are looking for except when we have obvious pathology, such as serious depression; even here it is sometimes compounded by intellectual deterioration. A psychotherapeutic technique, as well, must be describable in enough detail that it can be replicated by others. Psychotherapists working with older adults should have a realistic understanding of what areas of intervention are perceived as most necessary to their clients. It is simplistic to believe that one particular therapeutic approach will work for most patients.

Group techniques are particularly successful with older people because they experience similar kinds of reactions that may not be revealed and shared while alone. It is often assumed that older people who spend much time in solitude lose their ability to communicate and become introspective to the point of not being able to respond to interpersonal psychotherapy. It is amazing to find out how open to discussion and desirous of talking these people are. Here, careful therapy of any kind, whether it be supportive or insight-oriented, can be very helpful.

Where groups of older people naturally gather, one finds a kind of natural group therapy occurring. It generally is more supportive, although sometimes a hostile or envious member of the group will be angry and vindictive. Where people have experienced similar events, one does find empathy occurring, particularly when they are talking about their children and spouses. Insight is more difficult to attain; this requires a deliberately chosen group with facilitators or coordinators who have been trained in insight-oriented group therapy. It is surprising how well some older people take to insight therapy and use it with imagination. In fact, one occasionally sees rather dramatic changes in relationships between parents and children, or older persons and their friends, based upon an insight that they did not previously possess.

Collaboration among disciplines and specialists is as important in those working with older people as it is in those working with younger people. Although more and more professionals are being trained in geriatric psychiatry, psychology, and nursing, very often discussions of psychotherapy are superficial and more directed toward pharmacotherapy. Finally, the keynote advice in dealing with older patients is not to infantilize or in any way treat them in a childlike fashion, although older patients will sometimes respond in what seems to be a positive fashion to this kind of care. There is nothing more belittling, however, than to see very young therapists treating patients old enough to be their grandparents in what can only be described as a demeaning fashion. To reiterate, a thorough grounding in developmental psychology and a developmental approach to psychotherapy is extremely important.

Clinical Examples

The therapist was visited by a couple in late life who had decided that they wanted a divorce. It became apparent that the marriage had been an unhappy one for the last ten or so years; the partners argued and saw each other increasingly as an enemy rather than a partner. The wife complained that the husband, who was well off enough to retire from the business he started, spent his time drinking in a solitary fashion, did not travel with her as he had promised when they were younger, and belittled and abused her verbally. He, on the other hand, said that his wife would not respond to any sexual overtures, spent her time continuing the social activities of her younger days, and only nagged and argued with him.

The therapist's first approach was that of traditional marital therapy. After a period of months, it appeared that things had settled down well enough for termination to occur. The couple went away, only to be brought back by their children some months later with things even worse than before. This time, the therapist took a complete history with the children and as many of their spouses as could be present. A very different history revealed itself, much of it related to the developmental frame of reference.

The husband, in building his company, had decided to bring his two sons into partnership with him. They entered, learned the business, and very quickly built branches, modernized, and produced new technology. The father, the founder, found himself not understanding how things worked; he felt left out. The sons built him a magnificent office close to the front entrance and left him there, where he spent most of his time sitting alone and feeling rejected by his sons. He grew paranoid to the point of thinking that they were trying to ease him out and eliminate him from his company. The therapist was amazed to discover an identical type of story from the mother, who talked of her daughters loving her but, at their summer cottage, building a suite above the boathouse for her and her husband so that they would not be bothered by the grandchildren and their noise. She, too, felt abandoned and no longer useful.

The therapist was then able to see that both parents were at identical life stages with very similar life problems that had to do with acceptance of change and self-esteem. When this was presented to them, they came together; their understanding rejuvenated the marriage and gave openings for improvement in the marriages of two of the children.

The above example is one of marital therapy, but it shows how an understanding of life stages and life tasks can lead to a somewhat different therapeutic approach.

Patients who are often extremely successful and have been obsessional, hard-driving and monolithic in their ambition and thinking often find it hard to enjoy their success and life. They usually are superego-driven, content with successes for only a short while, if at all. It is not uncommon to see either an underlying dysphoria or a mild chronic depression that increases with age if not recognized and treated earlier. This often occurs in families; therapists who have dealt with families, particularly those where there is history of bipolar illness or unipolar depression, must be vigilant in watching their patients with this particular premorbid personality type so that they may recognize a more serious psychological impairment developing. This author has worked with up to three generations of the same family and has seen the pattern repeated in each generation on several occasions. This is also a developmental issue—but one that is reinforced both by family and probably with genetic predisposition. As these people age, sometimes starting as early as late mid-life, their depression tends to become more serious and overwhelming. As success grows, unhappiness becomes greater. This author has written (Prosen, Martin, and Prosen, 1972) about impulsive acting out in people like this. Although seemingly successful, they cannot enjoy their success and search for happiness via sometimes inappropriate behavior that can cause havoc in their own families.

A third patient, a professional whose bipolar father the therapist had worked with for some time, worked hard, as did his father, and was relatively happy and successful early in his life. As his middle age approached, he could not achieve enough satisfaction, also similarly to his father, and became more obsessional and increasingly depressed. The therapist, very much aware of the possibility of the onset of a bipolar illness in this patient, worked to get him to modify his life, both through psychotherapy and through choosing a different lifeline for himself. His development was discussed with him in detail. Ultimately, the patient did become depressed and even though it was very difficult during his depressive periods to work psychotherapeutically, he ultimately worked his way through a separation from his father and a realization that he was entitled to choose a different type of life and have different opportunities than his closed-off father. This resulted in a man who now began to age with both dignity and the ability to enjoy his work and his children, who have chosen careers (unlike his) in the arts and have been successful in young adulthood. The patient's first marriage failed; he married again, this time to a nonoedipal woman. The second relationship was noncompetitive and mutually supportive, in contrast to the first. One can see them aging together in a way that is enjoyable and creative.

A final example has two subtypes that this author has identified. The first subtype are the people who have spent a lifetime—often into old age attempting to understand their motivations, their relationships to others, and their ambitions. Life has often involved them in various attempts at psychotherapy, ranging from what might be called the more orthodox therapies sought from licensed practitioners to more esoteric and sometimes even spiritual and mystical ways of searching for answers. Sometimes these aging persons achieve the kind of peace that they seek, but more often than not they continue to pursue answers that are not available to them. They—whether professionally successful or not—enter old age and go through it feeling lonely, isolated, and particularly unable to take advantage of whatever enjoyment maturity, family, and grandchildren might bring. These people, because of depression, often receive pharmacotherapy: usually antidepressant drugs, often accompanied by antianxiety medications, as depression is often mired by phobic anxiety. These patients describe waking up in the morning or in the middle of the night, obsessed with fears and other nameless dreads, sometimes able to talk themselves out of them but often not, living with the specter of fear over their shoulders. They are difficult to treat and yet do respond to a warm empathic relationship and efforts to limit the force of their superego. Therapists here often take very direct positions in suggesting ways in which these patients can achieve more pleasure from their lives. Cognitive approaches are helpful.

The second subtype of this example is similar except that there seems to be an openness that leads to a continuing curiosity to understand themselves more and better. As they age, the curiosity actually increases so that they tend to read, pursue various quests, try different kinds of therapy, and incorporate bits and pieces from all that they learn so that, although they are inclined to periods of depression and unhappiness, they generally are able to grow beyond whatever limitations their earlier life imposed upon them. These are persons who are not overly defended, possess egos that still seem to have a fair degree of reliability and strength, and continue to desire evolution and growth. These are the few persons who enter psychoanalysis or intensive psychotherapy of a dynamic nature at an older age and approach it with eagerness, showing great satisfaction and gratification with each insight and, in some cases, showing surprising changes in their personalities.

GENDER AND AGING

Gutmann (1987) has talked a great deal about gender identity. He is interested in widespread cultural stereotypes about gender and age differences. He has, in particular, conducted cross-cultural studies and his work suggests, as is now more commonly believed, that as men age they become more passive, more nurturant, and, in some ways, more feminine. They remain identified as males but show less interest in sexual and aggressive behavior. Actually, Anna Freud (Freud and Sandler, 1985) pointed this out previously in a somewhat more oblique fashion. It is particularly important to understand the changing of gender identity in males as they age because the accepted prototypes of society do not readily allow this change to occur. The change is a desirable one in many ways and it is often accompanied by a more aggressive and socially stronger role for their spouses. In an intact couple where these changes are recognized and facilitated, the relationship strengthens. Where it is fought and not accepted, it leads to marital disharmony and to feelings of failure and inadequacy on both parts, but more commonly on the part of the male.

This discussion of aging is attempting to develop some new spins on age and again to consolidate a developmental view of the life span. This means discarding some of the older myths about aging and, in particular, doing away with the concept of an appropriate chronological age for retirement or indeed to become aged. This author has stated (unpublished paper) that aging and even maturation can be difficult to see. Physical structure tends to show the features of aging, but psychological structural changes are much less visible unless the signs are so obvious that they indicate without doubt some aspect of aging such as forgetfulness or perseveration. For example, studies (Sadavoy, Lazarus, Lissy, and Jarvik, 1991) do not in any reliable way show a decrease in reaction time with aging. Reaction time is commonly thought to decrease with aging; this relates to obtaining driving licenses or jobs that require dexterity.

To return to the concept of psychoanalysis and intensive psychotherapy in the older person, Sigmund Freud (1924) saw his theories and techniques as not applicable to older people. Abraham (1953) gave evidence for the successful treatment of older individuals with psychoanalysis. Rechtschaffen (1959) discussed the adaptations that had been made by various therapists in applying psychoanalytic practices to the elderly. He said that it might not have been the treatment of choice, but in many cases it worked. His review is one of the very important early writings on psychotherapy with the elderly.

THERAPY APPROACHES

As the percentage of the aging population increases rapidly, the need to train a solid, theoretically based and sometimes empirically based approach to therapy with the older person becomes increasingly important. As with the younger patient, generally health expenditures diminish for those older people in therapy. The major illnesses of the younger person, such as schizophrenia, still occur in the elderly, but depression increases in frequency and organic cerebral conditions, often related to underlying physical disease, are common. Even this latter will respond quite often to a combination of psychotherapy and pharmacotherapy, however.

The current focus on short-term care, including the willingness of insurance organizations to pay for brief "managed care" approaches, necessitates the learning not only of long-term analytic approaches, but also structured, goal-oriented, and short-term approaches. Here behavior is focused on bringing conflict to the surface as quickly as possible. Behavior modification can be successful. Depression often occurs from loneliness, grief, and mourning. Here, the therapist can be helpful in encouraging others to understand what is happening with the patient, and depression is much more, quickly relieved than is generally thought.

Marital and family therapy has already been mentioned, as has support to caregivers (elsewhere in this volume). These are significant, particularly in institutional settings. Settings where people live independently can still encourage support systems. Many of the above approaches are described as empirical. No mention has been made yet of the importance of relevant caregivers and therapists who understand the cultural aspects of the aging patient—especially when placed in a setting where there are not people of similar social and ethnic background. Training in psychotherapy has for too long dealt with the young adult or in specialized cases, the child. Training in geropsychiatry or geropsychology has too often dealt with nonpsychotherapeutic approaches. There have been biases against what is, perhaps subtly, seen as the waste of resources in doing psychotherapy with older people. Intervention is not only possible, however, but very rewarding. When talking about aging, we may be talking of a forty-year period which may extend from the late fifties to ninety or more. Even here, technique and even the site of therapy varies with age and needs great flexibility. Although transference difficulties are less likely when therapy occurs outside an office setting, the therapist must still be awareness of the possibility, especially in the aging patient with some sensory impairment who misidentifies the approaches and intentions of the therapist.

THERAPISTS' FEARS OF AGING

It is also worthwhile for therapists to work with older patients in terms of dealing with their own anxieties about aging and death. This is an existential concern which is ever-present. Therapy often brings in patients who have serious physical illness and the therapist has a need not only to deal with the issues of death himself or herself, but to make students aware of this. For example, it is important for teachers who work with medical students to introduce this concern into the curriculum fairly early. It is also important to remind all practitioners in the health care field, especially at a time when more limited periods are offered to deal with illness, that working with patients who are dying means being with them and their families right up to and past the time of death. Perhaps the potential for life can be strengthened and the immune system boosted by dealing with the patient's self-esteem. This author has found it particularly important to help patients express their aggression in a focused and, if possible, nondestructive fashion.

Fantasies abound in severely ill patients, whether they are younger or older, and these fantasies are often kept hidden because of embarrassment or shame.

SUMMARY

In summary, the tenet of this chapter is that life is continuously evolving and that it is best looked at from a developmental perspective. This perspective carries with it the potential for psychotherapy that may need reshaping depending upon the developmental stage of the person. Again, development and chronological age do not always go hand in hand, nor need they. Therapists must look to a flexible kind of therapy that is not standardized for biological age but is standardized more for where patients are in their own lives so that they can maximize future potential and growth. Creativity is possible even to the end and when it can be expressed, it brings hope and excitement and diminishes depression.

REFERENCES

Abraham, G., Kocher, P., and Goda, G. (1980). Psychoanalysis and aging. *International Review of Psycho-Analysis*, 7(2):147–155.

Abraham, K. (1953). The applicability of psychoanalytic treatment to patients at an advanced age. In K. Abraham (ed.), *Selected papers on psychoanalysis*, 73. New York: Basic Books,

Allman, L.S., LaRocha, O., Elkins, D.N., and Weathers, R.S. (1992). Psychotherapists' attitudes toward clients reporting mystical experiences. *Psychotherapy*, 29(4):564–569.

Austad, C.S. (1992). The wisdom group: A psychotherapeutic model for elderly persons. *Psychological Reports*, 70(2):356–358.

Baker, F.M. (1994). Psychiatric treatment of older African Americans. *Hospital and Community Psychiatry*, 45(1):32–37.

Boehnlein, J.K., and Sparr, L.F. (1993). Group therapy with WWII ex-POW's: Long-term posttraumatic adjustment in a geriatric population. *American Journal of Psychotherapy*, 47(2):273–282.

Bowling, A. (1993). The concepts of successful and positive aging. *Family Practice*, 10(4):449–453.

Brok, A.J. (1992). Crises and transition: Gender and life stages issues in individual, group, and couples treatment. *Psychoanalysis and Psychotherapy*, 10(1):3–16.

Butler, R.N. (1963). The life review: An interpretation of reminiscence in the aged. *Psychiatry*, 26(1):65–76.

Cremin, M.C. (1992). Feeling old versus being old: Views of troubled aging. *Social Science and Medicine*, 34(12):1305–1315.

Duffy, M. (1992). Challenges in geriatric psychotherapy. *Individual Psychology*, 48(4):432–440.

Erikson, E.H. (1950). *Childhood and society*. New York: Norton.

———. (1959). Identity and the life cycle. *Psychological Issues*, 1(1), Monograph 1. New York: International Universities Press.

Freud, A., and Sandler, J. (1985). *The analysis of defense: The ego and the mechanisms of defense revisited*. New York: International Universities Press.

Freud, S. (1924). On psychotherapy. In *Collected papers*, 249–263. London: Hogarth Press, Ltd.

Friedman, H.S., Tucker, J.S., Schwartz, J.E., et al. (1995). Psychosocial and behavioral predictors of longevity: The aging and death of the "Termites." *American Psychologist* 50(2):69–78.

Geller, J.D., and Farber, B.A. (1993). Factors influencing the process of internalization in psychotherapy. *Psychotherapy Research*, 3(3):166–180.

Gutmann, D.L. (1987). Reclaimed powers: Toward a new psychology of men and women in later life. New York: Basic Books.

Ionedes, N.S. (1992). A therapy program for Alzheimer's disease: An Adlerian orientation. *Individual Psychology*, 48(4):413–418.

Katz, R.S., and Genevay, B. (1987). Older people, dying, and countertransference. *Generations*, 11(3):28–32.

Keller, J.F., and Bromley, M.C. (1989). Psychotherapy with the elderly: A systemic model. *Journal of Psychotherapy and the Family*, 5(1–2):29–46.

Kercher, K., Kosloski, K.D., and Normoyle, J.B. (1988). Reconsideration of fear of personal aging and subjective well-being in later life. *Journal of Gerontology*, 43(6):170–172.

Kirshner, L.A. (1988). A model of time-limited treatment for the older patient. *Journal of Geriatric Psychiatry*, 21(2):155–168.

Mannig, D.W., Markowitz, J.C., and Frances, A.J. (1992). A review of combined psychotherapy and pharmacotherapy in the treatment of depression. *Journal of Psychotherapy Practice and Research*, 1(2):103–116.

Martin, R.M., and Prosen, H. (1976). Psychotherapy supervision and life tasks: The young therapist and the middle-aged patient. *Bulletin of the Menninger Clinic*, 40(2):125–133.

McCarthy, S.V. (1986). Perceptions of life after seventy. *Activities, Adaptation and Aging*, 8(2):39–47.

Natale, S.M. (1986). Loneliness and the aging client: Psychotherapeutic considerations. *Psychotherapy Patient* 2(3):77–93.

Newton, N.A., Brauer, D., Gutmann, D.L., and Grunes, J. (1986). Psychodynamic therapy with the aged. *Clinical Gerontologist*, 5(3–4):205–229.

Nobler, H. (1992). It's never too late to change: A group psychotherapy experience for older women. *Group*, 16(3):146–155.

Prosen, H., Martin, R., and Prosen, M. (1972). The remembered mother and the fantasized mother. *Archives of General Psychiatry*, 27:791–794.

Qualls, S.H. (1991). Resistance of older families to therapeutic intervention. *Clinical Gerontologist*, 11(1):59–68.

Rechtschaffen, A. (1959). Psychotherapy with geriatric patients: A review of the literature. *Journal of Gerontology*, 14:73.

Reich, W. (1974). *Character analysis*. New York: Touchstone Books.

Reynolds, C.F. (1992). Treatment of depression in special populations. *Journal of Clinical Psychiatry*, 53(9, Suppl.):45–53.

Reynolds, C.F., Frank, E., Perel, J.M., et al. (1992). Combined pharmacotherapy and psychotherapy in the acute and continuation treatment of elderly patients with recurrent major depression: A preliminary report. *American Journal of Psychiatry*, 149(12):1687–1692.

Riess, B.F. (1992). Some thoughts and material on age-related psychoanalysis of the aged. *Psychoanalysis and Psychotherapy*, 10(1):17–32.

Sadavoy, J., Lazarus, W., Lissy, F., and Jarvik, J.F. (1991). *Comprehensive review of geriatric psychiatry*, Washington, DC: American Psychiatric Press.

Schmid, A.H., and Rouslin, M. (1992). Integrative outpatient group therapy for discharged elderly psychiatric inpatients. *Gerontologist*, 32(4):558–560.

Solis, J., and Brink, T.L. (1992). Adlerian approaches in geriatric psychotherapy: Case of an American widow. *Individual Psychology*, 48(4):419–426.

Solomon, K. (1991). The psychodynamics of male chauvinism in an elderly man. *Clinical Gerontologist*, 10(3):23–38.

Sperry, L. (1992a). Aging: A developmental perspective. *Individual Psychology*, 48(4):387–401.

———. (1992b). Psychotherapy systems: An Adlerian integration with implication for older adults. *Individual Psychology*, 48(4):451–461.

Sprinkart, P. (1988). Rediscovered lives: Work with older people in the search for time past. *Journal of Gerontological Social Work*, 12(3–4):47–62.

Tallmer, M. (1992). The aging analyst. *Psychoanalytic Review*, 79(3):381–404.

Teri, L., and Logsdon, R.G. (1992). The future of psychotherapy with older adults. *Psychotherapy*, 29(1):81–87.

Weiner, M.B. (1992). Treating the older adult: A diverse population. *Psychoanalysis and Psychotherapy*, 10(10):66–76.

Wellman, F.E., and McCormack, J. (1984). Counseling with older persons: A review of outcome research. *The Counseling Psychologist*, 12(2):81–96.

Whitbourne, S.K. (1989). Psychological treatment of the aging individual. *Journal of Integrative and Eclectic Psychotherapy*, 8(2):161–173.

AFTERWORD

Aging in the Twenty-first Century

Postscript

Harry Prosen

The Future of Gerontology

The themes of a number of chapters in this book, particularly by Sperry, Gutmann, McAdams, Cadmus, McNeil and Sperry, Sperry and Wolfe, Heidrich and Ryff, and Thomas, offer many thoughts about the present state of gerontology as well as implications and predictions for the future. All agree upon the rapidly aging population and our epidemiological information readily shows us that we will easily have a third of the population over seventy years of age fairly early in the next century. It is self-evident that this population cannot be overlooked and it is also becoming more obvious that this population will not have enough financial resources to be able to retire in any complete way; nor will many wish to do so. A major thesis of this book has been the importance of seeing this long and sometimes prolonged last stage of life as a period of development, rather than mourning for lost life. There is implied hope in this book that spirituality as part of wisdom will grow with age.

Some have stated that old age can be a major period of development, and we have attempted to bring into the concept of developmental aging the realization of wisdom and its use to benefit all of society. This reverence for the wise elder was commonly accepted in many early societies—even the American culture at one time—more recently those older have tended to be discarded and looked at as outcasts. The reaction has been the development of powerful movements of aging groups, resulting in organizations such as the American Association of Retired People. There is a fundamental shift in the way we regard the aging person, with the power of the shift coming from the volume of aging persons, their demand for recognition, and the evidence of their involvement in all that goes on. For a large part of history, younger generations viewed the aged as keepers of truth, preservers of the culture and of society, approachers of the gods, and those to whom one looked for ultimate answers. The fact that the aging see themselves as not only less dependent and less desired is resulting in the empowering of this group. It will result (as is happening now) with the aging becoming a vigorous political group who will have their say no less than those younger. They will likely be altruistic—much more altruistic than the younger generations in terms of wanting good things for their children and grandchildren—but I doubt very much that this altruism will extend so far as to sacrifice what they are now coming to see as many extended years of potential development for themselves.

Our authors have tended to divide the aging into those who are guarded by optimism, retain good health and vigor, and continue to work to some extent, and those who tend to become hypochondriacal and deteriorate. The research that we are conducting is looking for ways of producing more of the former and fewer of the latter. Our prediction for the next century is that life expectancy will approach one hundred years of age, therapies and medical treatment will be viable and useful to this group, and society will accept ever-increasing contributions from the aging person. Matters of ageism will become important matters of legal precedent and there will be no "glass ceiling" for the aged.

The Future of Geropsychiatry and Geropsychotherapy

Articles in this volume by Pollock, Yesavage, Cox, Hay, Sperry, and Prosen also show that geropsychiatry will emphasize more mobilization both of the body and of the mind. We are now developing ways of enhancing memory, calming and looking with optimism toward the future, and feeling useful; one can see that the elderly will not permit themselves as a group to be seen as potential victims of euthanasia. Indeed, there will be no place for old people to wander away and die without troubling others. Geropsychiatry will grow as a specialty, with its particular special emphasis on how a different psychopharmacological and psychotherapeutic approach is needed for the elderly. Clinician-researchers like Pollock, who have done therapy with patients in their nineties and even in their hundreds will continue to work in this area. We will increasingly attend to psychological issues that affect the aged—they will likely not be different than those that affect the young, and psychotherapy of the aged will become just as important as psychotherapy of the younger.

To play the devil's advocate for a moment, I would suggest that perhaps geropsychiatry should be disbanded as a specialty, as should gerontology. That is not to say that we should neither look at the particular issues that happen in aging nor have specialists who can deal with the aging, but that these matters should be brought forth throughout medicine and the social sciences as normal. If indeed the aging become one-third of the population, then geropsychiatry and geropsychotherapy are not subspecialties, but an ordinary part of practice. We must escape the gerontopathological view of aging. The future of medicine and medical training, as well as specialty training, will be that the body and mind are a unity, that they change over time, and that the approach to them changes over time both in terms of psychotherapy, spirituality, and pharmacotherapy. The specialist needs to become less specialized and more generic and understand all developmental issues. We will deal more openly with dying and death and try to be sure that the physician, in particular, spends as much time with the patient who is aging, helping that patient live as "normal" a life as possible. We will see increasing retirement communities that are related to and built on university grounds, where the final stages of life will occur over a long period of time and where stimulation will be given until it is no longer possible for it to be received.

Training Implications

The training implications are profound. Psychiatrists will be trained, as will other gerontology professors, to meet the changes noted by Sperry, Gutmann, McAdams, Cadmus, Sperry and Wolfe, Heidrich and Ryff, Thomas, Yesavage, Cox, Hay, and Prosen. This means that, following the Eriksonian model, we will indeed see aging as a stage of life with its own particular substages, all the way from a childhood of aging to an adolescence of aging to an adulthood of aging to, finally, what may really be regarded as old age. It is hoped, however, that the educated therapist, in dealing with these other matters and with a proper respect of the elderly and the aging patient, will help to minimize true old age. On the other hand, we are finding that where true old age and physical deterioration do occur, there are many opportunities for specialists to draw out many aspects of, again, normal development. Development is lifelong.

CONTRIBUTORS

LEN SPERRY, M.D., Ph.D. is a professor in the departments of psychiatry and behavioral medicine, and preventive medicine, and executive director of the Foley Center on Aging and Development, at the Medical College of Wisconsin in Milwaukee.

HARRY PROSEN, M.D. is a professor and chair of the department of psychiatry and behavioral medicine, and senior advisor of the Foley Center on Aging and Development, at the Medical College of Wisconsin in Milwaukee.

ROBERT R. CADMUS, M.D., D.Sc. was a professor of preventive medicine emeritus at the Medical College of Wisconsin in Milwaukee.

GENE D. COHEN, M.D., Ph.D., is a professor of psychiatry, and director of the Center on Aging, Health and Humanities, at The George Washington University. He is also director of the Washington, D.C., Center on Aging. He was formerly acting director of the National Institute on Aging.

RICHARD H. COX, Ph.D. is a professor of psychology at and president of the Forest Institute of Professional Psychology in Springfield, Missouri.

DAVID GUTMANN, Ph.D. is a professor and director of the Older Adult Program in the division of psychology, department of psychiatry and behavioral sciences, at Northwestern University Medical School in Chicago, Illinois.

DONALD P. HAY, M.D. is an associate professor of psychiatry and associate director of geriatric psychiatry at St. Louis University Medical School in St. Louis, Missouri.

LINDA K. HAY, R.N., Ph.D. is an assistant professor of psychiatry and director of the Clinical Trials Unit at St. Louis University Medical School in St. Louis, Missouri.

SUSAN M. HEIDRICH, Ph.D. is an associate professor of nursing at the University of Wisconsin in Milwaukee.

DAN P. MCADAMS, Ph.D. is a professor of human development and psychology at Northwestern University in Evanston, Illinois.

CAROLINE MCNEIL is a scientific writer for the Public Information Office of the National Institute of Aging in Bethesda, Maryland.

GEORGE H. POLLOCK, M.D., Ph.D. is the Ruth and Evelyn Dunbar Distinguished Professor of Psychiatry and Behavioral Sciences emeritus at Northwestern University Medical School, and a clinical professor of psychiatry and behavioral medicine at the Medical College of Wisconsin in Milwaukee.

CAROL D. RYFF, Ph.D. is a professor of psychology and associate director of the Institute on Aging at the University of Wisconsin in Madison.

JEANNE L. THOMAS, Ph.D. is a professor of psychology and associate vice chancellor at the University of Wisconsin-Parkside in Kenosha.

PAMELA WOLFE, M.D. is an assistant professor of psychiatry and behavioral medicine at the Medical College of Wisconsin in Milwaukee.

JEROME YESAVAGE, M.D. is a professor in the department of psychiatry and behavioral sciences at Stanford University in Palo Alto, California, and formerly chair of the Council on Psychiatry and Aging of the American Psychiatric Association.

INDEX